W9-BWZ-672

"I AM A MAN"

Also by Joe Starita

The Dull Knifes of Pine Ridge

"I AM A
MAN"

Chief Standing Bear's
Journey for Justice

Joe Starita

St. Martin's Press ✖ New York

www.stmartins.com

Library of Congress Cataloging-in-Publication Data

Starita, Joe.
    "I am a man": Chief Standing Bear's Journey for justice / Joe Starita.—1st ed.
        p. cm.
    Includes bibliographical references.
    ISBN-13: 978-0-312-53304-5
    ISBN-10: 0-312-53304-7
    1. Standing Bear, Luther, 1868?–1939. 2. Ponca Indians—Kings and rulers—
Biography.   3. Ponca Indians—History. 4. Ponca Indians—Government relations.
I. Title.
    E99.P7S837 2009
    978.004'9752440092—dc22
    [B]
                                                                    2008029877

First Edition: January 2009

10 9 8 7 6 5 4 3 2 1

For Phil—a chief among his people, a warrior to the end

Contents

Acknowledgments

A good many people deserve a nod of the head and a tip of the hat for making this book possible. They include Rosetta Le Clair, Parrish Williams, Sandy Taylor, Larry Wright Jr., and Judi Morgan gaiashkibos—patient and kind Ponca voices whose generosity of spirit provided a good deal of understanding and insight into the history and culture of their people. To John Wunder and David Wishart—friends and colleagues whose expertise and careful reading of specific chapters helped flesh out intimate details and flush out historical inaccuracies. To Michael Farrell and Lynne Ireland—for their thoughtful commentary on how to prune, trim, and cut back on some unruly excesses in the early going. To Christine Lesiak and Christopher Cartmill—for sharing the obsession and the endless hours discussing its historical significance and contemporary relevance. To Will Norton—dean of the University of Nebraska College of Journalism and Mass Communications for his generosity and unwavering support. To agent Jonathan Lyons, for his

Acknowledgments

energy and persistence, and to editor Daniela Rapp, at St. Martin's Press, for her professionalism and editorial guidance.

And a special thanks to the two people whose contributions to this project can scarcely be overstated: To Kyle Wyatt, researcher extraordinaire who always returned with an arsenal of documents and an engaging smile, and to Roger Holmes, whose clear eye, steady hand, and sharp focus invariably kept all the moving parts moving in the right direction.

It seems to me an odd feature of our judicial system that the only people in this country who have no rights under the law are the original owners of the soil: an Irishman, German, Chinaman, Turk, or Tartar will be protected in life and property, but the Indian commands respect for his rights only so long as he inspires terror from his rifle.

—Brig. Gen. George Crook

"I AM A MAN"

1

On the Banks of
the Running Water

Somewhere along the flanks of the great river, not far from a valley once flush with buffalo, beaver, bald eagles, and yellow-shafted flickers, where two centuries ago the captain explorers looked out and saw both America's past and future, somewhere near these rugged chalk bluffs, lie the bones of a father and son.

For as long as anyone could remember—before the horses, fur traders, whiskey, fever, and the pus-filled spots; before the steamboat, glass beads, and another god—their people had lived in this ancient river valley straddling the border of what would become Nebraska and South Dakota. Here, amid one of the continent's most intricate blends of plant and animal life, the father and son were born into a complex culture that had sustained their people for generations. It was never easy, but they adapted and so they survived, living in dome-shaped earth lodges and buffalo-hide tipis, harvesting the rich floodplain, hunting wild game, and foraging for wild fruits and vegetables in the hills and valleys. Up and down the river valley, the mothers knew the plants that would help protect them from everyday ailments—blue-flag rootstock for earaches, cedar fruits and leaves for coughs, chokecherry bark for diarrhea, and the raw root of the milkweed for stomach trouble. Boiled oak and red elm bark treated irritable bowels, and wild black currant helped kidney problems. The mothers gathered cattail down to dress burns, and also used it as talcum for their babies and as padding for cradle boards.

Like their ancestors, the father and son had begun life in these cradle boards, carried along and upright wherever their mothers went, able to see and hear and participate in the world around them. In time, they eventually played all the hand games and the rough-field hockey; they came to know the rituals of the religious ceremonies, and the social dances, and the rules of the different warrior societies. They knew what the Buffalo Police would do if someone spooked the herd. They knew, too, that no one became a serious suitor without a good string of horses.

At night in the winter camps, they had heard the story of the giant beast covered in hair that their people had once seen in a cave farther down the valley. And they heard about the eighteen-inch spirits, the dwarfs with large heads and long hair who were said to live in the higher elevations where they often led astray unwitting trespassers. Years before, the people had tried to warn the captain explorers coming up the Missouri, had told them the spirit dwarfs would kill anyone who climbed the large mound to the north. But on a sweltering August day, Meriwether Lewis and William Clark hiked to the top anyway and reported no sign of enemy spirits.

Instead, their journals recorded what they saw at the summit: "From the top of this Mound we beheld a most butifull landscape; Numerous herds of buffalow were Seen feeding . . . the plain to North N.W & NE extends without interruption as far as can be seen." For men accustomed to the dense forests of the east, it must have been quite a sight, a sight that few whites had ever taken in—the endless sweep of sky and tallgrass prairie, the rich soil, an overwhelming variety of plant and animal life.

It was a sight the father and son knew well. For most of their lives—one long and one short—they had known the song of the meadowlark drifting across their river valley homeland. They knew what it meant to see the piping plovers and indigo buntings, the spotted sandpipers bobbing in the sandbars, and the beaver villages sweeping across the backwater channels. What it meant to touch the wind knifing through summer fields of Junegrass, switchgrass, foxtail, and side oats gamma. To smell the air from atop the rugged chalk bluffs dusted with the fingerprints of a thousand blizzards. To feel the power of Wakanda spilling through the jagged scars of the black winter sky in the Moon When the Ducks Come Back.

Century after century, perhaps beginning as far south and east as the Carolinas, their people had gradually followed a mosaic of waterways north and northwest. Never numbering more than a thousand, they slowly migrated across half a continent until they finally settled in a place that satisfied all of their needs, a place the explorers first saw in the early autumn of 1804. Here, along the banks of the fertile, wooded river, they flourished, building villages and raising children, their culture increasingly rooted in a landscape that came to define who and what they were. Even now, in the faces and voices of the elders, it is the same as it has always been: Their river valley homeland was a place the people could never imagine leaving—in life or in death.

Today, at ninety-six, Parrish Williams is the elder of his people. He has a thick thatch of swept-back white hair, a smooth, unlined face, a soft voice. He lives alone, deep in the woods, in a modest home, its walls covered in photographs of his eleven children, some in wedding gowns, some in football uniforms, some in uniforms of the Marine Corps. Until recently, he had never seen the river valley where the father and son were born and buried, where his own mother and father were born, a valley hundreds of miles north of his home on the flat Southern Plains. Two hundred years to the week after the explorers first saw it, Parrish Williams stood on the same high ground and looked out:

"Those hills—they looked like mountains to me. And all the green, the trees, all the way up to the top. And then the river. It was the most beautiful country I ever saw."

But back then, as the eighteenth century began to wind down, there were a good many things neither the clan chiefs and the Buffalo Police nor the medicine men and the warrior societies could have known, could have foreseen. They could not have seen that, in many ways, the fate of their people—and hundreds of thousands like them—was already being cast in distant lands they'd never heard of, across an ocean they were unaware of.

They did not know that, throughout the last four decades of the eighteenth century, three great powers from across the water—France, England, and Spain—had vigorously sought to strengthen their footholds in the lands of the western New World and its lucrative fur trade. Of the three, the French initially had the most success. Like the other nations, the French regarded the red people as an inferior race, one they needed to win over to tap into the source of the valuable furs, but—unlike the Spaniards—they had no intention of conquering and converting them, then killing them off if they resisted. Many of the French explorers, traders, and trappers were more sympathetic. They were more inclined to see the Indian as a child of nature and they tried harder to understand the strange new people and their different way of life. They often married into the tribe, lived with the tribe, and became the heads of mixed-blood families. Some never left. And neither did their names: Janis, Bordeaux, Montclair, Robideau, Bettelyoun, Belle-court, Bissonnette, Peltier, Picotte, La Flesche, Le Clair—names that would remain in families scattered across the vast fur-trading region for centuries afterwards.

Although France had formally lost the French and Indian War to the British in 1763, it refused to cede its western lands to the victor, secretly transferring them to Spain instead. Spain, meanwhile, was content to rely on contacts from France's flourishing fur trade to help drum up business throughout the region. So for many years, the native people of the Upper Missouri became accustomed to French fur traders and their Spanish landlords, who now controlled all of the Louisiana Territory.

But in the waning years of the eighteenth century, cash-strapped Spain was getting squeezed from all directions. First came the spread of Russian fur traders along the valuable California coast. Then, the British moved south and west out of Canada, setting up fur-trading posts along the Upper Missouri on lands claimed by Spain. Not long after, a bold French general came to view the Louisiana Territory, with its abundant supply of food, timber, and furs, as the key to rejuvenating his empire. So in the first year of the new century, Napoleon secretly traded the kingdom of Tuscany to Spain, and the lands between the Mississippi River and the Rocky Mountains once again passed into French hands.

Soon, however, the general's ambitious plan to colonize Louisiana with slaves was thwarted when a slave revolt decimated his French army in Haiti. His Caribbean troops were now in tatters, and the hated British an increasing threat. Desperate for war capital, Napoleon devised a different strategy: He would put the Louisiana Territory on the auction block—and get out of the messy New World real-estate business for good. All he needed was a willing buyer.

The third president of the United States had long been fascinated by the idea of finding a direct water route to the Pacific, of finding new commercial streams for American traders, and of diverting Indian interest from the British-Canadian fur trade. So it wasn't long before Napoleon Bonaparte and Thomas Jefferson cut a deal. By the time the treaty ink dried on April 30, 1803, the United States of America, still a few months shy of its twenty-seventh birthday, had scored the greatest real-estate coup in history.

For fifteen million dollars—thirty-three tons of solid silver—the Louisiana Purchase effectively doubled the size of the United States, instantly making the fledgling nation one of the world's largest. The newly acquired 529,920,000 acres, picked up for three cents an acre, sprawled from the Mississippi River to the Rocky Mountains, from Canada to the Gulf of Mexico. It was larger than Great Britain, France,

Germany, Italy, Spain, and Portugal combined, and would eventually comprise whole or parts of thirteen states. Within its 828,000 square miles lay endless swaths of prime forest and virgin prairie, vast deposits of valuable minerals, countless species of plants and wildlife.

Inside this expansive territory, there also lived dozens of Indian nations anchored to their lands, many clustered in villages along some of the tens of thousands of miles of creeks and streams and rivers. One of those rivers was well known to the father and son, to the people who had lived there for more than a century.

The Niobrara begins as a small stream in the high plains of Wyoming and flows clear and swift 535 miles east, growing steadily as it meanders across arid Sandhills, rugged canyons, rolling prairie, forests of pine and hardwood, and moist, fertile valleys before emptying into the Missouri near the high chalk bluffs. From source to mouth, it drains an area the size of New Jersey and Connecticut, and cuts through rock formations that include the fossilized remains of ancient beaver, horse, rhinoceros, and mastodon. At the time the father and son lived there, it is said that more timber flourished in the eastern sixty miles of the river valley than in all the rest of Nebraska.

The river is fed by an intricate network of springs, scores of waterfalls, the Ogallala Aquifer, and some 20,000 square miles of Sandhills. These undulating hills, the largest expanse of sandy dunes in North America, act as a giant sponge, absorbing rain and snowmelt, and storing it in underground reservoirs, which discharge the fresh water back into a lattice of tributaries and feeder streams. As a result, the river maintains a smooth, near-constant flow year round. The people called it *Ni obhatha ke*—Running Water.

In 1819, about ten years before the father was born, a U.S. Army explorer trekked through the general region on his way west. He labeled the lands between the Missouri and the Rockies "a region destined by the barrenness of its soil, the inhospitable character of its climate, and by other physical disadvantages to be the abode of perpetual desolation." He called it the "Great American Desert" and warned settlers it was foolish to try to live in such a dire wilderness. In the language of the father and son there was no word for wilderness, so their people would not have understood what Major Stephen Long meant. They had often gone as far as the Rockies and the Black Hills, had traveled the river's entire length, and when they looked up and down the Niobrara Valley, they saw the rich soil and fresh water, and the plant and animal life that had sustained them generation after generation.

In the river valley's central region, a subtle marriage of climate, geology, and topography, of moist air colliding with dry air, produces a kind of biological crossroads. In one thirty-mile stretch, six different ecosystems converge, sorting themselves out by variations in sunlight, soil, and moisture. Within a few miles, the people could pass through three kinds of forest—from eastern deciduous black walnut, cottonwood, and willow, to northern boreal oak, elm, and ash, to Rocky Mountain ponderosa pine. On moist terraces nearby, they could walk through tallgrass prairies of fertile bluestem, cross over to mixed-grass prairies on the north side of the river, and see the short-grass Sandhills prairie on the drier south side.

Then, as now, the unique blend of microclimates sustained some 160 plant and animal species—a distribution in which numerous western species reach their eastern limits along the river while eastern species reach their western limits. The diverse habitat supports Baltimore and Bullock's orioles, indigo and lazuli buntings, and yellow-shafted and red-shafted flickers. It nurtures white-tailed deer, wild turkey, pheasant, sharp-tailed grouse, mallards, blue-winged teal, and Canada geese. Some parts of the year, the river valley hosts whooping cranes, peregrine falcons, bald eagles, green herons, cormorants, and white pelicans. When the people lived there, nests of least terns and piping plovers were scattered on sandbars along the river, neighbors to numerous beaver and mink. At night, it was not unusual for thirty-pound channel catfish to emerge from holes in the deeper water to feed in riffles.

Today, the 100th Meridian splits the middle of the Niobrara River Valley—an imaginary line frequently used to distinguish between the eastern and western United States. Two centuries ago, a granite marker in the nation's capital noted the starting point for measuring the country's rapidly expanding boundaries. Back then, the line denoting the 1st meridian passed directly through the middle of the White House.

In 1804, the occupant of the White House was a restless, thoughtful, sixty-one-year-old lawyer and writer, a philosopher, amateur scientist, and accomplished architect who had long harbored dreams of a westward expansion. When he stood near the two-foot-high granite marker and looked west, past the Appalachians and his beloved Virginia, out toward the uncharted 828,000 square miles that lay beyond the Mississippi, the third president of the United States might well have imagined a place like the people's ancestral river homeland: one of ample water and timber, fertile soil, and abundant plant and wildlife—the type of place where a new kind of democracy could take hold.

At the core of Thomas Jefferson's vision for what the new nation might become was an almost mystical belief—nurtured by the ideals of the Enlightenment—in the powers of ordinary, everyday, salt-of-the-earth citizens. An aristocracy of talented citizens who could harness the young nation's potential, and build a new world order far removed from the detestable European monarchies of old.

Whenever his thoughts drifted west, Jefferson could envision the endless sprawl of sky and prairie, of river, valley, and forest as the working laboratory for his cherished notion of a new citizen-state. Here was the opportunity to build a democracy stripped of ceremonial splendor and centralized government, devoid of urban banking interests and crass industrialists. It would be a frugal republic shorn of bloated national debt and expensive standing armies, one that promised "equal and exact justice to all men, of whatever state or persuasion, religious, or political."

Jeffersonian Democracy would rest solidly upon two pillars: an educated citizenry and an agrarian society. A gentleman farmer and avid horticulturist, Jefferson devoutly believed informed tillers of the soil held the key to his country's future. "Educate the people generally," he had once said, "and tyranny and injustice will vanish like evil spirits at the dawn of day." Of agrarian virtue, he was equally certain. "Cultivators of the earth are the most valuable citizens," he had written in 1785. "They are the most vigorous, the most independent, the most virtuous, and they are tied to their country and wedded to its liberty and interests by the most lasting bonds." These new citizens would work on a neat grid of family farms sweeping from the Mississippi to the Rockies—the foundation for a stable, prosperous, industrious, moral America.

And now, as the new century began, most of the pieces were falling into place. Shortly after he assumed the presidency in 1801, Jefferson had tapped his friend and former Virginia neighbor to be his private secretary. Not long after, Meriwether Lewis moved into the White House and the two soon began brainstorming an expedition to the Pacific.

In January 1803, Jefferson secretly submitted his plan to Congress. Chief among the expedition's objectives, the president stressed, was to expand significantly the country's commercial opportunities. Expedition leaders would forge diplomatic ties with the various Indian nations and notify them that the United States had replaced France as their new ruler. By winning over the original inhabitants of the Upper Missouri, they would wrest control of the lucrative fur trade from the British and make American allies of the natives. They would also gather as much ethnographic information as possible and look for a water route to the Pacific. Congress approved $2,500 to finance the expedition and appointed Lewis to lead it. He in turn offered his friend, William Clark, the opportunity to walk into history.

On May 14, 1804, in a keelboat and two pirogues, the "Corps of Discovery" pulled out of St. Louis, leaned into the Missouri, and headed upstream. With the twenty-nine-year-old Lewis and thirty-three-year-old Clark leading the way, the eastern president's long-cherished dream was taking its first steps into western reality.

How exactly the people living in their Niobrara River homeland—and the many more like them—would come to share in this new reality had vexed the nation's leaders, including its third president, for a long time. For much of his life, Jefferson's views on the country's native inhabitants had swung back and forth, vacillating between soft, sentimental stereotypes and a hard-edged pragmatism.

As a romantic, he often viewed America's indigenous people as heroic, gifted orators, innocent children of the forest, unspoiled, and unwitting victims of history. He had known some of these people as a boy growing up in Albemarle County, Virginia, and loved the tales his father brought back from excursions into the wild. The young Jefferson excavated Indian mounds, was an avid student of Indian folklore and history, and spent countless hours collecting, cataloging, and studying Indian language and vocabularies. He had made it a point that Lewis and Clark, among their multitude of duties, were to return with linguistic records of each tribe they visited. And in his writings, Jefferson offered a more resolute defense of the nation's native people than all but a few of his contemporaries.

But over time, as president of a youthful, ambitious, expansionist nation, Jefferson came to view the noble savage differently. The native people possessed enormous tracts of land, land that needed to be transformed into a sturdy framework of industrious American farm families if the restless, young republic of four and a half million citizens was to fulfill its destiny. Jefferson had long advocated buying and settling Indian lands in an orderly, friendly, neighborly fashion. As far back as 1786, he had said, "It may be regarded as certain that not a foot of land will ever be taken from the Indians without their own consent. The sacredness of their rights is felt by all thinking persons in America, as much as in Europe."

Seventeen years later, on June 20, 1803, his formal instructions to Captain Lewis conveyed many of the same sentiments. "In all your intercourse with the natives," he wrote, "treat them in the most friendly & conciliatory manner which their own conduct will admit; allay all jealousies as to the object of your journey, satisfy them of its innocence, make them acquainted with the position, extent, character, peaceable & commercial dispositions of the U.S. . . . If a few of their influential chiefs, within practicable distance, wish to visit us, arrange such a visit with them . . . If any of them should wish to have some of their young people brought up with us, & taught such arts as may be useful to them, we will receive, instruct, and take care of them."

Converting wild, nomadic hunters into civilized, sedentary farmers offered natives the best chance to survive, Jefferson believed. In public remarks to his citizens, he had articulated those views clearly: "Now reduced within limits too narrow for the hunter's state, humanity enjoins us to teach them agriculture and the domestic arts, to encourage them to that industry which alone can enable them to maintain their place in existences and to prepare them in time for that state of society which to bodily comforts adds the improvement of the mind and morals."

In writing, he laid out, step by step, how such a transformation might occur:

> The plan of civilizing the Indians is undoubtedly a great improvement on the ancient and totally ineffectual one of beginning with religious missionaries. Our experience has shown that this must be the last step of the process. The following is what has been successful: 1st to raise cattle, etc., and thereby acquire a knowledge of the value of property; 2d, arithmetic, to calculate that value; 3d, writing, to keep accounts, and here they begin to enclose farms, and the men labor, the women spin and weave; 4th to read *Aesop's Fables* and *Robinson Crusoe* are their first delight.

Eventually, however, a sharp split developed between Jefferson's public and private views on the matter. Within the private confines of the White House, where romantic push evolved into pragmatic shove, he came to see the native people as an entrenched impediment in civilization's path—one that would have to be removed, ruthlessly if necessary, for Jeffersonian Democracy to prosper.

On February 27, 1803, two months before the Louisiana Purchase, more than a year before the Corps of Discovery left St. Louis, Jefferson wrote a long, detailed letter to William Henry Harrison, governor of the Indiana Territory. The governor, he said, had typically heard only the official, public version of the nation's Indian policy. "But this letter being unofficial, and private, I may with safety give you a more extensive view of our policy respecting the Indians."

The president began by stating that the goal of American policy was "to live in perpetual peace with the Indians, to cultivate an affectionate attachment from them, by everything just & liberal which we can offer them within the bounds of reason."

Then, in specific detail, Jefferson went on to tell the governor how to purge the eastern United States, one by one, of every remaining Indian tribe. Once they're lured onto a small piece of land "they will perceive how useless to them are their extensive forests," and want to give them up in exchange for government assistance to sustain their farms and families. High-pressure trading posts near Indian encampments, he said, would create debt to help leverage their lands. The government will "be glad to see the good and influential individuals among them run in debt, because we observe that when these debts get beyond what the individuals can pay, they become willing to lop them off by a cession of lands."

Gradually, Jefferson wrote, American settlements will squeeze natives out and they will "either incorporate with us as citizens of the United States or remove beyond the [Mississippi]." Resistance would be futile. "Should any tribe be fool-hardy enough to take up the hatchet at any time, the seizing the whole country of that tribe and driving them across the Missisipi [*sic*], as the only condition of peace, would be an example to others, and a furtherance of our final consolidation."

The sooner that consolidation was underway, he told the governor, the better. "The crisis is pressing. Whatever can now be obtained, must be obtained quickly. The occupation of New Orleans, hourly expected, by the French, is already felt like a breeze by the Indians. You know the sentiments they entertain of that nation."

In the next few years, often in secret meetings and private letters, Jefferson continued to push aggressively for the removal of all eastern tribes to the western lands. They could go voluntarily or involuntarily, but they had to go. Later, beginning with his Second Inaugural Address, he advocated that even lands west of the Mississippi were to be off-limits. In the end, the father of Indian removal came to believe that the ancestral inhabitants of the new republic either had to give up the old ways and adopt the new—or perish.

By then, Jefferson had long ago encountered the quagmire where philosophical theory met political reality. In theory, he had been an ardent, outspoken critic of slavery whose writings reflected moral outrage and indignation. But in reality, the staunch advocate of freedom and individual liberty maintained a large slave household. Eventually, he also reconciled his contradictory views on the Indian issue—views that would set in motion a century's worth of government policies that led to removal, reservations, reform, assimilation, and the end of one age-old way of life.

But in the spring of 1804, there was a vast, uncharted expanse between the Mississippi and the snowcapped western peaks to explore—and an opportunity to fulfill a presidential vision of what that land might become. Three years earlier, not long after taking office, Jefferson had conveyed it in a letter to his friend James Monroe. His dream, he wrote, was to look out one day and see an endless supply of rugged, self-sufficient citizen-farmers in such numbers they could cover "the whole northern, if not southern continent, with a people speaking the same language, governed in similar forms, and by similar laws."

By early autumn, the Corps of Discovery had pushed almost 850 miles up the nation's newly acquired river, its team of twenty-seven soldiers, several interpreters, a slave, a number of others, and the two captains struggling against the Missouri's stiff current by day and sleeping in wedge tents by night, alternating head to toe like sardines in a can.

Early on the morning of September 4, 1804, they arrived at a point where one river spilled into another, a point not far from high chalk bluffs and a broad, fertile valley. Clark noted in his journal:

> . . . this river is 152 yards wide at the mouth & 4 feet Deep Throwing out Sands like the Platt (only Corser) forming bars in its mouth, I went

up this river three miles to a butifull Plain on the upper side . . . this
river widens above its mouth and is devided by Sand and Islands, the
Current very rapid, not navigable for even Canoos without Great difficulty owing to its Sands; the colour like that of the Plat is light . . .

On that chilly, windy Tuesday more than two centuries ago, the explorers saw the Running Water for the first time and soon they would
view the village of the people who lived in the broad, fertile valley near
the confluence of the Niobrara and Missouri rivers. Although Jefferson
never met any of the natives, he might have been surprised by how much
he had in common with them. In a sense, they embodied many of the
qualities and embraced many of the values with which the nation's third
president now hoped to seed the western lands of the United States.

In the language of the father and son, the name of their people meant
"sacred head." By the time Lewis and Clark arrived, the Ponca were
gathered in a single village.

Inside their village, the women had built large, igloo-shaped earth
lodges, mostly of clay. The twenty-foot-long entryways ballooned into
thirty-four-foot-wide domed living rooms supported by a complex lattice of peeled cedar poles. Outside walls often were three feet thick at
the base and a foot-and-a-half on the roof, insulation for the scorching
summers and punishing winters of the Central Great Plains. Protecting
the cluster of village lodges on the perimeter was a wooden stockade
fashioned from cottonwood logs cut from dense groves along the river.

The Sacred Head People were avid horticulturists and dedicated
farmers. Outside the stockade, in rich bottomlands near the mouth of
the Niobrara, lay fields of squash, pumpkins, beans, tobacco, and a variety of corn. Beyond the fields, at river's edge, channel cat, carp,
bluegill, grass pickerel, and tributaries full of brown and rainbow trout
nourished the food supply. By the middle of the eighteenth century, the
Ponca had encountered the Comanche and began trading their bows
and arrows for Comanche horses. The horses eliminated the struggle to

run buffalo over a cliff, and soon the people had settled into a comfortable seasonal rhythm in their river valley homeland.

It began in late March and early April, when they planted their spring crops in the bottomlands ringing the main village. By late June, when the crops were in good shape, they packed up their tipis and left the earth lodge village, fanning out across the savannah for the summer buffalo hunt. Sometimes, they traveled as far west as the Black Hills, where the women and children stayed in Wind Cave while the men gathered elk and deer meat to supplement the buffalo, whose thin summer hides would become clothing, moccasins, and lodging. In late August and early September, the people returned to the mouth of the Niobrara to harvest their crops. Throughout the winter, smaller hunting parties went off for more buffalo, their meat now fatter, their thicker coats good for warm robes and bartering at the trading posts. By early spring, everyone returned to the village to help plant crops, and the cycle would begin anew. In between, there were trips south of the Platte for supplies of salt and visits to their friendly eastern neighbors, the Omaha and Otoe, and frequent jogs to the white fur-trading posts along the Missouri.

Over the years, as more and more French and Spanish came upriver, the Ponca began to learn a good deal about the new people. Among them, it had long been a point of pride that no one had ever killed a white man.

The Sacred Head People were considered fine horsemen and hunters and, from time to time, their war parties fought the Pawnee and powerful Lakota Sioux, traditional enemies bent on protecting their lands, their meat supply, and accumulating acts of valor in their raids on a smaller, weaker foe. But mostly, to the white fur traders and neighboring tribes, the Ponca were seen as friendly, industrious, self-sufficient, and trustworthy—a largely sedentary people, corn-growers who understood the rhythm of agriculture and possessed a vast knowledge of Niobrara plant and animal life.

But neither hunting and agricultural skills nor a sturdy stockade and plant knowledge could protect the Ponca from the pus-filled spots that began to cover them in the winter of 1800–1801. Before Lewis and

15

Clark embarked, the president had ordered them to bring smallpox medicine to the Indians and "instruct & encourage them in the use of it." But by the time the explorers arrived, it was too late for the Ponca—and many of the other tribes. A smallpox epidemic, fanned by the enclosed, clustered earth lodges, had swept through their village at the mouth of the Running Water three years earlier, ultimately wiping out half the tribe. The captain explorers described the Ponca as the "remnant of a nation once respectable in point of numbers." In the early September days of 1804, they estimated only about two hundred had survived.

Throughout large swaths of the open, arid Great Plains, prairie dogs had evolved to survive by living in colonies guarded by sentinels, thriving on grass and little water. Over time, pronghorn antelope developed keen eyes and hearing to detect predators, and large hearts and lungs to outrun them. With its shallow, flexible, widespread root system, the mesquite plant could survive little moisture and frequent fires.

Although the Ponca numbered no more than two hundred at the dawn of the nineteenth century, they, too, had long since adapted to the demands of the powerful plains landscape. They had lived in the Niobrara Valley a hundred years before the captain explorers arrived, and when disease consumed their enclosed villages, they began to rely on the tipi and tribal buffalo hunts. Despite the ravages of smallpox, the Ponca had become a sturdy, independent people, a close-knit tribe with an abundance of agricultural skills and a fierce will to survive.

Among them, in casual conversation, formal speeches, and at ceremonial events throughout their village along the river, it was not unusual to hear the same phrase—*Ne tah gau tha. Ne tah gau tha*—over and over. It was not unusual to hear "We want to live. We want to live."

In 1829, Jews were expelled from two Russian cities and the English Parliament granted religious freedom to Catholics. Andrew Jackson left for Washington on a steamboat to begin his presidency and Davy Crockett headed a congressional committee reviewing Tennessee's public land claims. After resigning as governor of Tennessee following an ugly marital breakup, Sam Houston became a citizen of the Cherokee Nation. The Tremont, the nation's first modern hotel, opened in Boston, and white rioters in Cincinnati drove out half the city's black population.

That same year, the father had been born along the banks of the Running Water. In the language of the Sacred Head People, he was called *Ma-chu-nah-zha*. By the time he was a young man, Standing Bear already saw that the old ways and new ways were on a collision course. In the years ahead it would be left to the Ponca chiefs to find a safe passageway through a new world order if the people were to survive. After all, the forces that were closing in were there for all to see. They had been building, decade after decade, throughout the first half of the nineteenth century.

Decimated by smallpox, and terrorized by Lakota war parties, the Ponca were forced to seek refuge with their friends the Omaha the winter after Lewis and Clark left. Eight years later, during the War of 1812, a number of Indian nations aligned themselves with Great Britain, greatly weakening American confidence in the fidelity of its native people. So when the war ended, the government renewed its efforts to win back their loyalty. On June 25, 1817, the Ponca signed the first of four treaties with the U.S. government, a treaty of perpetual peace and friendship, a treaty of mutual national recognition.

In October 1824, a group of thirty Ponca returning home from a friendly visit to another tribe was ambushed by the Brulé, one of seven sub-tribes of the Lakota. Only a dozen Ponca escaped. When the attack ended, all of their chiefs, mostly old men unable to flee, lay on the ground, including their head chief, Smoke Maker. Not long after, a government agent visited their village. The chief's distraught son came out to show him a medal the government had once given his father—a medal symbolizing the peace and protection the treaty had promised.

Months later, on June 9, 1825, the battered Ponca signed a second treaty. In exchange for Ponca acknowledgment of U.S. supremacy, the federal government again pledged to protect the Ponca, who also agreed the government had the right to control all trade with the tribe. In return, the United States promised to extend to the Ponca "such benefits and acts of kindness as may be convenient, and seem just and proper to the President of the United States."

By the 1830s, their village had become a regular stop for the crush of traders, frontiersmen, and artists steaming up the Missouri. George Catlin and Karl Bodmer both visited and left with canvasses of Ponca life and faces. In 1833, Prince Maximilian of Wied arrived and noted the aftermath of another smallpox epidemic two years earlier: "They formerly lived, like the Omahas, in clay huts, at the mouth of the river, but their powerful enemies, the Sioux and the Pawnees, destroyed their villages, and they have since adopted the mode of life of the former, living generally in tents made of skins, and changing their place from time to time."

Throughout Standing Bear's childhood, the squeeze from the Lakota to the west, an infusion of whites from the east, and the specter of disease all around never let up. Fifty years into the new century, the wild game began to rapidly disappear, and it wasn't long before the only buffalo on the plains lay in piles of bleached, white bones.

For Standing Bear, it was the beginning of many changes he could not have foreseen in a long life that would stretch through the rest of the century and into the next. Back then, the young man could not have known how his people would one day end up as trespassers on their river valley homeland—lands legally conveyed to them by the Great Father, then given away to the hated enemy without their knowledge or consent. He could not have imagined the cold steel at his back, the chains around his ankles, the dankness of the stockade, the swollen rivers they waded across in the spring, the coughing in the tents along the muddy bottoms of the Elkhorn, and the Christian ladies who would make his daughter's burial dress. Nor the summer flies and mosquitoes in the southern lands, and foraging for corn in the frozen fields of the north, chewing their moccasins, sleeping with the children in haystacks, and the bloody footprints they would leave on the agent's floor.

Back then, he could never have known about the Indian-fighting Army general who could no longer sleep, and the midnight message the general would deliver to the unusual newsman. About the bear-hunting frontier judge who had never cared for his people, and the silver-haired lawyer for the railroad that cut through all their lands. About all the church folk who would one day fill the wooden benches in the federal courthouse, where he would do what no other who looked like him had done before.

As a young man living along the Niobrara in the years when the buffalo first began to disappear, he could not have imagined the questions they would ask: Who was he? Where did he come from? Who were his people? What did they believe? Who was his god? Lawyers arguing about a constitution, amendments, legal rights, life, liberty, happiness, citizenship, equality, slaves, savages, false idols. How he would one day stand up and tell them about the color of blood.

And he could never have known the words of Bear Shield, just a boy of sixteen. What his only son would whisper to him that Christmas, lying in their tent, hidden among the trees along a river in another country. How the father, by fulfilling a promise, would force his captors to confront their own past, force them to provide a glimpse of what the future held for those who looked like him and the boy. For a brief moment in the last quarter of the nineteenth century, the aging chief of a small, obscure tribe from a remote river valley in a far corner of the Great Plains would hold up a mirror to the church elders and the prominent citizens, to the farmers and ranchers, to the teachers and generals and newspaper men, to all the judges and lawyers and senators and presidents and ask them: Who were they? What did they stand for? What were their values? What did they believe in? What did freedom and equality mean? What did it mean to be a Christian? To be an American?

Back then, there were a good many things the father and son could not have known before they began their long journey home, back to the high chalk bluffs near the banks of the Running Water.

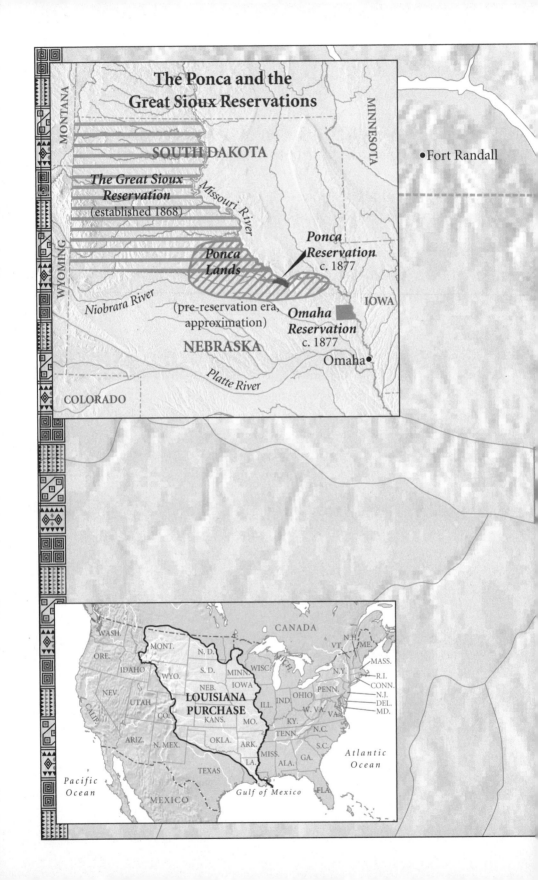

The Ponca and the
Great Sioux Reservations

MONTANA

MINNESOTA

SOUTH DAKOTA

The Great Sioux
Reservation
(established 1868)

Missouri River

•Fort Randall

WYOMING

Ponca
Lands

Ponca
Reservation
c. 1877

Niobrara River

(pre-reservation era,
approximation)

IOWA

Omaha
Reservation
c. 1877

NEBRASKA

COLORADO

Platte River

Omaha•

CANADA

WASH.

ORE.

IDAHO

MONT.

N. D.

WYO.

S. D.

MINN.

WISC.

MICH.

VT. N.H. ME.

N.Y.

MASS.
R.I.
CONN.

NEV.

UTAH

NEB.

IOWA

LOUISIANA
PURCHASE

ILL.

IND.

OHIO

PENN.

N.J.
DEL.
MD.

CALIF.

CO.

KANS.

MO.

KY.

W. VA.

VA.

ARIZ.

N. MEX.

OKLA.

ARK.

TENN.

N.C.

S.C.

Atlantic
Ocean

Pacific
Ocean

TEXAS

LA.

MISS.

ALA.

GA.

MEXICO

Gulf of Mexico

FLA.

The Niobrara Homeland
1877–1891

SOUTH DAKOTA

N
W E
S

Má-azì
(Ponca burial ground)

high chalk bluffs

Missouri River

Fish Smell Village
(until 1877)

Verdel

Ponca Creek

*Ponca's temporary
island home*

Niobrara

Niobrara River

Standing Bear's family
allotments after 1891

NEBRASKA

0   5 miles
0   5 kilometers

2

A Homeland Under Siege

Standing Bear could not believe it, could not believe what he now heard. Words that came like thunder from the distant chalk bluffs.

None of the people could comprehend the talk, the words of the interpreter. It was a frigid day, in the Moon When the Snow Drifts into the Tents. Without warning or notice, a strange white man from the East had appeared. Soon, his message spread through their villages clustered near the mouth of the Running Water: The Great Father wanted all of the Sacred Head People to move to another country: a place they had never heard of, far beyond the Platte River; far beyond the southern-most boundary of lands they had claimed as their own for generations. In the new country, the land and water were good. They would be safe and prosper. It would be best for them to go right away.

"We said to him: 'We do not know your authority. You have no right to move us till we have had council with the President . . . We do not wish to go,'" Standing Bear would say later.

"I Am a Man"

By late January 1877, when the white man from the East first arrived, Standing Bear and seven-hundred Ponca had abandoned their single encampment at Grey Blanket Village, gathering instead into two camps about five miles apart at the eastern end of their reservation. They were divided into nine bands, one chief for each band. White Eagle was the head chief. Standing Bear was second in command. His father, The Drum—or Old Drum as he was sometimes called—had been a chief and so Standing Bear, in the tradition of his people, had inherited the position, as would someday his young son, Bear Shield. The fundamental social unit of the tribe was the clan, a kinship group built along bloodlines, and each clan had a specific duty that helped maintain the quality of tribal life. For as long as anyone could remember, Standing Bear and his family had been members of the fifth clan—the Bear Clan. Each year, from the first winter frost until spring, the Bear Clan became the tribal leaders, responsible for overseeing the ceremonies, rituals, and social life of the camp.

The position of chief seemed a good fit for Standing Bear. He had shown leadership abilities at an early age and formidable powers later on. It is said his prayers once diverted a powerful storm that threatened to disrupt a sacred dance. Now near fifty, he had the bearing of a leader—sharp features, erect, dignified, square-jawed, thick through the shoulders and chest. During tribal celebrations and in everyday camp life, he frequently wore a bear claw necklace. The necklace usually was made and presented as a gift, often passed down from father to son, and it symbolized Standing Bear's power and tribal authority. The chief also had an easy grace, said those who knew him: a down-to-earth feel, a good-natured disposition.

Mark Peniska, the tribal chairman of Standing Bear's people in the early years of the twenty-first century, remembers hearing the stories from his grandfather. As a young boy, Grandpa Lee had met the old-man chief. "He always remarked about how outgoing and friendly he was. He had that common-man's touch, and because of that, people were naturally attracted to him. Plus, I guess he was a whale of a storyteller—even through an interpreter."

A Homeland Under Siege

Throughout much of the chief's life, his way with words had been an enduring trait, one noted by both his people and many of the white settlers surrounding their lands. Years earlier, one of their reservation agents had gotten to know him, and had sat in on a number of councils with the Ponca. He was "a very eloquent man, and very earnest speaker, and the well-wisher of his people," the agent said. "Standing Bear, in his speech—he was the most forcible speaker of the whole council, and I think the most eloquent of all the chiefs."

Standing Bear's first wife, Grae-da-we, had died about the time the great war between the North and South began. They had two daughters, one of whom—Prairie Flower—was now married and the mother of two young sons. Among his people, it was customary for a man to have one wife, but not unusual for a chief to have more than one. They had more duties, more obligations and responsibilities, and another wife could help with child-rearing, the cleaning and cooking, the extra meals, and the meetings and visitors that were daily events. The Ponca believed two wives would get along better if they were related, so, often the second wife was a blood relative of the first. By the winter of 1877, Standing Bear had two wives—Susette and her twenty-year-old niece, Lottie Primeau, who was French and Ponca. Susette was the mother of their only son, Bear Shield.

Standing Bear and his family all lived in frontier homes that had become commonplace in the Fish Smell Village, so named after a natural disaster one year killed many of the fish in the river and washed ashore many of the bodies. His family lived in a twenty-by-forty-foot log house made from trees he had cut with joints he had dovetailed for a sturdier structure. The family furnished their windowed, two-room home with two beds, two lamps, a table, a stack of dishes, and a stove Standing Bear bought for thirty dollars. Outside, he built a stable for his horses and a pen for his three hogs and two cows. His field was five-hundred yards long and he had acquired oxen, plows, harnesses, pitchforks, spades, and shovels. The fourteen-year-old Bear Shield often helped his father with the chores. More and more, the boy noticed, his father had taken to wearing white man's clothing—shoes, trousers, shirts, sometimes a hat.

Reflecting on the chief's homestead, the Ponca agent had forwarded a recent assessment of Standing Bear to his superiors in Washington: "He has always appeared to me to be a good man, and I think would make an excellent, even an exemplary, farmer if fair opportunities were offered, where there was no common enemy such as the Sioux to be dreaded."

On that bitterly cold winter day, January 24, 1877, United States Indian Inspector E. C. Kemble suddenly arrived with similar sentiments for the Sacred Head People. Among other things, he said, the Sioux would no longer be a problem in the new country far beyond the Platte. There, Standing Bear and the Ponca could farm in peace, on good land, protected by the government, far from their enemies in the North Country.

Two weeks earlier, Commissioner of Indian Affairs John Q. Smith had summoned Kemble to Washington where he received detailed written instructions on the government's plan for the Ponca. They were explicit:

> You are to proceed to the Ponca Agency, and after a conference with the United States agent, hold a council with the Indians upon the subject of their removal. You will give them to understand that their interests have been carefully considered, and that it is very desirous they should be established in a country where the circumstances of their self-improvement and maintenance, and the protection of person and property, are more favorable than in their present situation.

He told the inspector to feel out the Ponca about the new plan and, if they showed an interest, he was to take some of their leaders to the new country. There, they would look things over and select a new home. So, in mid-January, the inspector began making his way to the Niobrara.

Inspector Kemble, who lived at 228 East Fiftieth Street in New York City, knew little about Indians in general, even less about the Ponca specifically. Before becoming an Indian inspector, he had served two years as secretary of the Episcopal Church Commission. To bolster his shortcomings, Washington superiors ordered the Reverend Samuel Hinman, an Episcopal missionary at the nearby Santee Sioux Reservation, to accompany him to the Ponca Reservation. By then, it was not unusual to find missionaries scattered throughout Indian lands.

At the time of Kemble's visit, the United States had adopted a new approach to the Indian problem, one that came to be known as the Quaker, or Peace Policy. Championed by President Ulysses S. Grant, the policy was designed to eliminate rampant corruption in the Indian Bureau and to elevate the overall moral standing of its employees. Under the new plan, the Quakers and other Christian denominations would nominate agents to manage reservation affairs. The U.S. Army, meanwhile, would become the frontier's peacekeepers, protecting settlers from "marauding bands of hostile Indians," and confining tribes to their designated reservations. In the government's evolving flow chart, the President now got his information from the Secretary of the Interior, who got his from the Commissioner of Indian Affairs, who got his from the Indian inspectors, who, in turn, got their information from the church-based missionary agents.

At the time, the Reverend Hinman seemed like a logical choice to accompany Kemble. He had been a Santee missionary for a number of years and had lived among the Indians for seventeen years. He spoke both Sioux and Ponca and, for a while, Standing Bear's son, Bear Shield, had lived with the reverend and his family. Later, Episcopal officials kicked Hinman out of the church and off the reservation for embezzling and excessive drinking and for womanizing among his Santee flock.

But in late January, the reverend complied with the orders and accompanied the inspector to the Niobrara. Standing Bear and the other chiefs knew nothing about Inspector Kemble, the meeting in Washington, or the detailed written instructions. They knew nothing of any plan to move them to a new home. They were starting to make some progress in their old home and, after years of hardship, they were now eager to keep it going. They didn't want a place, Standing Bear said, "where we will be surrounded by Indians, and can not do as we want to—can not improve as we want to; we want to stay where we are surrounded by white people, where we can help ourselves."

Above all, the thought of leaving their homeland was unimaginable to the people. "We lived on our land as long as we can remember," the chief would later say. "No one knows how long ago we came here. The land was owned by the tribe as far back as memory goes."

When Standing Bear stepped outside his sturdy, two-room home in the winter days of January 1877, when he looked west across his frozen farm fields a mile south of the agency, he could imagine an ancestral homeland that once stretched five-hundred miles, from the Missouri to the Black Hills. What he saw now were a people who had adapted from earth lodge to tipi to wooden home, from the chase of the hunt to harvesting wheat, struggling to make it on a small parcel wedged between the Missouri and the Niobrara. Reflecting on the recent events of his own life, on the effort the tribe had made to survive those turbulent twenty years before the strange white man from the East suddenly appeared in their village, he must have found it hard to reconcile what had happened to the sprawling lands his people had lived on "as far back as memory goes."

Between 1778 and 1871, the United States entered into 374 formal treaties with Indian nations, treaties that had often reflected a fundamental arrangement: In exchange for large tracts of Indian land and safe passage for white settlers, the government set aside smaller tracts for tribes to live on and promised to provide food, clothing, shelter, and schools. If the Indians behaved, the government also pledged to protect them on their new lands, which they now legally occupied.

On March 12, 1858, with Lakota war parties an ominous threat, the buffalo disappearing, their people near starvation, the Ponca signed their third treaty with the government. In it, they gave up all claims to their remaining lands except for a small, isolated, hardscrabble tract a good deal west of their traditional homeland near the confluence of the Niobrara and the Missouri. On this new reservation, far removed from their old burial grounds and fertile cornfields, the government planned to "colonize and domesticate them." In exchange for most of their land, the government promised annuities for thirty years and $20,000 the first year to build homes, buy farming tools, and fence the land. The government also pledged a mill for their grain, another to saw timber, an interpreter, and a teacher to operate a school for ten years. And it promised to protect the Ponca in their new home against the chronic Lakota raids.

But there were problems from the beginning. The U.S. Senate took a year to act on the treaty, so none of the promised annuities arrived for more than eighteen months. While white settlers now farmed their fertile valley, the Ponca could coax little from the rocky, barren soil of their new lands. None of the farming tools arrived, there was no hay for their horses, and little timber. For heating fuel, they were forced to wait for the Niobrara to freeze over to cut trees on the river islands and haul the logs back to camp. When they went on a summer hunt, there were no buffalo. When they returned, the few crops they planted had failed. Their desperate agent managed to buy 500 sacks of flour, 180 pounds of beef, 100 sacks of sugar, 62 sacks of coffee, and 1,000 bushels of corn to keep them from starving in the winter of 1858.

The following summer, a large Lakota and Cheyenne war party, furious the Ponca had signed away their traditional lands to the government, laid waste to their hunting camp. They killed the Ponca's third-ranking chief, another chief, thirteen others, and kidnapped three children. Before leaving, they destroyed most of the Ponca tipis, drove off their ponies, burned their meat, and shredded their moccasins. When the survivors staggered back to their village, they asked the agent some questions: Why had the government failed them? Why were they not protected as the treaty promised? The sympathetic agent requested two companies of troops, but got no answer.

For Standing Bear and his people, the next decade proved even more disastrous. During four successive years, 1861 to 1864, their meager

29

crops and vegetable patches lay in ruins. What the drought didn't get, the grasshoppers did. Some families, who could now look out and see the sheep and cattle of the nearby white settlers, survived for days on half-dried corn stalks. Emergency government rations and surplus corn donated by the Omaha and Pawnee often kept them from starving.

With few horses, fewer guns, and Brulé Lakota war parties closing in, the people could no longer risk buffalo hunts. Often, they could not risk going out in their own fields. One spring, two women who had gone to plant seeds were found in the fields, both dead, both scalped. "When I go to my field, I have got to go with my rifle on my back; and when I work, I must keep one eye on my plow and one eye on those hills yonder," Standing Bear told their agent. "The Poncas have behaved well; quite as well, if not better than, under like circumstances, the same number of whites would have done," their agent reported. "If there are any Indians who deserve the charity of the government, the Poncas do." Although their pleas for protection continued, no government troops arrived.

On December 3, 1863, government troops encountered a small Ponca camp not far from their reservation. The hungry group of five Ponca women, five children, four men, and a young boy were returning home with a load of corn from their Omaha friends when some of the Seventh Iowa Cavalry arrived. At the time, while the Civil War occupied regular troops, groups of volunteer soldiers were paid to keep the frontier peace. The Seventh Iowa Cavalry was such a group.

That night, fifteen mounted Iowa soldiers rode into the camp, demanding to sleep with several of the women. Alarmed, the Ponca fled through the back of their tipis, escaping into the nearby woods. The soldiers destroyed the tipis, set their blankets and saddles on fire, shot up their cooking kettles, and threw away their corn. At dawn the next morning, the soldiers rode up while the same Ponca ate breakfast along the Niobrara. As one woman fled carrying her child, a trooper shot her in the side, the bullet lodging in the child's thigh. While she struggled to cross to the other side of the iced-over river, she was shot again. Not far away, two soldiers found a group of women and children hiding in the bush. They dismounted, walked up to the women, and shot three of them in the face. Then they turned their revolvers on a twelve-year-old girl, riddling her breasts at point-blank range.

When word reached their village, the outraged Ponca and their agent demanded an investigation into the murders of three women and a child, and compensation for their families. The governor of Dakota Territory said the Ponca should not have left their reservation without a pass. No arrests were made, no charges filed. In the official reports, it was described as "a very unfortunate occurrence." At the time, Indians had no standing in federal courts, no legal protection under state or territorial laws.

Still, the Ponca continued to honor the treaty of 1858. From the beginning, they tried to plant crops, lug timber from the river islands, get their sawmill up and running, build wood homes, educate their children, and get along with the government and white settlers. Year after year, their efforts were noted in government reports:

> Relying upon the ratification of their treaty and the adoption of timely measures to carry out its provisions in their favor, the Poncas proceeded, in good faith, to comply with its stipulations on their part by abandoning their settlements and hunting-grounds, and withdrawing to the small tract reserved for their future home . . .
>
> I cannot speak in too high terms of the uniform good conduct of this tribe. While many other Indians have been fighting the government and murdering the frontier settlers, this tribe and the Yankton Sioux have remained faithful to their treaty stipulations, and stood as a barrier between the hostile Indian and the white settler upon the frontier . . .
>
> The Poncas were peaceable and friendly people, disposed to be obedient, as they always were, to the President, and according to their knowledge willing and ready to work . . .

Years later, a U.S. Senate committee summed up twenty years of government contact with Standing Bear and his people:

In all accounts of the character of these Indians, and in all mention of them in official reports, they are described as among the most peaceful and quiet of all the Indians in the United States. Their disposition toward the United States has been uniformly friendly; they had never been known to cause trouble or disturbance, to make war upon the Indians or upon settlers; they were always ready to interfere between hostile Indians and the whites, and to ward off incursions of the Sioux and other wild Indians. They were deemed by the settlers on the Nebraska frontier as in some sense a defense to them . . . They cultivated the land, and many of them had farms of considerable size occupied in severalty, and altogether they presented one of the most encouraging and hopeful of all the fields for Indian improvement and self-support.

But each year throughout the first half of the 1860s, the pattern had remained the same: more drought, more grasshoppers, more tribes competing for fewer buffalo on shrinking lands, more hostile raids, more hunger, more desperation. And each year, Standing Bear and his people were forced to rely on the government for food and protection. Their only bargaining tool was what little remained of the ancestral homeland.

A few weeks before the Civil War ended, the Ponca signed their fourth and final treaty with the government. On March 19, 1865, a delegation of chiefs in Washington, D.C., agreed to give up 30,000 acres of their current reservation. As a reward for "their constant fidelity to the government and citizens," the Indian Office agreed to give them a new 96,000-acre reservation near the mouth of the Niobrara, their traditional homeland. The land they now legally occupied included their old burial grounds and cornfields. It also included several islands in the river.

Their new home also meant plenty of timber along the river and fresh meat from the large flocks of migratory waterfowl. Soon, the alluvial plain blossomed with grass and hay for the horses, and Ponca women nurtured robust crops in the fertile fields. The 1866 autumn harvest was bountiful enough that they gave the nearby Yankton Sioux a large share of their surplus corn. Eventually, buildings from the old agency were hauled to the new site where the high chalk bluffs and waterways offered better protection against the Lakota. And the nearby Missouri offered much easier access for the government-promised annuities.

But, again, it didn't last. Congress took almost two years to ratify the new treaty. Shortly after ratification, the annuities and government help pledged in the 1858 Treaty had reached their ten-year limit. There was no money left for the promised school, sawmills, harnesses, and plows, or the fencing to keep the horses and cows from eating their crops. As the 1860s wound down, severe hunger again stalked the seven-hundred Ponca in their two villages near the mouth of the Running Water.

In the years after the Civil War ended, the settlement of the West began in earnest. It wasn't long before the Great Plains was overrun with adventurers seeking fortunes in gold, mining, timber, hunting, ranching, and farming. In short order, large swaths of the grassland were plowed under and the prairie became a patchwork of telegraph lines and steel rails, cattle and barbed wire, more and more towns and villages, and an ever-expanding grid of ranches and farm homes—a prairie eventually swept clean of the once-vast buffalo herds.

To accomplish this, the government turned to the architects of the Union victory, men who could now apply Civil War battle skills to winning the West. Men who were often West Point graduates, and had distinguished themselves at Gettysburg, Shiloh, and Atlanta. Men who had some experience fighting Indians and had spent some time in the West. Men like George Crook. An 1852 West Point graduate, Crook had fought the Yakima in Washington Territory in the 1850s, before entering the Civil War as a brigadier general in command of an Ohio volunteer infantry regiment. Before the war ended, he had been at Antietam, led Union cavalry units at Chickamauga, and served under General Philip Sheridan in the Shenandoah campaign. But when he and the others crossed the Mississippi and headed west, they encountered a different kind of enemy.

"I Am a Man"

Year after year in the 1860s, from Minnesota to the Dakotas to Wyoming and Montana, government troops regularly clashed with a formidable adversary, a mobile confederation of superb horsemen, skilled fighters, and savvy chiefs who more than held their own in cavalry skirmishes. Most recently, the Lakota and their allies under Red Cloud and Crazy Horse had waged a relentless campaign against miners, settlers, the Army, and anyone else using a trail to Montana's gold fields that cut through the heart of their hunting grounds. On December 21, 1866, Crazy Horse led a decoy party that lured Captain William Fetterman and eighty men out of Fort Kearny, an outpost built to ensure safe passage along the Bozeman Trail. A few hours later, a larger force hidden in the hills slaughtered Fetterman and all his men.

On April 29, 1868, weary of the constant warfare, Lieutenant General William Tecumseh Sherman signed an historic treaty giving Red Cloud and the Lakota unprecedented concessions. The government, under the terms of the Fort Laramie Treaty, agreed to abandon its string of forts along the trail in exchange for peace. It also agreed to provide generous annuities of beef, flour, coffee, sugar, clothing, cooking utensils, and canvas tipis for each family. Most important, the treaty set aside the entire western half of South Dakota for the Lakota. The lands the Lakota now legally owned included their sacred Black Hills. They also included another 96,000 acres far to the east, lands near the mouth of the Running Water: They included the entire Ponca Reservation.

The Ponca had claimed these lands as their own "as far back as memory goes," lands they legally occupied according to a one-year-old treaty ratified by Congress. Now the lands had been given away to their larger, more powerful, more dangerous enemy, an enemy that had terrorized them for years for signing treaties with the whites. Unbeknownst to them, without notice or compensation, Standing Bear and his people had become trespassers on their own land—a development they would not be informed of until years later.

The Lakota had not asked for the Ponca land, didn't need or want it. But what the government later characterized as "a blunder" now gave the Lakota legal incentive to go after the smaller, weaker, peaceful tribe. So, for eight years, Lakota war parties, mostly Brulé, terrorized the besieged Ponca in their villages, destroying their crops, stealing their horses, slaughtering their livestock, killing and scalping the people whenever they could.

In early 1871, the Ponca had planted a good spring crop. The Lakota swept in and pulled up all of the corn, calling them women, saying they would not allow the Ponca to live like white people. In two treaties, the government had promised protection in exchange for Ponca land. But now the government had given away their land and furnished modern breech-loading rifles and ammunition to the enemy. When their agent pleaded with superiors to arm the Ponca for their protection, the requests were denied. There was not enough money for Ponca guns and ammunition. In the end, they were forced to go it alone.

And they did, year after year. In June 1873, a Brulé war party of more than two hundred came at them in two waves, one from the bluffs, another from down the Missouri. The Ponca drove them off. On another occasion, another two-hundred Brulé attacked their villages and were again driven away. "No other tribe on the continent would dare live where they did for a week," an Episcopal missionary reported.

During those years, despite the constant violence and state of fear, the Ponca kept trying to adapt to the changing world around them. They cut and hauled logs and helped build a church on their reservation and, more and more, began to attend church services regularly. The Reverend J. Owen Dorsey, an Episcopal missionary to the Ponca from 1871 to 1873, conducted the services. "The Indians were faithful in attendance upon service and shamed the whites. The morning service was held specially for them and they came in great numbers. I spoke in English. The afternoon service was designed for the whites and timed to suit their convenience; on an average not more than one employee was in attendance, sometimes two. . . ."

Still, no matter what they did or how hard they tried, the Ponca were always hungry. By the end of the summer of 1872, it had gotten so bad the commander of the local Army garrison dashed off an angry telegram on behalf of the Ponca. "Why they should be selected to

starve to death, while their hostile neighbors (the Sioux) are bounti-
fully fed and clothed is more than either the Poncas or I can understand," First Lieutenant Martin Hogan wired an Episcopal Church
official. "I found them with nothing to eat except boiled corn, and only
a sufficient supply of that to last them a few weeks. When that is gone,
unless something is done at once, they must and will starve to death . . .
The sin of the extermination of this people (if it must be) cannot be
laid to any parties connected with them here, and I sincerely hope that
it will be averted in time to save those who are responsible."

After a time, the constant raids and warfare, the hunger, isolation,
and sickness took a heavy toll.

In 1873, five years after his homeland had officially passed to the enemy, Standing Bear saw a people on the verge of annihilation. A people
who had not had a decent harvest in seven years. Who had no defense
against grasshoppers, drought, and hail. Who could no longer hunt
buffalo for fear of the Lakota. Who had lost most of their horses and
livestock in a spring snowstorm, and seen many of their buildings
swept away in a Missouri River flood. Who now walked around half-
naked, in tattered robes and blankets. He saw an impoverished people
overwhelmed by starvation and disease. That autumn, Standing Bear
could look out on the Missouri and see the steamships churning upriver, delivering food and weapons to the Lakota, fulfilling the promises of the Fort Laramie Treaty.

On November 6, 1873, their broken people desperate for a refuge,
the Ponca chiefs signed an agreement with the Omaha. In it, their old
friends, allies, and relatives agreed to sell part of their reservation to
the Ponca for a fair price. The agreement gave the Ponca a chance to
survive, to pull out of their villages and move farther south and east,
away from the constant Lakota raids. In Washington, the Commissioner of Indian Affairs strongly endorsed the plan. But not everyone
did. "The Nebraska Senators objected to that, saying they had Indians
enough already in Nebraska, and did not want any more," their agent

later explained. So the plan fell apart and, unbeknownst to the Ponca, a new one slowly began to take shape.

About two years later, the Ponca agent held two long councils with the chiefs. By the time the second one ended on September 23, 1875, Agent A. J. Carrier believed he had the consent of the chiefs to move their people south to the distant lands, ones far removed from the Lakota. When Standing Bear left the same council, he believed the agent had their consent to move his people only a short distance east, to join the Omaha on their lands.

As was often the case in such councils, a good deal depended upon the interpreters. The interpreter at the two councils, an Iowa Indian who lived among the Omaha, was a drunk and a troublemaker. The language barrier was another chronic issue, particularly when it came to conveying white concepts of geography. In the language of the Ponca, there was no word or phrase to describe the place where the agent said they had agreed to move, a place the government now intended to fill up with as many western tribes as possible. It was a place that didn't exist in the Ponca language and, at the time, it didn't exist in their minds. Nevertheless, the agent conveyed his version of the meeting to the Great Father, where it remained in limbo until about a year later, when another event quickly got it back on track.

By summer 1876, the nation was poised to celebrate its centennial. From Philadelphia to Washington, New York to Boston, the great cities of the East were flexing their patriotic muscle, unfurling flags, hanging bunting, building bleachers, warehousing confetti, lining up marching bands. Then, in late June, news began spreading like a fire across the open grassland about an incident along the banks of a remote river in the southeast corner of Montana Territory. About how George Armstrong Custer, the Civil War's impetuous boy-general, a national hero with presidential ambitions, had ridden out at dawn on the twenty-fifth, heading toward the river. And how later that day a group of half-naked savages armed with bows and arrows had taken on the world's finest cavalry, armed with the most modern weapons, and wiped out their commander and his five companies to the last man.

The Lakota had long been an intractable obstacle to westward expansion, and after Custer one thing seemed clear to the nation's leaders: The western territories could never be settled into a safe network of family farms and ranches until Sitting Bull and Crazy Horse and all of their followers were finally crushed, broken, and confined to reservations.

But the Lakota, a large and mobile nation, would require enormous amounts of food and goods to pacify. To deliver them by rail deep into western South Dakota was expensive. To deliver them by steamship along the Missouri's eastern edge, as far downriver as possible, was much cheaper. Businessmen in Yankton and Sioux City, with good contacts in the Indian Department, enthusiastically endorsed moving the Lakota to the Missouri, near where the Ponca lived on Ponca land, where the merchants would have a lucrative monopoly on furnishing the supplies. It wasn't long before plans were underway that excited the businessmen.

Seven weeks after the Little Bighorn, President Grant authorized $25,000 to move the Ponca from the Niobrara to the Indian Territory, lands that would one day become Oklahoma. This could be legally done, the act decreed, only "with the consent of said band." The Ponca were never consulted or informed of the public initiative, one that was quietly slipped into the Indian Department's annual spending bill.

Not long after the Lakota had taken out Custer, Spotted Tail and some of the other Brulé chiefs who had tormented the Ponca for years arrived on the Niobrara. They told Standing Bear and the Ponca chiefs they did not want their land, did not want any more warfare between the two tribes. So in July 1876, the Lakota and Ponca—unbeknownst to the government—signed a formal treaty, agreeing to live in peace, the Brulé on their lands, the Ponca on theirs. The two tribes would find a way to bury the past, so they could survive in the future.

Rosetta Le Clair knows the story of her people, understands what the different generations have had to do to survive. A member of the Buffalo Clan, she graduated from Haskell Indian School, married, raised a family and then, twenty years older than her classmates, began taking notes in college classrooms. After getting her degree, she started her own cement-finishing business. Today, at eighty, Grandma Rosetta, as she is called, lives alone, hundreds of miles south of the Niobrara, on property her family has had for more than a century. She's a Sun Dancer, attends all the annual powwows, and often conducts classes to teach the younger ones how to bead. She has heard the stories of her people many times and wants them to endure long after her. So she climbs in her Dodge Intrepid and drives to North Carolina for a conference, to Ohio for a workshop, to Illinois to speak to college students about history, about survival.

"All our fights were for survival, for hunting grounds, for good water, for timber. I have a Sioux scalp buried on my property, passed down by my family. It used to hang in my grandfather's house. My grandpa killed a Sioux and scalped him. But my grandmother told me, 'Bury it. Let it go back to dust.'"

By burying their past with the Lakota, Standing Bear and his people felt a renewed sense of hope in the late fall and early winter of 1876. Two government treaties said the Ponca still had legal claim to their land. The Brulé didn't want the land and had offered to give it back. The two tribes had signed a friendship treaty, pledging to let one another live in peace. No Ponca had ever consented to leave the Niobrara for distant lands. The local newspaper had begun to praise the Ponca as good neighbors and white settlers wanted them as a protective buffer against the dangerous Lakota. And many others continued to praise Ponca efforts to adapt and survive along the banks of their river homeland.

James Stevenson had spent a good share of his adult life in the American West, mostly as an Army colonel assigned to various research expeditions studying Indian character, history, manners, customs, culture, and language. During his career with natural history departments and the Smithsonian Institution, the ethnographer visited about sixty Indian tribes, including the Ponca. He described them as an industrious, self-sufficient, sober, law-abiding, and physically robust people who had an unusually strong attachment to their homeland. A people ideally suited to adapt from nomadic hunters to stable farmers. "I am very confident that, with ordinary management, they will rise in the scale of civilization quite readily and rapidly . . . they are naturally inclined to learn, and are disposed to cultivate the soil; and one of the most important and promising features in connection with these people is, that they are disposed to live together in permanent villages," Stevenson said after several summers spent observing the Ponca.

All in all, the Ponca had survived two difficult decades and by late 1876, their plans for better days seemed to rest solidly on the sturdy homes and fertile soil of their homeland. Back then, they couldn't know that other plans had gained too much momentum, had gone too far downriver, to be turned back.

William H. Hare, bishop of the Episcopal Church at the nearby Yankton Agency, had known the Ponca for a number of years, had visited them often, and observed their treatment. That fall, when he looked at the events unfolding in the winter after Custer, he saw a different picture than Standing Bear, one that he summed up a few years later. "It is the weak point in the government's treatment of the Indians; they themselves often say, the better they are the worse they are treated by the Great Father. Those who kill are well treated, while peaceable and good Indians are neglected."

Two days after he arrived, the strange white man gathered all the Ponca chiefs in the reservation church. During three council meetings on January 26 and 27, 1877, Inspector Kemble laid out the Great Father's plans. Seated by him were the Ponca agent, James Lawrence, the Reverend Hinman, and two mixed-blood interpreters. With each translation, the Ponca were more and more startled, more and more alarmed. Over and over, they said they had only agreed to move a short distance to their friends and relatives, the Omaha. They made it clear they did not want to hear about leaving for a new, faraway place, wanted nothing to do with what they now heard.

"It came on us like a thunder-clap," Standing Bear said. "We did not have any knowledge of what they had come there to say. All of a sudden they said, 'Pack up; the President says you must move.' . . . Where shall we go? The land all around us is covered with people. I said, 'This is our land; we were born here; we have lived here all our lives till now; we are growing old here, and we had hoped to die here.'"

White Eagle, the head chief, said he did not believe the Great Father would decide to move them without consulting the people first. He told the inspector they needed more time to think about it, to pray and ask for guidance. "Although I am an Indian," he said, "I want to tell God all about this before I do anything more. I want to know and see for myself what I had better do. I want to ask God to help me decide." The inspector said there was no time to waste, the decision had already been made. "The President told me to take you to the Indian Territory, and I have both hands full of the money which it will require to move you down there. When the President says anything it must be done. Everything is settled, and it is just the same as though you were there already."

White Eagle persisted:

The President told me to work, and I have done it. He told me not to go on the warpath, even if the white men took away my horses and cattle, or killed my people. I promised I would not, and I have performed my promise. Although other people often move from place to place, yet I have always stayed on our land. It is ours. My people have lived and died on this land as far back as we can remember. I have sown wheat and planted corn and have performed all my promises to the President. I have raised enough on my farm to support myself, and now it seems just as though the government were trying to drown me when he takes my land away from me. We have always been peaceful. The land is our own. We do not want to part with it. I have broken no treaties, and the President has no right to take it from me.

Eventually, the chiefs softened. The people did not agree, but the chiefs said they would at least go down to the other place and take a look. That's all. And they signed a paper that said as much. "That was the agreement," Standing Bear said. "That if we did not like the land we could tell the President so, and if we did like it we could tell the President so." At the end of the second meeting, the inspector telegraphed Washington. The Ponca would give up their reservation, he said, if ten chiefs could look at the Territory, were pleased with it, and could come to Washington to finish negotiations. Washington replied: The chiefs could come to see the Great Father only if they had already agreed on a new home and only if minor details remained.

As was often the case, it had been a confusing council. "Hardly one interpreter in a hundred is competent to interpret such language as you must necessarily use in a treaty or negotiation," the Reverend Hinman said later. And the competency of the two mixed-blood interpreters at the councils had long been a concern. One agent described them as "desperate characters; men of exceedingly bad reputation and habits." Nevertheless, when the final council meeting ended, the Ponca were not confused. They had agreed to go down and look at the land, and they intended to keep their word. "All the chiefs talked together, and said to each other, 'There can be no harm in going down and seeing the land, and if we don't like it we won't take it,'" Standing Bear said.

The next day, and from that day on, Inspector Kemble began to see it differently. He began to imply what his superiors were eager to hear—they had a deal. By agreeing to go down and look for a new home, he told his bosses, the Ponca had already consented to giving up their old one. All that remained now was to pick out a site. The inspector promised he would personally help the Ponca find a choice spot. He had been to the Indian Territory. There was plenty of good land there. Nothing would be left to chance. "I would sooner put my hand in the fire and burn it off," he said, "than to lead them into a country where there were swamps and disease, and where the climate was bad."

They left on February 2, 1877. Standing Bear, White Eagle, and the eight other chiefs rode in wagons from their Niobrara home, arriving in Yankton, South Dakota, two days later. There, at the request of the chiefs, Inspector Kemble bought civilized clothing to replace "all their native toggery." In Yankton, the inspector, the Ponca agent, and the ten chiefs boarded a train for Independence City, a small town in southeastern Kansas, where they took wagons for the final push into Indian Territory. Throughout the last leg in the open wagons, the wind and rain were relentless, the roads thick with mud. The large Ponca men jolted the wagons to their bumpers, bouncing roughly along the rutted roads. That night, at a shelter on the edge of the Territory, the chiefs stared glumly into the campfire. They left early the next morning for the Osage Reservation, passing through flat, sandy lands covered with rocks, the wind and rain turning colder.

They arrived among the Osage, their friends and relatives from centuries ago, about mid-afternoon, February 9. The Osage agent and all the chiefs were gone. No one had told them the Ponca chiefs were coming, so no arrangements had been made. No welcoming ceremony, no feasting, no exchange of gifts as was the custom. In the morning, it began to rain and blow harder, the rain turning to sleet off and on for the next four days. White Eagle was sick. He lay on the floor wrapped in his blanket, unable to move. The other chiefs looked out on the broken, stony land, and they looked hard at the people living on it. They were "without shirts; their skins were burnt, and their hair stood up as if it had not been combed since they were children. We did not wish to sink as low as they seemed to be," Standing Bear recalled. They waited a few days, then turned the wagons west to see the lands of the Kaw.

The Kaw were friendly and the Ponca chiefs spoke to them in the Kaw language. The Kaw chiefs offered the Ponca some of their land, said they could come down and live with them, as they had generations ago on the other side of the Mississippi. The chiefs saw the land of the Kaw was strewn with rocks, and they could see the river bottoms that gave rise to the sickness. Soon, they headed toward Arkansas City, a small town in Kansas just a few miles north of the Territory. When they arrived, Standing Bear spoke with several Pawnee. They told him the Territory had been hard on their people. They were poor, destitute, the climate unhealthy. Many were sick with the fever and chills. Since they came, malaria had wiped out half the tribe. And most of their horses had died.

By nightfall, Standing Bear and the Ponca chiefs had seen enough. On the evening of February 19, at their hotel in Arkansas City, they told Inspector Kemble and their agent they didn't like any of the land they had seen. They wanted to go to Washington and tell the president. The inspector said, no, they could not do that. They must first choose a new home in the Territory and agree to give up their old reservation to the government. Then they could go.

"They tried to make us say 'yes,' but we would not," Standing Bear said. "When we refused, they went out and slammed the door as hard as they could. After a while, they came back, and said, 'Hurry up and settle, and be quick about it, too.' We said to him, 'How shall we settle? In what way? We have already said we won't have either of these pieces of land that you have shown us. Now take us to Washington, as you said you would.' They just said again, 'Be quick, show yourselves brave, act like men.' "

The chiefs said no, the land was bad. They did not like it and they would not take it. They said they were tired and sick and homesick.

They asked the interpreter to tell the inspector, "If you won't take us to Washington, then take us home."

The inspector said no, he had no authority to do that.

Then give us some of the money set aside for our journey. We will take the train.

No, the inspector would not do that.

Then go tell him to give us a pass, a little money for food, a map to show us the way.

The interpreter knocked on their hotel door. No, there would be no pass.

No money for the train, for food. No map. Nothing.

"In dealing with Indians," the inspector later explained, "we must sometimes do as we do in dealing with children—must make allowances for peculiarities, such as childishness and indifference to their own welfare, and may have to decide for them what is best for them, and exercise a sort of peremptory influence over them, in order to bring them to see things correctly . . . as white men see them."

That night, the ten Ponca chiefs huddled in a hotel room, unsure what to do. After a while, Standing Bear said, "Let us start for home; although we do not know the road, let us go, anyway." Some of the chiefs argued to wait until morning, until it was light, to begin walking back to the Niobrara. White Eagle was still sick. So was another. Two others, the mixed-blood chiefs, were old men, both nearly blind. They decided to leave the two old-men chiefs behind, to stay with the inspector and the agent. The eight others would leave in the night.

About 8 P.M., the interpreter knocked on the inspector's door. "Well, sir, they have gone, as sure as shooting; the Indians have gone."

Ahead lay hundreds of miles of open prairie, frozen rivers and creek beds, snow and harsh winds. Lands they did not know, inhabited by strangers whose language they did not speak. They found the railroad depot and started walking, north to Wichita, sixty miles down the tracks. The two sick chiefs struggled to keep up and so they did not get far that first night. At dawn, they started again, but they were too weak and made it only a short distance the next day. They stopped along the way and sold a few tomahawks and some of their red clay pipes and pooled their pocket change until they had eight dollars and kept walking. After several more days, they made it to Wichita. They found a man at the depot who spoke Sioux, and they offered him some of their moccasins and the eight dollars for train tickets. He said if they came back early the next morning, they could ride for free. When the chiefs arrived, he had a message: "This man who brought you down here has sent me a letter in which he says that I must not take you on the cars, or let you go at all."

The day after the chiefs left, the inspector had telegraphed his superiors: "If their insubordinate chiefs are permitted to return to their people, there will be an end to all discipline among them, or to any control of the tribe by their agent. They should be arrested and held as prisoners at Fort Leavenworth, until such time as they shall consent to yield obedience to the orders of their agent. They have had no cause for their insubordination, having been treated with the greatest consideration and kindness since they left their homes." The message had been relayed to all the depots in the area and so the chiefs kept walking.

They left Wichita, heading north through Kansas, following the tracks as much as possible. Across the lands they traveled it had been a harsh winter, seventeen below zero one morning, six below on three others. "At night we slept in wheat-stacks; we crawled in among the straw and kept warm," Standing Bear said. "Our moccasins all wore out, and the soles of our feet got sore . . . the weather was cold . . . and some nights we nearly froze to death." In the frozen fields, they rummaged for hard corn by day and roasted it over open fires at night. One day, they met a Frenchman who welcomed them and let them stay overnight. He gave them loaves of bread, potatoes, butter, and a good supply of coffee. In the morning, he fed them breakfast and they left, walking north, into the winter wind. They walked three more days and arrived at a small town. They met a young white man there who spoke the Kaw language. He told them they were on the wrong road, that if they followed the railroad tracks they would find the Otoe Reservation at the end of the line. Some were barefoot now.

Eighteen days after leaving the inspector, they reached the Otoe Reservation, fertile lands spread across the valley of the Big Blue River straddling the Kansas-Nebraska border. The Otoe agent, Jesse Griest, watched them come through the agency door and into his office. He saw the bloody footprints on the floor and he and the Otoe took pity on them. The chiefs were too weak to walk, so they ate and rested for several days and afterwards, they made small gifts of their remaining tomahawks and beaded blankets. The Otoe gave each of them a horse and in mid-March they rode north, toward the Niobrara. They crossed the Platte three days later and after camping awhile, they rode on, heading for their old friends and relatives. They hit a late spring blizzard of blinding snow and heavy drifts that lasted several days, but they kept going, arriving at the Omaha Reservation in late March.

They were near starvation, discolored from frostbite, many of them sick. The Omaha took them in and when they had rested, Standing Bear told the story of their trip to the Indian Territory and their journey home and asked if they could help them so their land would not be taken from them. The Omaha missionary said he would copy down their story and send a telegram to President Rutherford Hayes. It would cost $6.25. The Ponca said they had no money. An Omaha man said he would pay. So on March 27, Standing Bear, several other chiefs, and the Reverend William Hamilton crossed the Missouri to Sloan, Iowa, and sent a telegram signed by the eight chiefs:

To the President of the United States, Washington, D.C.:

Did you authorize the man you sent to take us down to the Indian Territory to select a place for our future home to leave us there to find our way back as best we could, if we did not agree to go down there? This he told us, and left us without a pass, interpreter, or money, because we could not select one of three places, telling us that if we did not go there peaceably we would be driven by soldiers at the point of the bayonet from our present homes. We were so left, and have been thirty days getting back as far as the Omahas, hungry, tired, shoeless, footsore, and sad at heart. Please answer at once, for we are in trouble.

No reply came. After three days, most of the chiefs gave their horses to the Omaha, then turned north and west, walking the last forty miles home.

Standing Bear was not among them. On March 30, after waiting for the President to reply, he went farther up the Missouri, to the offices of the *Sioux City Daily Journal*. He brought with him a letter, written with the help of some of his Omaha friends, recounting what had happened since the chiefs left the Niobrara. The editor published the letter the next day, calling the plight of the Ponca "a story which has engaged considerable attention already, and which will engage considerable more if there are any persons in this country who believe that every human being, however humble, is entitled to the same justice claimed for themselves." After dropping off the letter, Standing Bear turned west and began walking toward the high chalk bluffs.

The Ponca chiefs didn't know that the inspector and his superiors had also exchanged a number of telegrams during the long walk back. The morning after the chiefs left their hotel room, the inspector left for Independence City. There, on February 23, he sent a telegram to his boss, the Commissioner of Indian Affairs: "Important to know at once if department will insist on removal of Poncas, even if they should withdraw their consent."

That same day, he received a response: "Removal of the Poncas will be insisted upon. Spotted Tail and Red Cloud must move this summer to Missouri River. Their presence will render further stay of Poncas at old location impossible."

Standing Bear and the seven Ponca chiefs had wandered across the frozen frontier wilderness for more than forty days and nights, crossing nine rivers and covering more than five-hundred miles to return to their home on the banks of the Running Water.

When they arrived back in their villages on April 2, 1877, Inspector Kemble was waiting.

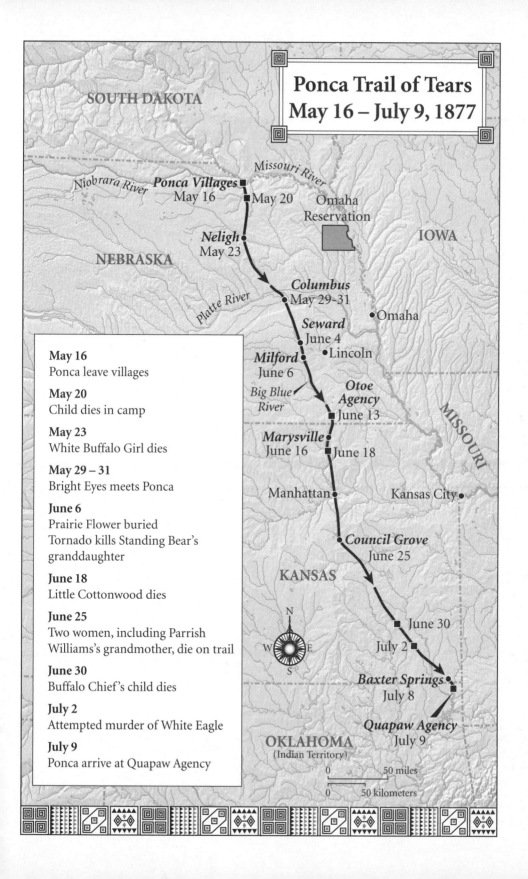

Ponca Trail of Tears
May 16 – July 9, 1877

SOUTH DAKOTA

Niobrara River
Ponca Villages
May 16
Missouri River
May 20

Omaha
Reservation

IOWA

Neligh
May 23

NEBRASKA

Platte River

Columbus
May 29–31

Seward
June 4
•Lincoln

•Omaha

Milford
June 6

Big Blue
River

**Otoe
Agency**
June 13

MISSOURI

Marysville
June 16   June 18

Manhattan•

Kansas City•

Council Grove
June 25

KANSAS

■ June 30

N
W   E
S

July 2 ■

Baxter Springs
July 8

Quapaw Agency
July 9

OKLAHOMA
(Indian Territory)

0   50 miles
0   50 kilometers

May 16
Ponca leave villages

May 20
Child dies in camp

May 23
White Buffalo Girl dies

May 29 – 31
Bright Eyes meets Ponca

June 6
Prairie Flower buried
Tornado kills Standing Bear's
granddaughter

June 18
Little Cottonwood dies

June 25
Two women, including Parrish
Williams's grandmother, die on trail

June 30
Buffalo Chief's child dies

July 2
Attempted murder of White Eagle

July 9
Ponca arrive at Quapaw Agency

Swiss painter Karl Bodmer captured the sacred chalk bluffs near the traditional Ponca village during an extended visit to the American West in the 1830s. *Courtesy of Joslyn Art Museum*

Standing Bear, seen here in a formal portrait taken in 1877 in Washington, D.C. *Courtesy of Nebraska State Historical Society*

Bright Eyes (Susette La Flesche) and her younger brother Woodworker (Francis La Flesche) as they appeared about the time of the 1879 East Coast speaking tour. *Courtesy of Nebraska State Historical Society*

White Eagle, the head chief of all the Ponca. *Courtesy of Nebraska State Historical Society*

Standing Bear, not long before his death in 1908, beside his home. *Courtesy of Nebraska State Historical Society*

Boston Daily Advertiser, November 3, 1879. The plight of Standing Bear and the Ponca set off a vigorous debate on the legal status of Native Americans—a debate reflected in the extensive coverage many of the nation's prominent newspapers devoted to Standing Bear's trial and his East Coast speaking tour.

The ten Ponca chiefs were photographed in November 1877 during a visit to Washington, D.C. Standing Bear is seated third from left, his brother Big Snake is standing far left. *Courtesy of Nebraska State Historical Society*

Brigadier General George Crook.
*Courtesy of Nebraska State
Historical Society*

THE PONCAS VICTORIOUS.

JUDGE DUNDY DECIDES THAT THEY ARE WRONGFULLY RESTRAINED OF LIBERTY.

OMAHA, Neb., May 13.—Some weeks ago H. Tibbles, assistant editor of the Omaha *Herald*, engaged counsel to sue out a writ of habeas corpus to release Standing Bear and his party, who were being returned to the Indian Territory by military force, having fled therefrom on account of sickness which was rapidly exterminating the tribe. J. L. Webster and A. J. Poppleton argued the case for the Indians without fee.

The New York Times, May 14, 1879.

U.S. senator Henry Dawes. *Courtesy of Nebraska State Historical Society*

Judge Elmer S. Dundy. *Courtesy of Nebraska State Historical Society*

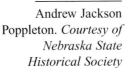

District attorney Genio Lambertson. *Courtesy of Nebraska State Historical Society*

Andrew Jackson Poppleton. *Courtesy of Nebraska State Historical Society*

Attorney John Lee Webster. *Courtesy of Nebraska State Historical Society*

Thomas Henry Tibbles. *Courtesy of Nebraska State Historical Society*

FOR THE PONCA INDIANS

THE SPEECHES IN STEINWAY HALL.

STANDING BEAR AND BRIGHT EYES TELL WHAT THEY KNOW ABOUT TREATIES— OTHER ADDRESSES.

The New York Times, December 13, 1879.

Standing Bear and his wife, Susette, are shown here with their orphaned grandson, Walk in the Wind, in 1877. *Courtesy of Nebraska State Historical Society*

Rosetta Le Clair and Parrish Williams stand on the porch of Williams's cabin in the woods outside Ponca City, Oklahoma. *Courtesy of Kyle Wyatt*

A towering bronze statue of Standing Bear rises against the backdrop of a sprawling oil refinery in Ponca City, Oklahoma. *Courtesy of Kyle Wyatt*

THE ABORIGINES.

Mass-Meeting in Their Interest at Farwell Hall.

Speeches by the Rev. Drs. Mitchell and Goodwin and Gen. Leake.

T. H. Tibbles, of Omaha, Relates His Experience with the Poncas.

The Chicago Tribune, July 1, 1879.

The first casualty along the Ponca Trail of Tears was White Buffalo Girl, a baby who died of pneumonia four days into the journey. At her grave site, her father begged local residents to treat his infant daughter's grave as though it were one of their own. For more than 130 years, the citizens of Neligh, Nebraska, and surrounding communities have honored his request by decorating her grave with flowers year-round. *Courtesy of Kyle Wyatt*

This ancient cottonwood tree stands at the site of the old Fish Smell village, the place where a government agent first informed the Ponca they would have to leave their beloved homeland for the Indian Territory. *Courtesy of Michael Farrell*

The Niobrara River was the main artery of the Ponca homeland. Only empty stomachs and soldier guns at their backs forced them from it. *Courtesy of Michael Farrell*

3

The People Turn Their Faces South

In the early spring of 1877, the white farmers and ranchers heard it for a long time. From their homes along the river valley, they could hear the sobs and wailing that came each night from the two villages below the high chalk bluffs near the Running Water.

For a while that spring, the women and children who had hidden in the woods during the day returned at night and stayed behind the locked doors of their homes, homes that closely resembled those of their white neighbors. Like Standing Bear's, they were homes the people had built themselves, from trees they had cut themselves and logs they had sawed into lumber at the reservation mill. They cut windows into the walls and, over time, furnished the rooms with heating stoves, dishes and plates, beds, tables, and chairs. By then, a good many of the seven-hundred Ponca living in the two villages had their own livestock, had acquired wagons, plows, harnesses, and some oxen to work their fields, and they had recently sold some of the surplus corn and wheat to their neighbors.

They had their own schoolhouse, their own Episcopal church, a minister, and many were now dressed in the same kind of clothing as their white neighbors.

That spring, Inspector Kemble was in a hurry to make it back to the villages before the eight chiefs. He knew the government had long ago given the same land to two different people. He knew one of them had to go. And he knew there wasn't much time. He had already gotten the word from Washington: The Lakota were moving to the Missouri in a few months. On February 27, 1877, as he rushed back to the Niobrara, another telegram arrived at his hotel in St. Joseph, Missouri: "Proceed to Ponca Agency and remove Indians without delay to Kaw Reservation." He told his superiors the Quapaw Reservation would be a better fit and he asked for permission to move the Ponca there instead. On March 7, the day the eight chiefs bloodied the Otoe agent's floor, he received a reply: "You have full authority to remove the Poncas to Quapaw Reservation."

Now it was official. He had his orders. He knew what would happen when the chiefs returned, what they would say to their people about the new country, the other things they would say, and so he wanted to get it moving, get it going as quickly as he could. The government was counting on him. The businessmen were counting on him. He made it back to the Niobrara three weeks before the chiefs.

Shortly after arriving, he sent the interpreters, two mixed-blood brothers with a history of whiskey trouble, into the villages. "Hurry and pack up. Be quick. Get ready and move." The people were frightened, confused. Some were angry and some panicked. They didn't know what to do. They said to the inspector: "We want to know all about this. Our chiefs were to attend to this matter for us. You took them away. What have you done with them? What has become of them?"

Day after day, the interpreters kept it up throughout the upper and lower villages, repeating the inspector's message again and again: You must move now. Gather your things and put them in the wagons: "If you don't hurry and move up, the soldiers will shoot you." Each day, the people became more afraid, more confused, angrier, unsure where to turn. Where were the chiefs? What had happened to them? The women and children took it the hardest. The white neighbors could hear them in the night and they, too, became alarmed. A few began to write letters and send telegrams to Washington, asking what was going on, what was happening to the people in the two villages.

The upper village was mostly mixed-bloods, about one-fourth of the tribe, who lived near the agency headquarters. Standing Bear and the full-bloods lived in the larger lower village near the mouth of the Niobrara. After a while, some of the mixed-bloods began to load up a few of their belongings. It disgusted the full-bloods who refused to obey the inspector's orders. "We will not put our things in the wagons," they said to the interpreters. "We will not let anybody else put them in. We will lock our doors. And if they get our things at all they will have to break open our doors."

Standing Bear's brother, Big Snake, spoke for the full-bloods. Large, stern, and barrel-chested, he was the soldier chief, the head of the military society, his strength and power feared and respected in both villages. He told the interpreters the people would not leave their homeland. They had no intention of packing up, of abandoning a place that was legally theirs for a place they knew nothing about. He wanted to make sure the inspector understood, so he paid him a personal visit. "I want you to get off from this reservation. Drop your words on the land here, and go across the river." The inspector was a little shaken.

By late March, the sentiments of some of the white settlers began to cross some of the desks in Washington. On March 27, the Commissioner of Indian Affairs sent a telegram. He, too, was a little shaken, unsure he was on solid ground. He wanted reassurance, wanted to hear from his agent in the field that the Ponca removal was proceeding properly, unfolding within the law. His telegram ended with two sentences: "Have they fully consented to go? Such consent must be obtained." Inspector Kemble replied a few hours later. The Ponca, he told superiors, had given "their unequivocal consent." The two old, blind, mixed-blood chiefs had consented, he would later explain and, as for the others, he did not "consider that the wishes of those eight chiefs should be respected." By not looking over all of the lands he had taken them to see, those chiefs "proved faithless to their tribe and their government." That same day, March 27, some of the eight chiefs who walked home rather than give their consent had crossed the Missouri to telegraph the President, saying they were sad at heart, they were in trouble, could he answer right away. They waited three days, but got no reply. The inspector got his immediately: "Proceed with removal."

When Standing Bear and the other chiefs arrived home that early April day, they found the removal already underway. They saw that a good many of the mixed-bloods had their wagons piled high with belongings. They saw the inspector and the interpreters on the move, shouting orders, yelling at them to keep filling their wagons, to be quick about it. Among their own people, the full-bloods, they saw that the elderly looked dazed, the women and children terrified. The young men came running to the chiefs.

"How did you find the country? What kind of land was it?"

"We told them it was a bad country. We would not take it."

When the people heard how the chiefs were treated, how they had gotten home, fear turned to anger, and the frightened inspector called a council. "If the President should speak to us, and talk kindly to us, and say, 'Do you consent to go,' I would think that was all fair," Standing Bear said. But "you are not doing that way, and I think you are doing this all on your own responsibility; I think you have no business to do it."

White Eagle, the head chief, stood and walked to the front of the room and spoke on behalf of his people. He said they had always honored their treaties, had worked the land and raised good crops, and had kept the peace with their neighbors. In years past, when the Lakota stole cattle and horses, the Ponca had fought them, returning the livestock to their white owners.

Then he turned to the inspector. "You profess to be a Christian, and to love God," he told him, "and yet you would love to see blood shed. Have you no pity on the tears of these helpless women and children? We would rather die here on our land than be forced to go. Kill us all here on our land now, so that in the future when men shall ask, 'Why have these died?' it shall be answered, 'They died rather than be forced to leave their land. They died to maintain their rights.' And perhaps there will be found some who will pity us and say, 'They only did what was right.'"

The next day, the inspector contacted Fort Randall. "My friends," he told the Ponca, "I have sent for the soldiers. They will be here this evening. If any blood shall be spilled, don't blame me; it won't be my fault."

It had been seventy-three years since the captain explorers first saw their village, sixty years since they signed the first peace and friendship treaty. On April 6, 1877, four days after the chiefs returned, thirty mounted cavalry made their way into the villages, and not long after, another thirty arrived, the first time U.S. soldiers had ever been summoned to enforce the peace on Ponca lands.

As soon as they arrived, the soldiers began milling about the villages on horseback, telling the people to put their things in the wagons. The people were unsure what to do, so the chiefs sent word to their friend, Solomon Draper, a lawyer and newspaperman who lived across the Niobrara about three miles away. The inspector found out and angrily sought out the chiefs. "He said lawyers were like vultures, hovering around to destroy us; that they would take all our money, and never do us any good," Standing Bear said. But the chiefs trusted Draper and they asked if he would help them. The lawyer, who also published the nearby *Niobrara Pioneer,* knew they were in a bad spot. He knew the decision had already been made, the preparations underway, the contracts let. He knew the Yankton and Sioux City businessmen were anxious to clear the way for the Lakota. And he knew how friendly the merchants had become with the inspector. Still, he said he would try.

So he crossed the Niobrara and confronted the inspector. He said it was dangerous to move northern people to southern climates. They could not adjust to the change. The malaria had killed many before and it would kill the Ponca, too. "I told him that those Indians were ignorant, and in a helpless condition; and if he had any regard for their wishes or their welfare, he certainly, in his position, ought to intercede with the department for keeping them there, instead of trying to accomplish their removal against their wish."

Inspector Kemble said the removal was too far along. It would look bad to back down now. "The dignity of the government," he said, "demanded that it should go ahead." The lawyer told him he had examined the treaty. The language was specific—the Ponca had clear title to their lands. They were the legal owners of their reservation. Could the inspector at least delay the removal, give him ten days to prepare a legal defense of the Ponca homeland? No, he could not. The inspector said the lawyer had no authority to represent the Ponca. He told him it was illegal for him to be on their reservation. And if he persisted, he would arrest him. So the lawyer went back across the river.

Soon, the inspector, the interpreters, and the sixty mounted cavalry began to tighten the circle on the frightened mixed-bloods. They moved through their village, yelling at those who refused to go, who would not pack up their things, to fall in line and fill their wagons: "If you don't the soldiers will fire on you." Throughout the second week in April, the mixed-bloods steadily weakened. "Take them," Standing Bear said. "They don't belong to the tribe anyway. They are partly white. They are not Poncas." The full-bloods crowded around their chiefs, and the chiefs told them: "Lock your doors, and when they go to get your things they will have to break open your doors; and when the white people hear of this they will prevent our land being taken away from us in this way."

In the mornings, the women and children began to leave their homes, fleeing into the woods, hiding from the soldiers in the trees and bushes. The men guarded the homes, some staying inside, some walking around outside, patrolling the village. The soldiers rode around, telling the men to hurry up, to go inside and pack up their belongings and put them in their wagons. The men refused. After dark, the women and children crept back into their homes. For a long time, it was mostly the women and children the white settlers heard during the night.

When the full-bloods would not pack up their things and put them into the wagons, the inspector sent the interpreters through the villages with a new message: No more food. No more rations. If they wanted to eat, they must pack up and cross the river—then they would get food. But they refused. "He wanted us to agree to go down to the Indian Territory," said Standing Buffalo, one of the eight chiefs who walked home. "We would not agree to it, and so he tried to starve us into it." When they ran out of food, the chiefs began to sell off some of their ponies and bought food from their white neighbors. When that ran out, they lived mostly on sweet corn. The old people, the women, and children ate first. Still, they refused to leave their homeland.

So the inspector focused again on the mixed-bloods. In the beginning, he had offered their chiefs gifts and trinkets, then money if they would get their people in line. Now, he offered food if they would finish packing the wagons, cross the river, and begin the long journey south. By April 15, most of the mixed-bloods in the upper camp had been broken, had packed their wagons, and were ready to go. Escorted by forty troopers, they began the slow trek down to the river. They had started late and by the time they arrived, there wasn't enough light to cross, so they were forced to camp that night near the large full-blood village. By morning, the full-bloods had convinced many to turn back.

The next morning, only 170 of the 700 Ponca began crossing the Niobrara. John Springer, an Omaha Indian farmer, stood on the other side watching the mixed-blood group moving down toward the river. He saw the angry inspector and the wagons piled high and the soldiers come down the banks, and watched them push the heavy wagons through the current, and he saw how the old people struggled to wade across the swift, shoulder-deep waters. Eventually, they all made it to the other side, where they set up a temporary camp. "Then he gave them rations," Springer said.

The inspector then turned to the full-bloods in their large village on the other side of the river: It was useless to resist. Everyone must go. But they would not go, not agree to leave their homes and move away from the Niobrara. "We said to him: 'This land is ours. It belongs to us. You have no right to take it from us. The land is crowded with people, and only this is left for us,'" Standing Bear said.

Not long after, another soldier detail arrived in the full-blood camp. Standing Bear and Big Snake "had utterly defied and disobeyed orders," the inspector said. They were "inciting disturbance on the reservation" and "imperiling the peace of the reservation, and preventing the removal of those who were willing to go." The inspector ordered their arrest and the soldiers moved in. They tied up the two brothers, put them in a wagon, and drove them to the jailhouse at Fort Randall.

By then, the chaos and fear, the panic and weeping that had swirled about the camp for weeks had long since gotten the attention of more and more citizens in the surrounding communities. Throughout the early spring, local newspapers devoted extensive coverage to the plight of their neighbors in the two villages along the river. The *Sioux City Daily Journal* recounted the long journey home by the chiefs, the telegram sent to the President, and their impending removal in a front-page editorial: "They know that they have conducted themselves peaceably and honestly; that they have made great progress toward civilization; that they are comfortably located; that the advantages of these facts they are about to lose; and that in order to deprive them, deceit and subterfuge have been resorted to, and violence has been threatened." The *Niobrara Pioneer* published a front-page editorial under the headline "Swindled Poncas—An Act Too Base to Be Recognized by Honest People in a Free Land Like Ours." The Reverend Alfred Riggs, the missionary at the Santee Sioux Agency twenty miles away, sent an angry letter to the paper. "To move them without their legally conveying their title to the Government, is an act too base for any but a Turk or Russian to commit in this age of the world," he wrote.

Earlier, Riggs had sent a telegram to the Secretary of the Interior. He said the Ponca were being forced off their land without their consent and "great wrong will be done these Indians and more disgrace accrue to our country by such ruthless disregard of our obligations." He asked the secretary to delay the removal until an investigation could sort things out, but received no reply. The Knox County Commissioners unanimously endorsed a resolution asking the President to explore alternatives "that will prevent this great wrong and injustice to the Poncas." Some of Yankton's leading citizens wrote the governor of Dakota Territory, who was visiting Washington, urging him to bring up the matter with the President. He did. The president referred it to the Indian Bureau.

Soon, the Commissioner of Indian Affairs was again uncertain, was again having doubts and second thoughts about the wisdom of removing the Ponca. The emotional response of so many white settlers and citizens made him question what was happening to a small tribe in one small corner of the American West. On April 17, Commissioner John Q. Smith telegraphed the inspector:

> Have too little information to decide what should be done. How many Indians refuse to go? What proportion of influential members of tribe refuse? Will those already started go on if others remain? What is your recommendation?

The inspector, irritated, angry, and disgusted, promptly wired back: "I leave for Washington this afternoon to fully explain the situation." The local businessmen who had the lucrative contracts with the Lakota offered the inspector a ride to Yankton and he accepted.

With Standing Bear and Big Snake in jail, the depleted mixed-bloods straggling on, and the frustrated inspector headed east to press for removal, the desperate full-bloods went looking for help, for someone to plead their case in Washington. Once again, they turned to their old friend, the lawyer-newspaperman. Their head chief went to see Solomon Draper in his office across the river.

"My friend, I want you to go to the Great Father," White Eagle said.

"I have no money," Draper replied.

"My friend, I have thirty-two horses. I'll give them to you."

"Well, bring them to me."

White Eagle did and the ponies were sold at auction for about ten dollars each. The lawyer told the chiefs he would take the money, go east, and see what he could do. That spring, Attorney Draper and

Inspector Kemble both left for Washington about the same time to see the same men about the same problem.

When the two men reached the nation's capital in late April 1877, the Secretary of the Interior had been in office seven weeks. At age forty-eight, Carl Schurz had arrived in Washington as a newly minted cabinet member with a colorful past. Born in a castle near Cologne, Germany, he got swept up in the German revolution of March 1848, was arrested, imprisoned, and later escaped. He fled to England, married and, in 1852, left with his new bride for the United States, eventually settling in Wisconsin. There, he joined the Republican Party, vowing to oppose slavery and help the many German-Americans in the area. While his wealthy wife started the nation's first kindergarten classes, Schurz climbed swiftly through the Republican ranks. Abraham Lincoln appointed him Minister to Spain in 1861, but he asked to come home a year later to join Union forces in the Civil War. He rose to brigadier general and fought at Gettysburg and Chattanooga. Not long after the war ended, Schurz became Washington correspondent for the *New York Tribune* and later the editor of the *Detroit Post*. With the help of his good friend Joseph Pulitzer, he was elected U.S. senator from Missouri in 1869.

By the time he reached the Interior Department eight years later, the Indian issue had become a tug-of-war between the civilian and military wings of the government. General William Tecumseh Sherman, among others, believed the solution to the nation's Indian problem was to confine the western tribes to enclosed reservations under strict military supervision. There, they would gradually die off of their own barbarism. Others, Schurz included, tilted toward the older beliefs: using agriculture, education, and religion as guiding forces that would eventually kill the Indian, but save and civilize the man. Neither side consistently prevailed and the dueling philosophies often bred confusion, uncertainty, and indecision within the ranks. But in April 1877, Custer had given the military the stronger hand.

The People Turn Their Faces South

After the Little Bighorn, the Army began a relentless campaign to crush and contain those bands of western tribes that had not yet succumbed to the hunger and cold and military strikes that began to stalk them wherever they turned. In the fall of 1876, General George Crook, commander of the Department of the Platte, had assembled a fighting force of more than two thousand men to go after those Lakota and Cheyenne who still refused reservation life, who had helped annihilate Custer and 211 of his men. In late November, the soldiers attacked a sleeping Cheyenne village in northern Wyoming, destroying the camp, wiping out the winter food supply, and making off with more than five-hundred horses. The pressure continued on Lakota villages scattered along the mountain creeks and streams throughout the winter.

On May 6, 1877, riding at the head of a two-mile procession that stretched across the high plains of western Nebraska, Crazy Horse led 899 of his starving people into Fort Robinson and surrendered to Crook. Two weeks earlier, about the same time the inspector and the lawyer were heading to Washington, Dull Knife and Little Wolf rode into the fort and stopped in front of Crook, shook his hand, and surrendered 554 of their starving Northern Cheyenne. Not long after, orders arrived for Crook from his superiors: The Northern Cheyenne were to be moved to the Indian Territory. They, too, refused. They said they would never go, would never leave their homeland, that they would die first. Crook, who was sympathetic to their plight, who did not always agree with his Washington superiors, patiently explained they had no choice, at least for now.

While Crook dealt with the Northern Cheyenne on the western Plains, Inspector Kemble met with the Commissioner of Indian Affairs in Washington. The commissioner was unsure what to do with the Ponca full-bloods who still refused to leave their lands. He couldn't make a decision and he didn't want to go it alone. So the two men went to see the Secretary of the Interior for advice. The inspector laid out the case, told him the facts, gave him all the information, and asked him what he should do. Schurz told him to make his case in writing. So the inspector did. "I am of the opinion," he wrote, "that no time should be lost in compelling those who are holding back to join their brethren now en route to the Territory. Good faith to the latter, not less than the best interests of the refractory portion of the tribe and the preservation by the government of authority and respect among all the tribes on the Missouri River, as well as its own proper dignity, demand that this should be done."

But the Secretary of the Interior was still unsure what to do. So he told the Commissioner of Indian Affairs to consult with the General of the Army, to see what he advised. The commissioner did. General Sherman said he agreed with the inspector. Then Interior Secretary Schurz said he agreed, too. So the inspector left their offices and returned to his hotel.

Shortly afterwards, Attorney Draper arrived and met with the Interior Secretary and the Indian Commissioner. During three days of meetings, he told them the Ponca had been treated unfairly, the inspector was not telling the truth, and the Indians had not consented to leave their lands, that they overwhelmingly opposed it. He told them their white neighbors did not want to see them go, that they had always been good friends, that they were a valuable buffer between the settlers and the Lakota. He asked them to stop the removal, to send out a delegation of their own choosing—one that could investigate and give them the facts, that would tell them the truth.

For two days, the Interior Secretary and the Indian Commissioner were uncertain what to do. They went back and forth, unable to give the lawyer an answer. Finally, they said they had reached a decision: The removal must go forward. The reports of their authorized agents in the field could not be ignored. The reports were the basis for government decisions. And the reports said a number of Indians had been willing to go and had already left. "To stop and reconsider the matter now would bring the department into disrepute; they could not do it with dignity."

Inspector Kemble and Attorney Draper both left Washington about the same time, headed for the same western lands. On his way back, the lawyer got sick and spent three weeks recovering in Ann Arbor,

Michigan, where he sent a message to a friend back in Niobrara. The friend told the chiefs the bad news. On April 24, the inspector got a message from his boss: "General Sherman has ordered two companies from Fort Sully to the Ponca Agency."

Not far from Fort Sully, down the Missouri a little ways, Standing Bear and Big Snake were taken from the jail at Fort Randall in early May to appear before a military tribunal of eight officers.

"The commanding officer said: 'I have received four messages telling me to send my soldiers after you. Now what have you done?'" Standing Bear later recalled. "Then we told him the whole story. Then the officer said: 'You have done no wrong. The land is yours; they had no right to take it from you. Your title is good. I am here to protect the weak, and I have no right to take you; but I am a good soldier, and I have to obey orders.'

"He said: 'I will telegraph the President, and ask him what I shall do. We do not think these three men had any authority to treat you as they have done. When we own a piece of land, it belongs to us till we sell it and pocket the money.' Then he brought a telegram, and said he received answer from the President. The President said he knew nothing about it. They kept us in jail ten days."

The commanding officer sent a reply to the President, asking him to cancel the removal orders. Then he released Standing Bear and Big Snake.

While the two brothers were in the stockade, Indian Agent E. A. Howard had arrived in Columbus, Nebraska, from Hillsdale, Michigan. He was sent there by the Washington office with instructions to help move the Ponca and he expected to find the full camp ready to go. When he got to Columbus on April 28, no one was there. Later that day, the Ponca agent, James Lawrence, finally arrived with the mixed-blood group—170 Indians and their forty-six wagons. Trudging through intermittent rain, snow, sleet, and mud, the group had taken two weeks to travel 110 miles. "In this I was disappointed," Howard told his superiors, with "more than three-fourths of the tribe having refused to leave their old reservations in Dakota, stating . . . that they preferred to remain and die on their native heath, in defense of their homes, and what they claimed to be their rights in the land composing the reservation upon which they were living, than to leave there and die by disease in the unhealthy miasmatic country which they claimed had been selected for them in the Indian Territory."

Two days later, Inspector Kemble arrived from Washington and ordered Agent Howard to return to the Niobrara to organize the final removal of the full-bloods. It would be Howard's job to pack them up and move them down. The inspector, meanwhile, would take command of the mixed-bloods, turning them south for the long march to Indian Territory.

When Standing Bear and Big Snake finally made it back to their people, they found a village overwhelmed with turmoil and confusion, the poison of a three-month standoff in the air wherever they turned. The women and children were hungry and scared, and the old people were weak. The young men had turned angry and hopeless, their white neighbors frustrated and helpless. Still, the Ponca refused to be quick, to pack up and go.

"It was like a man throwing a rope around a steer, and trying to pull the steer one way, while the steer was trying to pull back," Standing Bear said. "There was such a struggle all the time. They were trying to pull us off the reserve, and we were trying to keep from being pulled off."

The new agent, Howard, arrived on the Niobrara in early May. He stayed on the other side of the river and sent word he would like to meet with the chiefs. They refused. He sent word again. The chiefs said they would agree to a council. On May 8, Standing Bear, White Eagle, and the other chiefs met the agent at a remote spot along the banks of the Niobrara. He patiently explained they must agree to leave their lands, that four more companies of soldiers would soon arrive, that they came with firm orders from Washington. "I know you have been treated unjustly, and I feel sorry for you," he told them, "but I cannot help you. The President has sent me to take you down. I will do all in my power to make the journey comfortable for you so that you may not suffer."

White Eagle spoke for the chiefs. "It is good when men meet as friends and talk kindly to each other," he told Howard. "You have spoken the first kind word we have heard for a long time. We had made up our minds to resist and die on our own land rather than go to a strange one to die." He told the agent they would go and meet with their people and let him know what they wished to do.

White Eagle and Standing Bear gathered the men of the tribe for a long council. "My people, we, your chiefs, have worked hard to save you from this," White Eagle told them. "We have resisted until we are worn out, and now we know not what more we can do. We leave the matter into your hands to decide. If you say that we fight and die on our lands, so be it." When he finished, no one spoke. The men rose in silence and began walking home, thinking about how they should answer their chiefs.

When they arrived at their homes, they saw that the soldiers had rounded up all of the women and children and were standing guard over them. They saw that mounted troopers had ridden to their homes, knocked down the doors, removed their household utensils, and piled them in wagons. They had taken their plows, mowers, hay forks, grindstones, all the farming implements of any kind and everything too heavy to load in a wagon—equipment and machinery they had worked hard to pay for—and locked them in a large warehouse. When they finished, the soldiers pointed their bayonets at the people. "We told them we would rather die than leave our lands," Standing Bear said, "but we could not help ourselves."

The weather had turned cold and rainy and so the transportation and logistics were slow in coming together. The Ponca spent the last few nights in their barren homes and each night it was the same as it had been for many nights before, only a little louder now. John Springer, the Omaha Indian who lived along the Niobrara, had heard it throughout the spring of 1877. "The Indians were crying the whole night, because they did not want to go. Men and women, too, crying all night."

Early on the morning of May 16, the men and women and children of the lower village solemnly began to gather on the banks of the Running Water with their horses and wagons and household goods. Days of rain had swollen the Niobrara and its current ran swift and cold, so the chiefs asked the agent to help get the old and the sick to the other side. The quicksand made it too dangerous for horses to pull the heavy wagons across, so all the wagons were emptied, their contents ferried over on the shoulders of young Ponca men, the wagons pulled across by hand and ropes. Many of their thirty-five oxen and five-hundred horses struggled to make it across. Every now and then, the powerful current swept some of the mounted troopers off their horses and some of the Ponca men waded in after them, pulling them to safety. The effort to cross had taken all day, and they were exhausted and some were sick by the time they and their livestock and their belongings finally made it to the other side by late afternoon. "We were now happily ready for a forward movement," the agent reported.

From the beginning, the inspector had insisted on making the journey overland instead of taking a steamship down the Missouri, so the Indians were forced to use their own wagons and there weren't enough for what was needed. When Standing Bear and his son, Bear Shield, and more than five hundred of their people stood on the far bank at 5 P.M. that day, they could look across the Niobrara and see the accomplishments of the last few years: 236 homes they had built themselves, eight mowers, two reapers, their school, their church, a sawmill, a flour mill, and most of the household goods and tools they had accumulated through the years.

In their eight-hundred-square-foot home, Standing Bear and his family of eight left behind four chairs, three lamps, two bedsteads, two washtubs, a washboard, a heating stove, a cooking stove, a table, a valise, crockery and knives and forks. Outside, they had abandoned 4 cows, 4 hogs, 3 steers, 21 chickens, 2 turkeys, a stable, a cattle shed, 130 bushels of corn, 100 sacks of wheat, a plow, ladders, garden rakes, 3 axes, 2 hatchets, and 20 joints of pipe.

That night, a severe thunderstorm blew across the makeshift camp on the far side of the river, and heavy rains pounded their canvas tents throughout the next day and night. The following day was cloudy and cold and the rain kept coming, and they could do little but stay in their tents while the agent and the soldiers made final preparations for the long journey. At dawn on May 19, another downpour drenched the camp, but the clouds broke a few hours later and the agent was ready to begin.

So at 10 A.M., on a damp, chilly morning in the Moon When Summer Begins, Agent Howard gave the order to break camp and soon a long train of livestock, twenty-five mounted soldiers, and the Sacred Head People turned their faces south, moving up the banks and over the bluffs above the Running Water, starting down a long road they had never traveled before.

The weather had been unusual for so late in the spring—some snow, some sleet, the heavy rains, and the cold nights and mornings in their tents—and some of the people began to worry about the old and the young. They marched twelve miles of the six-hundred-mile journey the first day and pitched their camp by a creek. The next day, a Sunday, it rained hard all morning and the roads were bad, so they stayed put on the damp creek bottom all day. That afternoon, the second day after they left the Niobrara, a child died in the camp.

They continued on, breaking camp at seven on the third morning, marching thirteen miles across roads thick with mud until they reached the small village of Creighton, where they stopped for the night and to bury the child. They left again at seven the next morning and, with no rain and good roads, they marched all day, twenty-five miles, pitching their tents not far from the Elkhorn River near Neligh, Nebraska. The morning of May 23 opened with a light drizzle that turned into a blinding, two-hour deluge. A steady rain continued throughout the day, forcing the Ponca to remain in camp. That afternoon, a baby girl died of pneumonia in her tent.

Black Elk and Moon Hawk did not know what to do for their daughter. The next morning, they asked the agent for help and he asked the town carpenter to make a wooden cross for the dead girl. The mother could not bear to go and so later that morning the father spoke through an interpreter to the handful of local citizens gathered by the oak cross on a hill north of town:

"I want the whites to respect the grave of my child just as they do the graves of their own dead. The Indians do not like to leave the graves of their ancestors, but we had to move and hope it will be for the best. I leave the grave in your care. I may never see it again. Care for it for me."

Today, at the Laurel Hill Cemetery north of Neligh, high above the Elkhorn River Valley, several thousand graves sweep across a rolling hillside, the final resting place for pioneers, farm families, Civil War veterans, the first sheriff, the first county commissioner, scores of businessmen, judges, mayors, Lydia Jones and her baby, who both died during childbirth in 1874, and Joseph Bowlsby, who was born in New Hampshire six years before Thomas Jefferson helped write the Declaration of Independence and who died in Neligh on July 11, 1877, at age 107 years, four months, and eleven days. Along a fence line on the western edge of the sprawling cemetery, on a small knoll covered in jack pine, cedar, box elder, and red-winged blackbirds, lies a simple stone marker in a potter's field overlooking the fertile river valley: "White Buffalo Girl, died May 23, 1877, aged 18 months, daughter of Black Elk and Moon Hawk, of the Ponca Indian Tribe en route to their new home." A colorful bouquet covers the base, the only grave in the cemetery allowed to have flowers year-round.

For more than 125 years, the citizens of Neligh and surrounding communities have kept fresh flowers on the grave. Sometimes it is mothers and daughters who arrive with a wreath or floral decoration on Memorial Day. Sometimes it's a veteran's group or schoolchildren. Other times, the flowers just appear. No one really knows where they came from, only that they are always there, week after week, month after month, year after year. Levern Hauptmann, the vice president of the

Antelope County Historical Society, has spent his eighty-one years in Neligh and doesn't remember a time when he couldn't see flowers on the potter's field grave. "I suppose a little of it's guilt," he said. "But mostly it's the Christian thing to do. We promised this man a long time ago that we would respect the grave of his daughter and we always have."

After burying White Buffalo Girl, the orders were given to break camp and at 10 A.M., Standing Bear, Bear Shield, and 530 Ponca packed up and headed for the Elkhorn River. They had lost two children in five days and a number of other women and children were getting sick. The heavy rains had left the roads under two feet of water and washed out the bridges at the Neligh crossing, so they marched eight miles and spent the day repairing the roads and bridges farther down across the flats until they finally got everyone into camp late that evening. They marched twenty-eight miles the next two days in cold, damp air, and the nights turned colder when they could find no firewood. On May 27, the morning came in with a chilly, misty rain and they made it eight miles down Shell Creek before a drenching downpour forced them to stop and make camp.

More and more were getting sick now. They did not have the right clothes and protection at night against the constant rain, and Standing Bear's adult daughter was among the sickest. Tuberculosis had filled Prairie Flower's lungs, and the mother and father could do nothing to help the shallow breaths and her struggle for air. There were no doctors and no medicine to stop the bacteria from spreading and neither she nor the many other sick in their tents along the dank creek bottom could be moved comfortably. The agent wanted to leave at five the next morning, hoping by nightfall to be in Columbus where there was medicine and a doctor, but a lashing thunderstorm overwhelmed the camp, delaying their departure two hours. After seven miles, the roads gave out, and they spent two hours cutting willow branches and scavenging for wheat straw and packing them on the roads to make them passable, then marched another seven miles before camping that night, ten miles from Columbus.

"I Am a Man"

Before leaving the Niobrara, White Swan, one of the eight Ponca chiefs who had walked home, wrote a letter to his brother on the Omaha Reservation, saying the soldiers would soon march them south to the Indian Territory. He told him about when they expected to be in Columbus and asked if he would come to say good-bye. His brother, Joseph La Flesche, one of the last recognized chiefs of the Omaha, got the letter in time and he shared it with the oldest of his four daughters.

She was a twenty-three-year-old poet whose childhood dream had been to teach Omaha children in their own school on their own reservation. So she spent six years at the Elizabeth Institute for Young Ladies in New Jersey, working hard, getting good grades, devouring Shakespeare, teaching part-time to help pay for her education. After graduating from the girls' boarding school in June 1875, she returned home and was told she could not teach on the reservation. One day at the agency office, she found a copy of the "Rules and Regulations" governing reservation employment. In one section, it said Indians should be the preferred teachers, so she wrote a letter to Indian Commissioner Smith, saying she was qualified and would like to apply for a teaching position at the reservation school. The commissioner told her she could not teach without a certificate, so she asked the Omaha agent for permission to leave the reservation to take the exam for her teaching certificate. The agent refused to give her permission, so she got one of her father's best horses and rode twenty-eight miles to Tekamah, where she asked the superintendent of schools to give her the exam. He gave her the hardest reading and arithmetic sections, but she passed anyway, got the certificate, and rode back home. She sent the certificate to the Commissioner of Indian Affairs, who told her she couldn't teach without a certificate of good moral character. So she wrote Miss Nettie Read, one of her teachers at the New Jersey school, who sent her a number of letters attesting to her good moral character. She sent the letters to the commissioner and heard nothing for several months. So she wrote him again, saying she would take her story to the newspapers if he didn't respond.

Not long after, the commissioner approved her position and she became the first Indian teacher on the Omaha Reservation. They gave her a small, dilapidated building and twenty dollars a month, so she gathered up some children, scrimped and saved, and eventually bought a small organ to teach them music, and then started a Sunday School for her students. The reservation's census rolls identified her as Susette La Flesche. Her people called her *In-shta-the-amba*. In a few years, she would be known to many whites—from Chicago to Boston, New York to Washington—as Bright Eyes.

In late May 1877, Bright Eyes, her father, and about ten other Omaha packed up and headed for Columbus. They arrived several days before the Ponca, so they camped and waited. Early on the afternoon of May 29, they saw the long line of wagons and horses and oxen coming slowly across the flats of the Platte River toward Columbus. The young poet and schoolteacher was among the first to reach them. "We met them on the road," she said. "They were crying, the men as well as the women—all were crying."

That night, the Omaha stayed with them in their camp and Bright Eyes heard the stories. Some of the Ponca had slipped away and gone back home. They had begun leaving from the beginning, stealing away at night, and heading back to the Niobrara, hiding among the Yankton and Santee Sioux, so many that the soldiers started counting them at each bridge crossing, calling out their names, checking to see who was missing. Still, they kept leaving, one family, then another, while they all camped on Soap Fork outside Columbus. The people told her they had fought it as long as they could, had resisted to the end, but it was no use. The government was too strong. Had they kept it up, they would have all died.

It was cold and muddy and they stayed in camp three days while the agent got more food, five-thousand yards of canvas for new tents, and repaired the battered wagons and harnesses. By June 1, Captain Fergus Walker and his twenty-five soldiers had turned around and headed back to the Niobrara. Bright Eyes and her father turned east and headed back home. At eight o'clock that morning, Standing Bear and the Ponca turned south, struggling across the soggy flats of the Platte, heading for their new home. They traveled fifty miles in four days, marching over muddy roads, past the village of Ulysses, through the rain and across the Big Blue River, camping along Lincoln Creek about four miles northwest of Seward on the evening of June 4.

Many more had fallen ill and the lymph nodes on the necks of some of the children had swollen and broken through the skin. Many others had breathing problems, the dank, enclosed tents helping spread the tuberculosis. Prairie Flower could not get her breath, and the mother and father could do nothing. They had hoped the pure water from nearby Shogo Springs would help her and the others, but it didn't help. They broke camp at seven o'clock on June 5, heading for the small village of Milford on the Big Blue, fourteen miles away. About two o'clock that afternoon, the chief's daughter stopped breathing.

The agent paid fifteen dollars to arrange a Christian burial and the next day the citizens of Milford offered their help. Mrs. Mary Welsh made a new cloth dress for Prairie Flower, and Mrs. Borden cleansed her body and prepared it for burial. Mr. Borden, the local carpenter, made a coffin, and a number of Mennonite women brought fresh flowers to the grave. Throughout the journey, Agent Howard kept a daily journal, meticulously noting the weather, how far they traveled, road conditions, the sick, the dead, and a variety of personal observations. "It was here, in looking upon the form of his dead daughter, thus arrayed for the tomb," he wrote on June 6, "that Standing Bear was led to forget the burial service of his tribe, and say to those around him at the grave that he was desirous of leaving off the ways of the Indian and adopting those of the white man."

After the burial, the chief and his weary, worn-out people remained in their river camp outside Milford while the agent arranged for more supplies. About 5 P.M., the skies above the Big Blue River suddenly turned black and a fierce southwest wind whipped in off the plains. The agent wrote in his journal:

It was a storm such as I never before experienced, and of which I am unable to give an adequate description. The wind blew a fearful tornado, demolishing every tent in camp, and rending many of them into shreds, overturning wagons, and hurling wagon-boxes, camp equipage, &e., through the air in every direction like straws. Some of the people were taken up by the wind and carried as much as three hundred yards without touching the ground . . . The cries of the people, mingled with the terrific thunder and tumult of the storm, made "confusion worse confounded" and I earnestly hope to be spared any similar experience in the future.

The sharp lightning bolts, deafening thunder, and deluge of rain and hail continued with unabated fury for four hours. When it ended, the camp was in ruins, several were seriously injured, and another member of Standing Bear's family was dead. The wind had toppled a boiling kettle of water and scalded to death his infant granddaughter. Her body was taken to Milford, where she was buried beside her aunt.

After the storm passed, a Milford doctor arrived to tend to the sick and injured. In an obituary forty-three years later, the *Milford Review* recounted for readers the trip Dr. George W. Brandon had made to the devastated Ponca camp:

Darkness began to veil the sky and peel after peel of murderous thunder filled the air. The savages went into a wild revelry of a war dance and made ready to wreck vengeance upon the pale face village. A messenger was sent post haste for Dr. Brandon to come and dress the injured. He arrived upon the scene, the infuriated Indians were dancing the war dance, brandishing their firearms and tomahawks, slashing with scalping knives, howling with frenzy, frantic with rage, ready to start their bloody slaughter. The ghastly scene lit by the dying embers of the camp fires and vivid flashes of lightning was enough to turn the stoutest of hearts. It was with great difficulty that savages were quieted and the pale face medicine man finished his errand of mercy.

The storm forced a two-day delay while the agent arranged for repairs and more supplies, and the people tried to put their camp back together. The tornado had taken its toll in other ways, Agent Howard noted. "It has also had a depressing and bad influence on the hearts and minds of the Indians, which on account of their superstitious nature, is hard to dispel."

They broke camp on June 8 and moved on—seven miles, twelve miles, fifteen miles—along mud-caked roads, across swollen creeks, over flooded rivers, past Crete and DeWitt and Beatrice. A woman's thumb was accidentally cut off and a doctor came to treat her and the many sick. Wolf Creek was washed out, and they built a bridge of driftwood and got everyone across. They camped one night near the Otoe Agency, where Standing Bear and the other chiefs found refuge four months earlier, and their old friends made a gift of ten ponies. The rains kept coming and they were forced to stay near the Otoe two days waiting for the creeks to recede.

Near Beatrice, Agent Howard summed up the conditions in a letter to Indian Commissioner Smith. "In consequences of these extraordinary storms small creeks have been suddenly swollen to the magnitude of raging rivers, carrying away bridges and rendering the fording of them almost impossible; and altogether the roads have been rendered to the worst condition possible for the elements to make them, causing great hindrance and delay for the Indian Train. The continuous storms have also caused much annoyance and no little suffering to the Indians, especially to the women and children who were poorly prepared to meet such a condition of the elements."

They kept moving, crossing into Kansas by mid-June. A wagon toppled, severely injuring a woman. They ran out of food on the sixteenth and went to Marysville for emergency rations. Little Cottonwood died on the eighteenth and four families bolted from camp, heading back to the Niobrara. The agent rode nine miles to overtake them and escorted them back to camp. A severe storm swept through that night, flooding most of the tents and equipment. The roads were impassable, so they buried Little Cottonwood and stayed in camp.

They left at six the next morning and kept pushing—ten miles, twelve miles, fifteen miles, eleven miles—stopping near Manhattan, where a doctor came with medicine. Two women died on June 25 and were buried the next day. They kept moving—nine miles, seventeen miles, eighteen miles, seven miles—past Emporia, the weather turning hotter, more humid each day. On June 30, a child of Buffalo Chief's died. They placed it in a coffin, buried it, and kept going, stopping at noon on July 2 because there wasn't enough water to continue in the scorching heat.

That afternoon, one of the people tried to kill White Eagle. "For about two hours, the most intense excitement prevailed, which was heightened by continued loud crying by all the women and children," the agent reported. He gave the assailant, Buffalo Track, a pass and food and ordered him to return to the Omaha Reservation, where most of his relatives lived. They left at six the next morning, pushing south—eighteen miles, seventeen miles, fifteen miles, another fifteen miles—through searing heat, the clouds of greenhead flies attacking the horse teams and swarming the oxen until their legs began to buckle.

Inspector Kemble and his group of 170 mixed-bloods were already in the new place, having arrived about a month earlier. "The Indians moved with cheerful alacrity," he informed superiors, and upon arriving they "appeared exceedingly well pleased with their new home." It had cost $8,199 for their fifty-nine-day journey, more than double the original estimate. "As it turned out," he noted in his final report, "it would have been considerably cheaper to have moved the tribe by river and rail than by land."

Standing Bear and Bear Shield and the five-hundred full-bloods were getting close now, so they kept moving through the heat and humidity of southern Kansas, twelve miles on July 7, another twelve miles on July 8, until they were just north of Baxter Springs, near the border of the Indian Territory. The final push began at 6 A.M. on July 9. Seven hours and eleven miles later, they passed through the last town in Kansas. About 1 P.M., as they approached their new home, a place they called the Warm Country, a storm came in off the Plains, catching them in open land.

"The wind blew a heavy gale and the rain fell in torrents," the agent reported, "so that it was impossible to see more than four or five rods distant, thoroughly drenching every person and every article in the train; making a fitting end to a journey commenced by wading a river and thereafter encountering innumerable storms."

During their fifty-five-day journey, Standing Bear and the Ponca had walked across two states and six-hundred miles, said good-bye to the Omaha and the Otoe, and survived two tornadoes and an attempted murder. By the time they arrived, they had lost nine of their people and their homeland.

Most days, Parrish Williams sits in a comfortable chair in his modest home near the banks of a river six hundred miles south of the Niobrara. His shoes are two sizes too big and he uses a gnarled walking stick to get to the kitchen table, where he studies tribal land records, or to fetch a fresh pack of Marlboros from the bedroom, or to see who's knocking on the door of his cabin in the woods. Above his comfortable chair, draped in a blinding blue robe, Jesus stands alone in the green hills of a beautiful country, arms outstretched, smiling.

The old man's voice is steady and calm, earnest, rising a bit when he gets excited, but not too much. In his matter-of-fact way, Grandpa Parrish sits in his easy chair, recounting spats he and his brothers and sisters had in the years Woodrow Wilson occupied the White House and what his mother said to quiet them and a wild shoving match a couple of girls had one time in the spring of 1925. As the elder of his tribe, it is his job to keep the past alive for the children, the same way it had been done for him, so he remembers the stories he first heard as a young man growing up on this same land in the years after World War I.

Back then, they would sometimes take their dinner in a thick grove of cottonwoods along a bend of the Salt Fork River. Afterwards, he liked to listen to the stories his father and grandfather told. The boy asked questions sometimes, but mostly he just listened, and he learned some things about his people back in the cottonwoods that he's never forgotten.

His grandfather belonged to the clan that made things grow. He knew the plants and herbs, and when Parrish was a child, his grandfather would come to the cabin and take care of him and his brothers and sisters whenever they had colds or the flu or sore throats. "Sometimes he would boil the plant or cook it and other times we would just eat it raw. My grandfather was our doctor."

The old man's father was born in 1872 on the Niobrara. His father's mother and grandmother were born there, too, and five years later, all three made the journey south. "They told them to pack only what you can carry—nothing more. Leave all your homes and the other things and all your land behind. That's what they told them." The phone rings. He takes his walking stick, takes his time, answers it, and settles back in the chair. On another wall, there's a portrait of Standing Bear in a blue robe, eagle feather, and bear claw necklace, hand outstretched, staring intently inside a room filled with soldiers and citizens and well-dressed ladies.

Over the years, he asked his father what it had been like on the Niobrara, what their camp was like, how the life was up there, what his memories were of their homeland. But his father could never remember anything about that life. His earliest childhood memory always came back to the same place.

During the long trek south, his father's mother had no wagon, so she had walked most of the way through the first five weeks of the journey to the Warm Country. On June 24, 1877, while they were camped three miles southeast of Manhattan, Kansas, a doctor came to attend to the sick. The next day, the first anniversary of the Custer fight, two women died during the fifteen-mile march. One of them was his father's mother.

"I Am a Man"

"My great-grandmother wanted to grieve when she saw her daughter had died. While she was sitting there grieving, they came along and pulled her up off the ground and forced her to keep marching. My father saw all of that.

"He probably cried. He was only five years old."

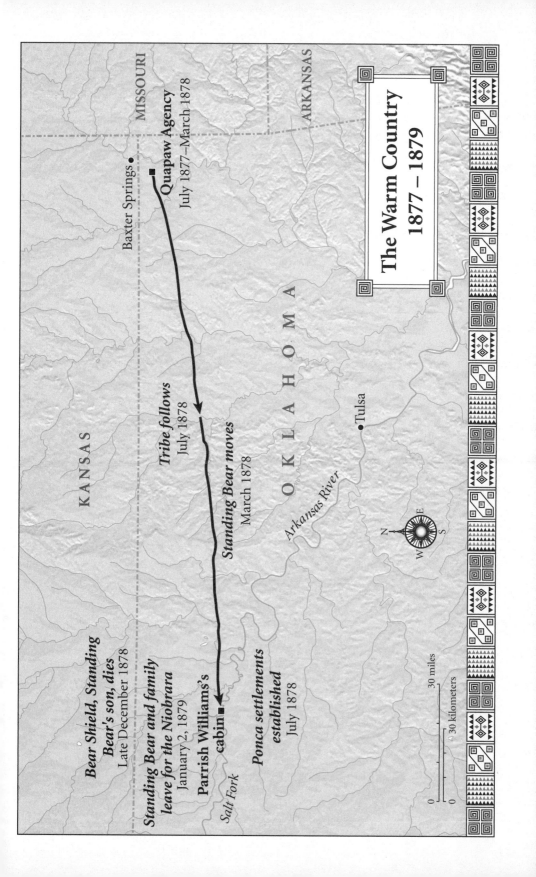

The Warm Country
1877 – 1879

MISSOURI

Baxter Springs •

Quapaw Agency
July 1877–March 1878

ARKANSAS

KANSAS

Tribe follows
July 1878

Standing Bear moves
March 1878

OKLAHOMA

Tulsa •

Arkansas River

N
E
W
S

Bear Shield, Standing
Bear's son, dies
Late December 1878

Standing Bear and family
leave for the Niobrara
January 2, 1879

Parrish Williams's
cabin ■

Ponca settlements
established
July 1878

Salt Fork

0   30 miles

0   30 kilometers

4

Life and Death in
the Warm Country

In 1877, Russia declared war on Turkey and Queen Victoria was proclaimed empress of India. Rutherford B. Hayes became the nineteenth President of the United States although he lost the popular vote, and Billy the Kid gunned down an Arizona blacksmith.

Thomas Edison announced he had invented a machine that could capture sound, and Maryland militia killed nine Baltimore and Ohio Railroad workers in a day of rioting. The All England Croquet and Lawn Tennis Club hosted its first Wimbledon match and Tchaikovsky's *Swan Lake* made its debut.

That same year, after recovering his remains from the Little Bighorn, the U.S. Army buried George Armstrong Custer with full military honors at West Point. At Fort Robinson, Nebraska, a soldier bayoneted Crazy Horse in the side and the Lakota war chief bled to death on the floor of an agency office. His parents left with the body on a travois and headed north, hiding it in the bluffs of his homeland.

Nine hundred miles away, on the dusty lands of the Southern Great Plains, the business of removing western tribes from their native lands and resettling them within designated boundaries was in full swing.

The idea of setting aside an "Indian Country" west of the Mississippi had been around for most of the century. Spurred by the desire of the nation's third President to clear out the eastern tribes for white settlement, it began shortly after the Louisiana Purchase and would unfold in three stages during the next eight decades. In 1804, Congress had approved negotiating removal treaties with eastern tribes and for twenty years a number of Indian nations gave up their lands and began to drift west, voluntarily and haphazardly, into a vaguely defined region of the Great Plains far beyond the reach of white settlements. Twenty-six years later, with passage of the 1830 Indian Removal Act, resettlement became official and the forced removal of the nation's native inhabitants began in earnest. Congress firmed up the boundaries, specifically setting aside those lands west of Missouri and Arkansas for the remaining eastern tribes. In time, those lands became commonly known as the "Indian Territory."

The first resettlement stage occurred in the spring of 1838 when President Andrew Jackson, ignoring an earlier U.S. Supreme Court decision upholding Cherokee land rights, ordered Army troops to forcibly remove more than 15,000 Cherokee from their prosperous villages and fertile Georgia farmlands, lands long coveted by white settlers. Before reaching the Indian Territory six months and six-hundred miles later, more than one-fourth of the tribe had died of disease or starvation. Soon, the Choctaw, Chickasaw, Creek, and Seminole joined the Cherokee in the southern portion of the sprawling Indian Territory. The "Five Civilized Tribes," as the government called them, had to build new homes, cultures, and governments, and learn how to adapt and survive. By 1845, more than 100,000 eastern Indians had been removed to the western lands, the remnants of their nations scattered within designated borders that gradually began to shrink as more and more whites crossed the Mississippi.

Life and Death in the Warm Country

About a decade later, the Kansas-Nebraska Act of 1854 spawned the second resettlement stage, one marked by a new round of treaties that began to concentrate more and more Indians on less and less tribal land—a squeeze that helped open up eighteen million acres for white settlement. By the end of 1854, the once-vast Indian Territory had shrunk to what would one day become the state of Oklahoma, most of which was owned by the Five Civilized Tribes. But in 1865, because the five tribes had supported the Confederacy during the Civil War, the government canceled its earlier treaties with them and negotiated new ones. These treaties forced the five tribes to either give up or sell a good portion of their western lands, lands the government then set aside for the numerous western tribes that would soon arrive during the final resettlement wave.

From the beginning, the basic intent of the 374 treaties signed during a ninety-three-year span was to acquire Indian land, and they had been an overwhelming success. Between 1853 and 1857 alone, fifty-two separate treaties enabled the government to acquire 174 million acres of Indian land. "In no former equal period of our history have so many treaties been made, or such vast accession of land obtained," George Manypenny, the Commissioner of Indian Affairs, remarked in 1857. Now, during the 1870s, the boom years were on, years in which all that land—the Great American Desert—quickly began to bloom into Jefferson's long-cherished dream. Europeans by the tens of thousands joined the western cavalcade, sweeping across the land with plows and pitchforks, horses and harnesses, leaving robust fields of corn and wheat in their wake. The transcontinental railroad bound east coast with west, creating frontier settlements overnight and ready markets for the nation's fertile midsection. Texas cattle were moving north along the trails and spilling out of railheads from a spider web of steel lines, pushing deeper and deeper into the old hunting grounds. Soon, the hold-out tribes, the ones that had not yet agreed to give up the old ways and the old lands, that had refused to live inside designated boundaries, came to be viewed as the final obstacle in the path of an agrarian-based democracy. And it wasn't long before they encountered a weapon they could no longer fight, one far deadlier than the Springfield rifles, the Colt pistols, and the artillery fieldpieces.

Throughout the 1870s, annihilating the Indian food base became an instrument of government policy, a policy General Philip Sheridan bluntly articulated to Texas lawmakers in 1875:

> [Buffalo hunters] have done in the last two years, and will do more in the next year, to settle the vexed Indian question, than the entire regular Army has done in the last thirty years. They are destroying the Indians' commissary . . . Send them powder and lead, if you will, but, for the sake of a lasting peace, let them kill, skin, and sell until the buffaloes are exterminated. Then your prairies can be covered with speckled cattle and the festive cowboy, who follows the hunter as a second forerunner of an advanced civilization.

In short order, the guns of professional buffalo hunters, railroad contract workers, and sportsmen from near and far were unleashed from the Dakotas to Texas, the Rockies to the Missouri. Between 1871 and 1883, more than fifteen million buffalo were slaughtered, the herds that once stretched 120 miles reduced to a few hundred straggling survivors. For the remaining tribes, the sobering choice arrived quickly: accept reservation life and government rations—or starve.

Far to the east that decade, the architects of federal policy had all come to share the same vision. If they wanted to sweep the western land of its remaining obstacles, to finally complete the vast grid of family farms and ranches, they needed to fill the Indian Territory with as many tribes, friendly or unfriendly, as possible. So throughout the 1870s, the Comanche and Apache, Sauk and Fox, Potawatomi and Shawnee, Otoe and Missouri, Kaw, Osage and Peoria, Wichita, Kickapoo and Pawnee, Kiowa, Nez Perce and Wyandot, Cheyenne and Arapaho all arrived in the Indian Territory during the third and final resettlement wave. By the decade's end, tribes that once moved freely across much of the western lands had been clustered and confined within 58,000 square miles, 7 percent of the original Louisiana Territory.

Their new home, its proponents argued, would now become a working laboratory where native people could be transformed into productive citizens, where they would be shorn of their savage customs and become educated, Christian farmers, where they would give up their language, customs, and religion and gradually assimilate into the greater advanced society about them. "The true remedy for these evils," the Commissioner of Indian Affairs, Ezra Hayt, said of the restless, discontented tribes in 1877, "is their immediate removal to the Indian Territory, where 58,000 square miles are set apart for the use of Indians; where they can be fed and clothed at a greatly diminished expense; and where, better than all, they can be kept in obedience, and taught to become civilized and self-supporting."

To its detractors, the Indian Territory in the last quarter of the nineteenth century had become something else—a sprawling waste dump where the refuse of Indian cultures was deposited on desolate reservations overseen by ignorant bureaucrats, neglectful commissioners, crooked inspectors, corrupt agents, drunken mixed-blood interpreters, plundering subcontractors, land-grabbers, cattle rustlers, and whiskey peddlers, a place General Sherman once defined as "a parcel of land set aside for Indians, surrounded by thieves."

The Indian Territory also had another defining characteristic: Throughout the 1870s, as had been true from the beginning, those forced to live on the reservation lands of the Territory had no legal rights in U.S. courts. On their lands, there were no federal laws protecting Indians from crimes committed against them or punishing them for crimes they committed against other Indians. They could not sue a white man in federal court for stealing their horses, or rustling their cattle, or raping their wives. But they could murder one another, steal an enemy's horses, and abuse another's wife without fear of encountering a federal hanging judge. Although Indians could not leave their reservation without permission, the government could move them about the country, from place to place, at any time, without any legal restrictions. Indians could lose lands they had title to without compensation and they had no legal means to prevent the loss or recover their land. Unlike white immigrants and, now, former slaves, Indians lived in a land where the first article of the Constitution specifically excluded them from becoming citizens of their country. As far as the law went, they had no legal identity and so no one could say for sure who or what they were. Were they a people? Conquered subjects? Independent nations? Government wards? Potential citizens? All of their lives, they had existed in this legal limbo, in a kind of shadow world, as far as the United States government was concerned, a government that had never defined the legal status of the people who had been on the land centuries before the Constitution was written.

This state of affairs had increasingly come to bother others, especially the church folk and missionaries who lived and worked among the Indians, people who were trying to instill the concepts of civilization and justice in their native flock. In his annual report to superiors, William H. Hare, a bishop of the Episcopal Church who lived at the Yankton Indian Agency, noted his frustration in trying to square the practice with the preaching:

> Civilization has loosened, in some places broken, the bonds which regulate and hold together Indian society in its wild state, and has failed to give the people law and officers of justice in their place. This evil still continues unabated. Women are brutally beaten and outraged; men are murdered in cold blood; the Indians who are friendly to schools and churches are intimidated and preyed upon by the evil-disposed; children are molested on their way to school, and schools are dispersed by bands of vagabonds; but there is no redress. This accursed condition of things is an outrage upon the One Law-giver. It is a disgrace to our land. It should make every man who sits in the national halls of legislation blush. And, wish well to the Indians as we may, and do for them what we will, the efforts of civil agents, teachers, and missionaries are like the struggles of drowning men weighted with lead, as long as by the absence of law Indian society is left without a base.

Life and Death in the Warm Country

By mid-summer 1877, after eight decades of removal and resettlement, thirty-two tribes numbering 73,301 Indians had come to live within the 58,000 square miles that became Oklahoma. On July 9, another 523 Indians were added to the Territory's census rolls.

After weathering the punishing storm south of Baxter Springs, Standing Bear and the Ponca full-bloods passed out of Kansas and into the Territory, getting their first glimpse of the new homeland on a sultry Monday afternoon in early July more than a century and a quarter ago.

Inspector Kemble described their new land as a beautiful country, one the mixed-bloods who had come down with him were delighted with. "As well they might be," he said, "for, instead of its being a marshy country, it is on one of the most favored sections of the Indian Territory; so desirable, indeed, that there are very few white men who would not take all the risks of fevers to secure a hundred and sixty acres there." Outside of the fever and chills, typical of the area, he said he had never heard anyone complain that it was an unhealthy country.

When Standing Bear and the full-bloods looked out upon the new lands, they did not see thick groves of cottonwoods, sloping hills, freshwater streams, and a floodplain bearing the fruit of plow and seed. They did not see any sturdy wooden homes furnished with tables and chairs, dishes, and heating stoves. They saw no tool sheds, gardens, harnesses, and plows. They saw no sawmills or flour mills, no church or school. No reapers, mowers, grindstones, or hay forks. No fences or livestock.

Instead, they looked across the Quapaw Reservation lands and saw an inhospitable prairie, a hot and humid patchwork of stony fields and marshy swamps. They saw there were no homes and no agency headquarters, only an aging commissary, a few scattered mission buildings, and a dozen crude log huts for the Quapaw. They saw that the mixed-bloods, who arrived a month earlier, had set up their camp on a small knoll on the south end of the new lands, so that night they began to set up their camp along a creek bottom on the north end, sleeping on the ground in tattered canvas Army tents.

They awoke the next morning, the beginning of an unusually severe hot spell, and felt a kind of heat and humidity they had never experienced in the north country. It swamped their creek-bottom camp for several days, giving rise to clouds of mosquitoes and swarms of greenhead flies that began to engulf their camp and their horses. From the beginning, a feeling began to stir among many in the makeshift camp, and for many, it was a feeling that never left.

"The water was bad, and the ground was bad," Standing Bear said. "Everything was strange. A great many of our people were sick."

When Agent Howard looked upon the ragged tent city strewn along the creek bottom, when he looked across the Quapaw lands where the people now lived, he saw it much the same as Standing Bear.

"It is a matter of astonishment to me," he wrote his superiors in Washington, "that the Government should have ordered the removal of the Ponca Indians from Dakota to the Indian Territory without having first made some provision for their settlement and comfort. Before their removal was carried into effect an appropriation should have been made by Congress sufficient to have located them in their new home, by building a comfortable house for the occupancy of every family of the tribe. As the case now is . . . no houses have been built for their use, and the result is that these people have been placed on an uncultivated reservation to live in their tents as best they may."

In its haste to clear the way for the Lakota to move to the Missouri, the government had neglected to arrange for Ponca housing, clothing, food, water, farming equipment, and medicine. They had also been placed on their new land without the knowledge or consent of the owners, the Quapaw, who were neither compensated nor consulted about their old friends and relatives moving in with them in the summer of 1877. The Sacred Head People had been herded south, marched into Indian Territory, and dropped off at the northern end of someone else's reservation, lands to which they had no legal claim and where, once again, they had become trespassers. The lands they did have a legal claim to, a 96,000-acre reservation conveyed by treaty and ratified by Congress, had been given away. The Ponca received no compensation for their old lands, so they had no money to support themselves on their new lands.

And the government had no money for them, either. Getting the Ponca from the Niobrara to the Indian Territory had used up all of the $40,000 Congress set aside for their removal as well as all of their $8,000 in annual annuities—payments for a specific number of years that were designed to sustain the tribes until they could become self-sufficient. So for more than a year—through the first summer, winter, and spring, and into the second summer—the Ponca lived in canvas tents on someone else's barren land in the northeast corner of the Warm Country.

It wasn't long before word of their arrival and whereabouts drifted north to Baxter Springs, the Kansas border town three miles away. Like the greenhead flies that covered their horses, whiskey peddlers soon began to swarm over their camp, something they had not experienced in the northern lands. Their frustrated agent suggested forming an Indian police force to keep the peddlers at bay, noting in a report to superiors that frontier justice wasn't likely to help. Shortly after arriving, he wrote, several Ponca had already gotten drunk "having procured the liquor through the agency of a worthless white man at Baxter Springs. I immediately had the vendor arrested under a statutory law of Kansas prohibiting the selling, giving, or delivering of intoxicating liquors to an Indian. On the trial of the case the proof of guilt against the prisoner was made positive, but the court (justice,) at the request of defendant's counsel, charged the jury that the law was unconstitutional, and that a conviction could not be had against the prisoner for the offense charged, and the jury returned a verdict, under the charge of the court, of not guilty."

But for Standing Bear and his family, for the 681 Ponca and their 197 families, for all of the full-bloods and mixed-bloods now gathered in their two camps on Quapaw land, there soon was something far worse than the whiskey peddlers and greenhead flies, than the heat and humidity, the poverty and their worn-out canvas tents. They had long feared it above all else and within weeks, it began to overwhelm them. Their agent, too, had feared it and he had made it clear in his first report to the Commissioner of Indian Affairs.

I am of the opinion that the removal of the Poncas from the northern climate of Dakota to the southern climate of the Indian Territory, at the season of the year it was done, will prove a mistake, and that a great mortality will surely follow among the people when they shall have been here for a time and become poisoned with the malaria of the climate. Already the effects of the climate may be seen upon them in the *ennui* that seems to have settled upon each, and in the large number now sick.

The fear had stayed with Standing Bear ever since he had spoken with the Pawnee five months earlier, shortly before the chiefs decided to walk home that night rather than consent to moving their people to the Territory. By 1875, the government had removed 2,376 Pawnee from their colder northern lands. Two years later, 855 Pawnee men, women, and children—36 percent of the tribe—were buried in the Warm Country. Already, nine Ponca had died on the journey down, and eight more, weakened and vulnerable from the long march, died within six weeks of arriving. The tattered tents along the dank creek bottom helped spread the malaria and there was no money for the quinine that could help, so fresh graves became a common sight. The Ponca "have already lost 36 by death, which, by an ordinary computation," the Commissioner of Indian Affairs wrote in his summary report for 1877, "would be the death-rate for the entire tribe for a period of four years." Tuberculosis had taken Prairie Flower on the march down and now one of Standing Bear's four surviving daughters had the fever and chills, the malaria, in their tent on the bottomlands. So did the mother and grandmother of his wife. Many more had it, too.

"Up in our own land we lived in houses made of wood, that kept out the snow and rain, and kept us warm in winter," Standing Bear would say later. "Many of us had two stoves each, to keep the house warm; but when we went to live down there we had to live in tents, that let the rain and snow get in, and we had no stoves; and so a great many of my people got sick and died."

And they were hungry, all of them, almost all of the time. When the inspector cut off their rations up on the Niobrara, they had been forced to sell many of their horses to buy food and to pay for the lawyer's trip to Washington. In the Territory, the greenhead flies and poison weeds soon killed many of their surviving ponies and horse thieves made off with the rest. The oxen they had brought quickly died of disease and they had arrived too late to plant anything and there were no farm tools to break ground. Wherever Standing Bear looked, he saw the same thing, and he felt what many of the others did.

> When we got there the Agent issued no rations for a long time. For months we had to beg of the other tribes. We were all half-starved. This was all different from our own home. There we raised all we needed. Here there was no work to do. We had nothing to work with, and there was no man to hire us . . . Sickness commenced, several died. All my people were heart-broken. I was like a child. I could not help even myself, much less help them.

That summer, the hunger was everywhere, in the old homeland in the north and in the new one in the south. In mid-July, a herd of 2,200 Texas longhorns was driven across the Missouri, but nine drowned during the crossing. Several Ponca, who had avoided going south by hiding among the neighboring tribes, dragged the animals out by their horns and invited the Santee to a feast, a temporary relief from the hunger in the north country. But in the south, there was no relief.

By the end of their first month in the Warm Country, the feeling infected all of the people. "Reports from the Poncas state that large numbers of them are sick, and that they are greatly dissatisfied with their new location," the *Niobrara Pioneer* told its readers on August 16. A week later, the chiefs had a council with their agent, begging him to help them go home before the fever and chills took everyone. They demanded he arrange a meeting in Washington, where they could plead

91

their case to the Great Father face to face. Already, thirty-six Ponca had either stayed behind or slipped away to live among the Omaha and Santee up north. The others, Agent Howard told his superiors, "are getting restless and somewhat troublesome in the premises."

In early November, Standing Bear, nine chiefs, and their agent boarded a train and traveled across the eastern lands of the United States until they reached the nation's capital. They stayed at the Washington House, where they were given large rooms with comfortable beds and chairs, and one night they were escorted to the National Theater where they saw a performance of *Pink Pajamas*. On November 9, the Ponca chiefs met with President Hayes at the White House, telling him of their long journey south, detailing their life in the Warm Country, begging him to let them return to their Niobrara homeland. He said he would think it over and they would meet again soon.

Although the President was sympathetic to what he had heard from Standing Bear and the other chiefs, their request collided head-on with prevailing government policy: to fill the Indian Territory with as many Indians as possible. And it also harbored another risk the government did not want to take, one summed up later by Interior Secretary Schurz: "If we begin to move the Poncas . . . back to the North, on the ground of dissatisfaction or discontent, there are other tribes that will become discontented, if they are not now. The Pawnees . . . would probably demand to be returned north; and so it would spread from one to another."

The next day, the chiefs again went to the White House and met with the President, Schurz, and the new Commissioner of Indian Affairs. Six weeks earlier, amid widespread complaints the Office of Indian Affairs was rife with corruption, incompetence and inefficiency, Schurz had fired Commissioner John Q. Smith and replaced him with Ezra Hayt. During ceremonies in the Cabinet Council Chamber, the President thanked the chiefs for honoring their treaties and living peacefully among their white neighbors. "There is none of their blood on your hands," he told them. "You have always listened to what the government of the white people said to you, and you have done what you were told to do. You have therefore my sincere and hearty sympathy, and I will do all I can to help you."

But he said he could not allow them to return to the north country. "He thought now that we were down there we had better stay," Standing Bear said. "He told me to go back and hunt for some good land, and he would have our things sent to us; that we should be treated well, and he did not think we would be sick any more, after a little. We would soon get used to the country, and then we would not be sick. I said in reply that I could only obey his orders."

Before leaving, Standing Bear and the Ponca were invited to the offices of the Interior Secretary, who presented each of the chiefs with a medal bearing the image of Thomas Jefferson. Secretary Schurz told them that because they had been a good friend to the white people, the government was now their friend. "You shall have no reason to say that we treat Indians who are our enemies better than Indians who are our friends," he said. He encouraged them to return to the Warm Country with a good heart and good cheer, to select a new land the same size as the old one, with ample timber and water, and to cultivate it with courage and energy. "Work will make you prosperous and contented, and you will soon forget the country you have left."

On November 17, 1877, the chiefs boarded a train and headed west, leaving Washington with a presidential pledge that they could choose a new piece of land, that when they selected it, the government would supply them with cattle and farming equipment and the material to build homes like the ones they had up north. But when they arrived back among their people, winter had begun to settle in on the Southern Great Plains.

It was too late now to look for new land, so the Ponca began to scatter across the northern end of the Quapaw Reservation, fanning out, setting up their canvas tents anywhere that promised relief from the rain and sleet, the snow and cold. They had no stoves and there was little wood and no matter where they set up the tents, they could not stop the fevers and shaking chills, the nausea and vomiting, the yellow skin and sunken eyes. They had never lived like this, alone, on separate tracts of land, away from the main camp. And Standing Bear did not know how to help them, what to do.

"The whole family would be sick and no one knew it. In some of these families persons would die and the others would not be able to bury them. They would drag them with a pony out on the prairie and leave them there. Men would take sick while at work and die in less than a day . . . There were dead in every family. Those who could walk around were sick. Not one in the whole tribe felt well."

They lived and died until spring, when the search for a new home began.

His sturdy log cabin with carefully dovetailed corners lies just across the river from a large hill, a prominent earthen mound offering the only interruption to an otherwise flat landscape extending for miles. Grandpa Parrish has put away his tribal land records for the day and finished a roast beef sandwich and a bowl of peaches. He likes the easy chair this time of afternoon, the Oklahoma basketball game on the TV, the warmth of the propane heater below the portraits of the Christian savior and the Ponca chief. And he likes to tell the stories, the ones he heard from his father and grandfather when they were taking their dinner in the cottonwoods in the early years of the twentieth century.

The old man's voice gets a little more excited than usual when he tells the story of the seven young Ponca who left the Quapaw lands in the early spring of 1878, venturing far to the west, looking for a new home for their people.

When they got to the west, they found that the soil was too sandy, so they began walking back home to the Quapaw country. One night, they were eating supper, and they saw this hill. They told my grand-mother, who was their cook, to meet them at the bottom of this hill the next day and to cook the meal there. So they did, and after sup-per they climbed up to the top of the hill. When they got on top, they looked down and what they saw looked just like the Niobrara homeland—one river emptying into another. They said, "We'd like to pick this country; it's similar to our homeland in Nebraska." They went to gather rocks and stacked them on top of one another on that hill until they were about eight to ten feet high. And then they went back to the Quapaw country. When they got there, they told the chiefs, "We think we found the land that's suitable for us to live. Go to this place and look for a hill with rocks on it and see for yourself. It's good land with water, timber, and a lot of good grass." The chiefs went and agreed that it was good land and so we all moved to this place.

Rosetta Le Clair listens to the old man's story about how their people came to the land near where the Salt Fork River empties into the Arkansas River, land they have both lived on all their lives. Her grandfather, Little Standing Buffalo, came down on the long march from their northern homeland near the confluence of the Niobrara and Missouri, so she has heard the stories from her own people many times. "My grandmother said when Standing Bear and the others first came down here, they chose their main headquarters to be between the two rivers, so they would have water on both sides. My grandmother said no tornado or strong wind would come into this area because it was between the two rivers."

Standing Bear's daughter did not survive her first winter in the Warm Country. Neither did his wife's mother and grandmother. He had been one of the chiefs who had gone out and found the rocks on the hill and in March 1878, without informing the agent or waiting for permission, he gathered his three surviving daughters, his two wives, and his son and left the infested bottomlands, pushing west to the lands near the confluence of the Salt Fork and Arkansas. They had no money, no medicine, no farming equipment, few horses, and little food, but it didn't matter. Within a month, several hundred others abandoned the Quapaw Reservation and headed west, joining Standing Bear and his family, looking for a fresh start on the land between the rivers.

That May, the President made good on his pledge to help Standing

Bear's people find a better home in the Indian Territory. Congress set aside $45,500 to move the rest of the Ponca from the Quapaw Reservation and help resettle them on the new land near the rivers. By then, the new Indian Commissioner had fired E. A. Howard, the agent who had moved them from the Niobrara, for being incompetent. A few months later, his successor, A. G. Boone, was fired for incompetence. The new Ponca agent, William Whiteman, a lawyer from the border town of Baxter Springs, arrived to take charge in early July, and he soon began to organize the remaining Ponca for the long trek to the new land.

On the morning of July 21, 1878, they loaded their tents and their belongings, supplies, some farming equipment, and the old and the sick in their remaining wagons and headed west, moving slowly across the dusty roads in temperatures that ranged from 95 to 100 degrees each day. One of the horses died of exhaustion near Arkansas City, but eight days and 185 miles later, the rest of the weary caravan made it safely to the large bend of the Salt Fork River, not far from the hill where the stones had been placed.

About the same time, six-hundred miles north, the Lakota were leaving the old Ponca homeland on the Niobrara. They had come down for the winter, received their supplies on the Missouri, and decided they did not like the land and wanted to go back home. So in late July, they packed up and left, moving several hundred miles across the prairie, back to the lands where their ancestors lay buried. The Ponca lands were now abandoned, the fertile valley untended, their old homes and buildings empty. The government plan to relocate the Lakota, to cut shipping costs and keep a closer eye on them, had failed. And soon more than a few Ponca began to wonder why the good land and the buildings should stay empty, why Standing Bear and his people could not return home. Bright Eyes, the young Omaha Indian poet and schoolteacher, was struck by what she read in the local papers. "I was surprised to find that the white settlers around the reserve opposed the Poncas being taken away, and that they thought it was an outrage. I was surprised, because I heard that the white settlers hated the Indians and wanted to get their lands."

Life and Death in the Warm Country

When the rest of the Ponca finally arrived near the junction of the two rivers in the Indian Territory, they found the land was good, the best they had seen and, in appearance, the closest to what they had left. The soil was sandy, but covered with sage and a thick coat of buffalo grass, good for grazing in many areas. There were networks of fresh springs running out of the river bluffs and abundant heating fuel from the thick stands of cottonwood, oak, walnut, and pecan. In the beginning, there was only an aging commissary, but the President again delivered on his pledge and soon there were cattle, a sawmill, some shops, a school named for their head chief, White Eagle, and some farming equipment.

But for the second year in a row, they had arrived at a new home too late to break ground and plant crops and so they were again forced to rely on government rations through the fall and winter of 1878. The new home also posed another problem they had encountered before: The Ponca did not own any of the land where they were now running cattle, cutting timber, building shops, and starting a school. They lived on lands owned by the Cherokee, lands that a treaty allowed the government to use to resettle other tribes. But the Cherokee were the landlords and they could evict the Ponca if they did not pay for the land. And although Congress had been asked to provide money for them to buy the land, no money had been approved more than a year after the request. So for the third time in eighteen months, the Ponca found themselves squatters on someone else's property, with no money or legal rights to make a claim.

They also had no homes and so they again lived in tents on the new land, clustered in one large village near the agency headquarters. Standing Bear was not among them. He and his family lived away from the main village, in the woods, out of sight of the agent and all the visitors. That fall, Commissioner Hayt arrived from Washington to visit the Ponca and tour their land. "There is probably no finer location for an Indian settlement in the Indian Territory, and in all respects it is far superior to their old location in Dakota," he wrote Interior Secretary Schurz. The commissioner acknowledged the Ponca had died in large numbers during their first four months in the Territory, which was inevitable, but said they had acclimated and could now expect to be as healthy as anywhere else. The one downside, he reported, was the attitude of one of their chiefs. Standing Bear "was constantly grumbling, and held aloof from the other chiefs, and seemed full of discontent, which he took no pains to conceal." The agent said he expected Standing Bear would leave if he got the chance. "It was not thought expedient at that time to put him in confinement, as one chief out of ten or twelve was hardly of sufficient importance to deal with in that manner."

Before leaving, the commissioner commended the Ponca for their determination and exemplary work habits, traits strongly endorsed by his boss back in Washington. Hard work and a good attitude, Secretary Schurz believed, could prevent disease. "Indolence and sulkiness are apt, if they do not breed disease, at least to aggravate it," he said. And hard work could also cure homesickness. "A man who is vigorously at work is much less apt to become homesick than one who sulks in his tent and broods over his troubles."

When Standing Bear looked inside his tent in the fall of 1878, he did not see two of his daughters, his grandchild, his mother-in-law, and his wife's grandmother. He saw that no matter where they had lived—on the creek bottoms of the Quapaw Reservation, on the fertile lands between the Salt Fork and the Arkansas, in a large village or alone in the woods—they could not escape the mosquitoes that had stalked them across the Warm Country for fifteen months. That fall, when he looked across the new land between the rivers, he did not see that they had acclimated at all, only that many more again had the fever and chills, the yellow skin, and they were dying now in greater numbers than ever before.

From the beginning, the diseases they had never known and could not fight often came to the tents of the chiefs. They killed two of the chiefs and their principal chief, White Eagle, lost his wife and four children. "One week after my wife died, one of the children died; two weeks afterward another child died; and along toward winter another child died; and three days after that another died," White Eagle said. "Better to go back to the old reservation and not have so good houses, and live in them, and have health in them, than to have good houses and fine things down in the Indian Territory, and be sick all the time, and all die."

By the end of the second summer, another forty-five had been lost, many of them buried quickly and without honor in the strange new land. It had never been their way to treat the dead in such a manner and it made Standing Bear feel sick and helpless, something few in the other culture understood. Colonel James Stevenson, the Smithsonian ethnographer who had lived among them for several summers, was one who did. He observed that among the Ponca, emotional bonds to people and places had been developed to an unusually high degree. "Their attachment to their homes, their old hunting-grounds, the places where they have buried their dead . . . is very great." And so was the attachment to their relatives.

From the time they left the Niobrara, throughout the first winter, the first summer and all of the second, the Ponca found interpreters and wrote the Omaha numerous letters, letters telling them about the journey south, the new life, how they were surviving, how many were sick, how many had died, how they missed their homeland, and how much they missed their friends and relatives. The Omaha, in turn, responded with many letters to the Ponca, letters letting the people in the south know that disease and desolation had spread across the northern lands as well.

"My sister's husband, as your son is dead, my heart is always sad. As you and your child made great efforts in helping me with my farm while you were here, and till you went to that land, I was grieved when I heard of his death. This one, my wife, is always crying. I have been walking with a heavy heart ever since I heard it. I have nothing left me but the horses which carry the wagon."

"Depend upon God. Remember Him. For if, instead of remembering God, you love this world alone, you shall be sad—you shall surely be sad in the future . . . Now I have written enough on this subject. When you write, send me word how many have died of the Pawnees whom I know. And write whatever you wish to write to me. Write to me how many horses you have."

"I wish to hear how you are. I wish to hear whether you and your people are in good health and are prospering. Since you left the land, we ever think of you throughout the day . . . Your younger brother, Heqaga-jinga, is dead. He was a very stout-hearted man. The men and chiefs are very sad. Even the women and the young men are sorrowful. What vegetable we planted are good. We have plenty of wheat, and we have done very well in raising corn."

"Please tell my father, Ceki, that my brother-in-law is dead. Say, 'It is reported that your mother's brother is dead.' The people usually die in five days. The sickness is bad. I send to you seven days after the death of my brother-in-law. The woman whom I married came near dying."

"Grandchild, I send you two words. I have shaken hands with the Dakota, Spotted Tail. It was for no special reason that I shook hands, yet it was good . . . Though I always remember you, no matter what happens, yet I am sad when anything unpleasant occurs. I say that Wakanda shall decide for me about my affairs."

Throughout those first few years in the Warm Country, some of their Omaha friends and relatives also came to visit. One spring, Bright Eyes took a train to Wichita and then a stagecoach south to see her aunt and uncle on the new Ponca land between the rivers. She was shocked at how sick her aunt was and the house they lived in—a little shack of rough boards and dirt roof with no heating stove, one of six shanties the Omaha would not have as "chicken houses." She saw that most of the people still lived in canvas tents and kept the few starving horses that had not died or been stolen tethered close to their tents. She saw many Ponca vomiting from the salty water and wondered why their shanties and tents were scattered so far apart. The men told her the agent forbid them to live close together for fear they would plan an escape. The women told her the government had sent them many wagons, but the agent refused to issue them because he feared they would use them to flee. The government had sent plows, but there were no oxen and not enough healthy horses to break much ground. They could not speak English and there was no school to teach them. They were unable to work, to plant, or to build a home, and they felt increasingly isolated and frustrated, squatting in their tents, tending to the sick, on someone else's land.

"I have often heard Indians say, 'What is the use of doing anything? If I make a fine farm and build me a good house, and fix up everything comfortable and nice, the government will take it away, and some white man will get the benefit of it. What is the use of my doing anything?' I have heard Indians say that again and again," Bright Eyes said. She left after a week.

Throughout much of the fall of 1878, Standing Bear stayed alone in his camp along a tree-lined stream, well hidden from the agent's view. The prospect of spending a second winter in the leaky canvas tents worried him. And it concerned others, too. Their new agent, Whiteman, conveyed his fears to Washington in his first annual report: "The season thus far since our arrival here has been a very sickly one . . . coming from a northern latitude, where such diseases are unknown, with their systems unacclimated [sic], the malaria has been peculiarly fatal to them, and many deaths have resulted." The chronic sickness and inability to fight it, he noted, have "greatly discouraged and made them dissatisfied with this location, and they express a strong desire to go back to their old reservation in Dakota."

He urged the Commissioner of Indian Affairs and the Secretary of the Interior to make good on the government pledges that had helped lure the Ponca away from the Niobrara. He asked them to establish the size and boundaries of their new lands, to grant them legal ownership of their own reservation. "They seem to have lost faith in the promises of the government, and often say the 'Great Father' has forgotten them; by the time he again remembers them none will be left to receive what he has promised them." The agent asked his superiors to invite the chiefs to Washington during the coming winter months to discuss their concerns and as a show of good faith. "I think it would contribute greatly toward a restoration of good feeling," he said, "and to remove the spirit of discontent and dissatisfaction which now pervades their minds."

That fall, the feeling that had been with Standing Bear for a long time was not confined to his tent back in the trees on the Southern Plains. Among the Lakota, Crazy Horse and Sitting Bull had known the feeling and it had been with Dull Knife and Little Wolf of the Northern Cheyenne for many years. They were also entrusted with the welfare of their people and each year throughout the 1870s, many of the chiefs of the Northern Plains had found the decisions more and more difficult. They could stay on the open plains and fight, or surrender to the government. They could die with honor in their native country, or die of disease on a reservation hundreds of miles away. They could persist and face physical annihilation, or give up and risk cultural annihilation. Not long after his people were captured at the end of a 1,700-mile freedom flight, thirty miles from the safety of the Canadian border, Chief Joseph and his Nez Perce survivors were brought to the Warm Country. It wasn't long before he, too, knew the feeling. "When we stand on the hill," the chief said, "we look with one eye toward Washington Territory, and with the other toward the grave yard."

Grandpa Parrish has seen enough. The old man grabs his weathered walking stick, pads across the wood floor in his oversized moccasins, and clicks off a small color TV, Oklahoma comfortably ahead at the half. He grabs the worn-out armrests of his favorite chair and eases back down into a tangle of leather creases. He reaches for the red-and-white box of Marlboros on a TV tray by the chair, and sits and smokes by the warmth of the propane heater, quietly surveying the color photos on the walls of his living room. He's worried about his children, he says, and the children of the others. At his age, he knows there aren't many trips left to the cottonwood grove, down to the bend in the river out back. "I'm the oldest of my tribe, and the young don't really know the customs anymore. What happens when I'm gone? When I'm gone, who are they going to ask? I don't know."

He's been a good leader, a good elder, a good father. No one could say otherwise. Still, he worries. "We all used to live together. Now, there's one person on the land, but they have lots of children. Where are they all going to live when they grow up? It makes me sad to think about it. That's why I'm doing the research. I'm trying to get forty acres back, so we can get at least one more generation some homes and some land to live on."

The old man takes only a few puffs, then crushes out the cigarette. He scans the living-room walls—the kids at homecoming, running with the football, twirling a baton, on leave from the Marines, at the wedding altar. He likes to talk about them, thinks about them all the time. And he will say, over and over, how worried he is that they will forget, that one day there won't be anyone left who remembers. He lights another cigarette and looks up at the walls, staring blankly for a while at the oil portrait of the chief. "His boy got sick that October."

Standing Bear could not see how it got into the blood, into the liver and the kidneys. But he could recognize what happened once it did, what he had seen so many times in so many of the others—the high fevers and chills, the shaking and vomiting and nausea, the sweating and list-lessness. It visited everyone in the camps, but it had come most often to the old and the young. By the winter of 1878, it had taken 158 of his people, one-fourth of the tribe. And he could see now that it had come to his only son.

All that fall and into the winter, he could see how sick the boy was, the boy who would inherit his position and pass along the traditions to his children, and wherever he looked now, he could see how it had all changed so quickly. The lands they left had created their values and be-liefs, had helped forge their connection to the world around them and to the world beyond and had given them the strength to survive, but he saw no sacred rocks in the Warm Country, no sacred trees or hills, no rivers or streams. He did not know some of the animals and did not see the same plants they had used in the north country. And the place he had buried his father, the place where Wakanda lived, was hundreds of miles away. He was a chief, the second in command, and month after month, the answers had become more and more difficult. He didn't know how they could overcome the yellow skin and hollow eyes. He didn't know how many of the new ways they would have to adopt to physically survive or how many of the old ones they had to retain to culturally survive. And he didn't know what it meant to be Christianized and civilized by people who had taken their land, stolen their horses, starved their elders, liquored up their men, murdered their women, and abused their children. As fall turned to winter in 1878, the one thing he did know was how sick his boy was, how it was everywhere now, and the feeling that he'd had for a long time overwhelmed his canvas tent along the tree-lined creek between the two rivers.

"Sometimes I thought I had better gather up my people, send them on ahead, keep my warriors in the rear, and endeavor to retreat to the mountains, and if the soldiers came, all die fighting . . . I could see nothing ahead, but death for the whole tribe. I was much sorry for the little children who were so very sick. They would moan, and we had no medicine and no way to help them."

That winter, shortly after Christmas, Wakanda called the boy home.

5

Going Home

The agent didn't think he would do it—not then, not in broad daylight, not in this kind of cold and wind. And not with so much snow.

But the agent didn't know what the boy had said to his father, what he had asked him to do in his last few hours, in the last few days of the year. And he didn't know what the father had said to his only son, a boy lying on the stiff ground in their tent along the river in the winter of 1878. Before the end came, the father made sure the boy had heard his words.

So on the second day of the new year, Standing Bear gathered eight men and twenty-one women and children and they began loading four old wagons in their hidden camp near the mouth of the Chikaskia River. It had been building for a long time. Without the agent knowing, they had met in councils, debating in strong words throughout the fall and early winter. In the end, most of the other chiefs were against it. Many were sick. They were cold and hungry and weak, and the few horses they had were in much the same way. Standing Bear did not agree. He persisted, speaking forcefully and eloquently during the secret meetings around the council fires back in the woods. It was their second winter and still they lived in unheated tents. Outside, he had seen enough of the inch-long greenhead flies and the clouds of mosquitoes. He had tasted the salty water, and watched their oxen and five hundred of their horses die. And now, eighteen months later, one-fourth of the Sacred Head People had come to rest in the soil of the Warm Country, a land six hundred miles from their old burial grounds. The councils finally ended and when they did, a distance had developed between the chiefs, the two sides unable to agree anymore on what was best for their people. During the last few days of the year, Standing Bear had listened carefully to his son, he had heard his last words, and the words of the council no longer mattered.

On the afternoon of January 2, 1879, the thirty Ponca men, women, and children in the camp eight miles from agency headquarters finished loading their belongings in three covered wagons and a light spring wagon. On the road ahead, the morning came in at nineteen below zero with a steady north wind. They hadn't much in the way of winter clothing and it was coming down harder as the two worn-out horses stood motionless in the blinding snow. The boy was dressed in his best clothing and the chief gently placed him in a box and carefully lowered the box into the back of one of the covered wagons. When everything was ready, the father and mother stood behind the horses and the wagon, then turned their faces north and began walking away from the Warm Country, heading toward *Má-azì*, to the high chalk bluffs near the Running Water. Their boy was going home.

"We told the agent often that we were going to come away . . . Where should we start out to go to except to our own land, to our old home?" Standing Bear said. "We didn't think of doing anything else; we thought only of that, all the time."

For months, they had set aside some of their weekly rations, gradually building up a food supply, and an annuity payment in late December provided twenty dollars cash for the thirty Ponca on their journey north. Seven of them had been very sick when they left, and the cold and wind grew steadily worse the farther north they went. During their first three days on the open plains, the temperatures up ahead plunged to twenty-two below zero, fifteen below, and eighteen below. On the fourth day, January 6, steady gales of seventy miles per hour dropped the wind chill to forty-one below, temperatures that freeze the skin in ten minutes, so they couldn't travel far that day. After they left Indian Territory, the chief decided to abandon the traditional route and swing farther west, hoping their trail would be harder to follow. For Standing Bear, the routes were familiar. It was the third time in less than two years the fifty-year-old chief had set out on foot to cross Kansas and Nebraska.

As Standing Bear, his two wives, and the twenty-seven Ponca made their way across the frozen lands of southern Kansas, the commander of the Department of the Platte faced a crisis in the northwest corner of Nebraska. The previous fall, three-hundred Northern Cheyenne under Dull Knife and Little Wolf had walked off their reservation in the Indian Territory, heading for their Montana homeland. In mid-October, cold, hungry, and exhausted in the Nebraska Sandhills, the two chiefs made a decision: The younger, healthier ones would stay with Little Wolf and continue on. The old and the sick, and most of the women and children, would go with Dull Knife and seek refuge with Red Cloud and the Lakota. Dull Knife's group was captured about a week later and marched to Fort Robinson, where they eventually were told a decision had been made.

Each year, General Crook had found the decisions more and more complex, his orders more and more difficult. He told his superiors the latest ones would not be easy to carry out. He didn't know if his men had the heart for it. The Northern Cheyenne, he wrote, "repeated their expressions of desire to live at peace with our people, but said they would kill themselves sooner than be taken back to the Indian Territory. These statements were confirmed by Red Cloud and other friendly Sioux chiefs, who assured us that the Cheyennes had left their Reservation in Indian Territory to avoid fever and starvation and that they would die to the last man, woman, and child before they could be taken from the quarters in which they were confined." But the orders remained firm, so in late December, Crook tried again. "At this time, the thermometer at Fort Robinson showed a range of from zero down to forty below . . . The captives were without adequate clothing, and no provisions had been made to supply it . . ." Still, the orders stayed the same. On Christmas Eve 1878, Crook telegraphed his superior, Lieutenant General Philip Sheridan: "It would be inhuman to move them as ordered." Sheridan replied he would forward the concerns of food and clothing to Washington. But the orders stood. The Indians were to be moved south as soon as possible.

On January 3, when the post commander told Dull Knife that he and his people were to be marched back to the Territory, the chief stood and faced the soldiers. "I am here on my own ground," he told them, "and I will never go back. You may kill me here, but you cannot make me go back." That afternoon, the 149 Northern Cheyenne barricaded themselves in their barracks. On the evening of January 9, after five days without food and heating fuel, three days without water, they broke out, fleeing for the protective bluffs of the White River, the soldiers in pursuit. When it ended, sixty-four Indian men, women, and children were dead. "Among these Cheyenne Indians," Crook later wrote, "were some of the bravest and most efficient of the auxiliaries who had acted under General Mackenzie and myself . . . and I still preserve a grateful remembrance of their distinguished services which the Government seems to have forgotten." For a long time after, the decision to march them south, and the desperation that led to their deaths, kept Crook up late into the night.

Farther south, three weeks into the snow and cold of Kansas, the Ponca had used up the twenty dollars and the small amount of rations they had stockpiled, and some of the children were sick. They were all cold and they didn't eat for two days and so Standing Bear began to beg for food, relying on the kindness of frontier strangers, strangers who were poor, too, and didn't have much to give.

In eastern Kansas, he walked up to the house of a white man and motioned for him to come outside. When he did, Standing Bear pointed to the children. The man didn't seem to understand, but then he looked at their ponies and saw how thin and sickly and weak they were. He left and soon returned with his boys, who brought some hay and a large bag filled with corn. The white man watched as the Ponca emptied some of the corn, shelled it, parched it, and gave it to the children. When he saw how hungrily they ate it, he seemed to understand for the first time, and he went to his house and came back with flour and meat and some coffee. They thanked him, then turned the wagon carrying Bear Shield to the north and kept moving across Kansas, grateful for how kindly the white settlers treated them along the way, for all the bread and cornmeal and flour and coffee they gave them.

"None of them refused to give us anything when they saw we were hungry, except two places, and I don't think they had much themselves," Standing Bear said.

During the severe, early January cold spell, Agent Whiteman didn't venture far outside his new two-story, eight-room home. So six days passed before he discovered the Ponca had left. When he did, the agent sent an urgent message to his superiors in Washington, asking them to alert the agents at the Omaha and Otoe reservations in Nebraska. Standing Bear and his group had left without his permission and if the agents saw them, he said, they should immediately arrest them. He recommended a detachment of soldiers march them back south to Indian Territory.

When Standing Bear crossed into Nebraska, he made sure the Ponca stayed far west of the Otoe Reservation. They kept moving and after thirty-nine days they reached the Platte, camping and resting there for the night, then continuing again in the morning. They headed north and a little east, moving as fast as they could, getting closer.

Years later, General Crook's aide-de-camp summarized the Ponca's winter flight across Kansas and Nebraska, noting their determination to reach the old lands. "Application for permission to do this was refused, and thereupon a portion of the band tried the experiment of going at their own expense across country, walking every foot of the way, molesting nobody, and subsisting upon charity. Not a shot was fired at any one; not so much as a dog was stolen," wrote Lieutenant John G. Bourke.

For several weeks, Bright Eyes had been waiting, had been expecting them ever since her uncle sent a message from the Indian Territory that Standing Bear and the others had gone away. In early March, she and her father, Joseph La Flesche, got the word. On March 4, after a journey of sixty-two days, Standing Bear and the Ponca arrived in the northeast corner of Nebraska. They were camped west of the Omaha Reservation, resting up, just a few days' journey from their Niobrara homeland. After a while, Standing Bear sent runners from his camp to the Omaha to try to find out what was going on with the Omaha agent. The runners returned and said the agent had spoken kindly, had asked the Ponca to come and visit and he would see what he could do for them.

Not long afterwards, La Flesche and some of the Omaha went to visit Standing Bear's camp. For the second time in two years, they were shocked at what they saw—faces hollowed from hunger and skin blackened from frostbite, gaunt children, ragged clothes, emaciated horses, and so many sick. One man wore a string around his neck tied to a sack containing the bones of his grandchild. The Omaha gave them food and told them to rest up. They said they would try to help them.

It was early spring and the Ponca were anxious to work, to break ground, to try to grow some crops of their own. But they no longer had any land in the north country and so the Omaha held a council with their agent. They asked him to let Standing Bear have some land, to let his group become a part of their tribe as they were centuries ago, to let Standing Bear and his family come and live with them. All the Ponca wanted, they said, was to farm their land and be left alone. The agent said he would not give any advice on the matter, that Standing Bear could continue on to the Niobrara or come to the Omaha—the choice was his.

Standing Bear chose to stay awhile, to get his sick and hungry people rested and back on their feet. The Omaha gave them some land and some seed, and the Ponca who were not too sick began to break ground and plant, something they had always done in the north county in early spring. It was something they hadn't done for more than two years and it felt good.

"I stayed till one hundred and fifty-eight of my people had died," Standing Bear said later. "Then I ran away with thirty of my people, men and women and children. Some of the children were orphans. We were three months on the road. We were weak and sick and starved. When we reached the Omaha Reserve the Omahas gave us a piece of land, and we were in a hurry to plough it and put in wheat."

Not long after they began planting, Standing Bear was summoned to a meeting. "When we got there the Omaha agent said: 'Wait here; the President has sent me word that there is a man going up to the Niobrara country, and if he comes to the Omaha Reserve you can go up with him; you must stop here till I can send him word and hear from the President.' So we stayed." They stayed in their camp behind a hill near the La Flesche home and broke more ground and put in more wheat, resting up, feeding the children, trying to get the sick healthy again.

One Sunday morning, after they had been there about three weeks, Bright Eyes said, "One of my sisters looked out of the window and said that some soldiers had come."

The Omaha agent had gotten the word the day Standing Bear arrived and he immediately telegraphed the Commissioner of Indian Affairs. That spring, as the grid of family farms and ranches throughout the American West grew larger and stronger, as more and more tribes settled into the Warm Country, no one in Washington wanted to see a small group of disgruntled Ponca break free, a group whose actions might encourage others to do the same. The national policy of uprooting Indians from their native lands to clear the way for white settlement had gone unchallenged for almost half a century and, as far as the architects of Indian policy were concerned, it wasn't going to be challenged in the early spring days of 1879.

So, in short order, the news of Standing Bear's arrival moved quickly up the chain of command and the decision came back down just as fast. After hearing from Omaha Agent Jacob Vore, the Commissioner of Indian Affairs promptly told the Secretary of the Interior, who informed the Secretary of War, who told General Sherman, who passed it on to Lieutenant General Sheridan in Chicago. On March 17, the orders landed on the desk of General Crook at Fort Omaha: A military detail was to arrest Standing Bear and the Ponca, and march them back to the Indian Territory, posthaste.

Six days later, Lieutenant William Carpenter and six men of the Ninth Infantry arrived in the Ponca camp behind the hill near the La Flesche home. The Omaha knew why they had come. As word began to spread, they streamed in from across their reservation, flocking to the blacksmith shop and the agency headquarters, watching and waiting, many screaming and wailing in the commotion that followed the arrival of the soldiers in the Ponca camp. One of the Ponca men, Long Runner, would not go, would not obey the orders. When a soldier put a gun to his head, Long Runner said to kill him, he would rather die than go back. "He tried to jump up and get his gun," Bright Eyes said. "Then he drew his knife; then the soldiers handcuffed him; they put him in irons and took him down near the blacksmith shop, where they were camping; my brother was there nearly all night with him. They had him tied. The next morning, early, he was shaking with the chills. He was so sick he could not eat his breakfast; but they kept him handcuffed, and the soldiers stayed there guarding him with a bayonet."

Later that day, in their makeshift camp on Omaha lands, Standing Bear spoke to the soldier chief. He told him the Ponca were in their own country now, and they never wanted to go back. They had separated from the rest of their people, had come away to live in peace, to support themselves by working on their own land, just like the white settlers. "He stated that he had always been a friend to the whites," the infantry leader said, "and that on one occasion he found a poor soldier on the plains in midwinter, with both feet frozen, and nearly starved to death; that he carried him in his arms to camp and took care of him for several weeks until he died. 'And now,' said he, 'you, a soldier, come here to drive me from the land of my fathers.' "

Like Bright Eyes and her relatives, the lieutenant, too, was struck by the appearance of the people he had come to arrest, the people who were to be marched back to the Warm Country. "They were in a pitiable condition from the effects of chills and fever. Over half of the adults suffered from this disease on the march to Omaha, and, notwithstanding the best medical treatment while prisoners, many are still in feeble health. Before leaving their camp, the women and children cried piteously at the prospect of going back to the Indian Territory."

The Reverend James Owen Dorsey was also there that day and the Ponca came to see him, to ask for his help. "My friend, you know us," Standing Bear said to him. "We can't live down there where the Great Father put us. We came here to live and work the land." In the end, the lieutenant did not believe he could march the Ponca south, and did not have the heart to do it. He decided to let their chief speak to his superior, to the commander of the Department of the Platte.

On March 27, after a two-day march, Standing Bear and the twenty-five Ponca healthy enough to walk arrived at Fort Omaha, where they set up camp just south of the fort's main entrance. The fort's commanding officer, Colonel John King, surveyed the prisoners, then filed a report to superiors. He noted the many who were sick and concluded "it will be necessary for the entire party to remain here for a few days so that their ponies may recuperate sufficiently to enable them to proceed on their return to the Indian Territory."

That night, the eight Ponca men, seven women, and eleven children huddled in their three lodges outside the fort. Three months earlier, they had left their reservation in the Warm Country without a pass, without the permission of their agent, and now, in a few days, they would be taken back through the lands they had walked across, back to the place where many of their relatives were buried, where many more were crippled by disease and homesickness. Because they had left illegally, the government seized their belongings, forbade the Omaha to offer them sanctuary, and cut off their annuities. Standing

Bear gathered the splintered remnants of his small band and told them they had gone as far as they could, it was useless to resist anymore. They were powerless, they were too weak. They had no weapons to fight the government. In their lodges late that night, he saw how many were sick—all of them: men, women, and the children—and he knew what would happen now. "My efforts to save their lives had failed."

In the dark, early morning hours of March 30, 1879, a visitor quietly made his way to the offices of the local newspaper. After a long talk, the assistant editor of the *Omaha Daily Herald* bid good night to his visitor and finished putting the paper to bed that Sunday morning. After a few hours' sleep, he set off on a brisk four-mile walk, passing citizens on their way to church, reflecting on what the visitor had told him, thinking there might be a decent story in the three Indian lodges clustered just south of the main entrance to Fort Omaha.

In his thirty-eight years, Thomas Henry Tibbles had walked a good many roads before taking the one that now led to Standing Bear's lodge at the edge of Omaha. Born in Athens, Ohio, in 1840, Tibbles ran away from home while still a boy and was picked up by an immigrant train sent west by Henry Ward Beecher in his antislavery quest to settle Kansas and make it a free state. In the summer of 1856, the sixteen-year-old boy joined Jim Lane's Free-State Militia, fighting for the abolitionist cause in Kansas Territory where he was captured by pro-slavery forces during a border skirmish. Sentenced to be hanged, he escaped when abolitionist forces rescued him, although a musket ball tore off part of his ear during the fight. After the bloody two-year border war, he enrolled at Mount Union College in Ohio, where he took traditional liberal arts courses and several religion classes, and became a popular campus speaker. Three years later, at the outset of the Civil War, he put away his books and joined Union troops as a scout, trying to break up gangs of horse thieves led by Charles Quantrell in Kansas and Missouri. The Quantrell gang eventually captured him, tortured him, and hung him from a tree, but comrades found him and cut him down. After the

Civil War, he married, became an ordained Methodist preacher, and set out on horseback to spread the gospel throughout western Missouri and along Nebraska's Republican River Valley. In time, he grew disenchanted with Methodist restrictions, joined the Presbyterians, and built a church and congregation in Omaha. Later, he spent a few winters among several Indian tribes along the Missouri and, in 1874, after a grasshopper plague wiped out most of the crops, he caught a train for the East Coast, lecturing and raising money for hungry farmers and their families back on the plains. Three years later, Tibbles retired from the ministry and turned to pen and paper as a means to deliver the word, as a way to achieve social justice.

Standing Bear had little to say to the strange white man with the pen and paper who suddenly appeared in his camp that Sunday morning, telling the interpreter he would not agree to an interview until after his meeting with General Crook the next day. The reporter persisted, telling Standing Bear his paper did not publish on Monday, so no article would appear until after the meeting. Still, the chief believed the general would be insulted if he spoke to a reporter first. He again declined. Flustered, Tibbles wasn't sure what to do. Years ago, while wintering with the tribes along the Missouri, he had been initiated into their Soldier Lodge Society, and as a last resort, he flashed some of the society's hand signs. It is said the chief recognized them, and after a while, he had a change of heart.

For the next three hours, the reporter and an Omaha Indian interpreter, Charles Morgan, sat and talked with Standing Bear, his wife, and several Ponca gathered in the chief's lodge. The newspaperman did not know the full story, had not heard many of the details, so he asked a lot of questions and patiently recorded the answers in his notebook.

The first to speak was Buffalo Chips. He spoke slowly, telling the reporter how the Ponca knew years ago they would have to trade the gun for the plow to adapt, to survive on the Great Plains. "The game is gone, never to come back. I look everywhere and I see none. It has vanished away like a dream when I wake from sleep. But the ground is here. It can never vanish away. From the ground the Indian must live." The

Ponca knew that, he said, and so they began to learn from the white settlers, raising crops, building wooden houses, sending their children to school. "Eight days ago I was at work on my farm which the Omahas gave me. I had sowed some spring wheat, and wished to sow some more. I was living peaceably with all men. I have never committed any crime. I was arrested and brought back as a prisoner. Does your law do that? I have been told since the great war that all men were free men, and that no man can be made a prisoner unless he does wrong. I have done no wrong, and yet I am here a prisoner."

Buffalo Chips said he was confused, that many of the Ponca had felt the same way for a long time. "Why does the government insist on feeding me? If they intend to always feed all the Indians I should think they would eat all the government had. I seem to be blind. I cannot understand these things. Here I am, and those who are with me want to go to work and raise grain to live on next winter. We don't want to live on the government. We want to support ourselves." And he said he would never go back to the Warm Country. "It would be better for the government, better for us, to stand us out there in a line, bring the soldiers, and tell them to shoot us all. Then our miseries would be ended, and the government would have no more trouble. It would be better that way."

Standing Bear spoke next. He recounted how the Ponca and Omaha were once a part of one tribe and spoke a similar language, how they had come to the plains, watched the game disappear, and taken up farming. How the Lakota raided their fields, stole their horses, and killed their people. How the Ponca eventually were taken from their lands and marched to the Indian Territory, where they had nothing to do but sit still, be sick, starve, and die.

His son, he said, was a good boy. He had done all he could to help him, to educate him in the other ways, so that when he himself was gone, the boy would know how to read and write and earn a living from the land, that he would have the skills to survive in the new world. He said his son was the reason they left the Warm Country.

"My boy who died down there, as he was dying looked up to me and said, 'I would like you to take my bones back and bury them where

I was born.' I promised him I would. I could not refuse the dying request of my boy. I have attempted to keep my word. His bones are in that trunk."

It was late afternoon, the sun slipping into the western prairie. The preacher turned newsman put the notebook in his pocket and broke into an energetic walk. He had an idea, and after a mile, he began to jog along the dark and deserted roads leading back to the city. He had not eaten and he felt a little weak, but he kept running until he reached the First Presbyterian Church, where the evening service was about to begin. Afterwards, the Reverend William Harsha let him speak to the parishioners and when he finished, he jogged to the First Congregational Church, where the Reverend Alvin Sherrill let him speak to his parishioners between the opening hymns. At 11 P.M., Tibbles made it back home. He ate and then sat down at his writing desk, transcribing the words he had heard in Standing Bear's lodge until shortly after 5 A.M.

Shortly after noon the next day, March 31, 1879, the commander of the Department of the Platte summoned Standing Bear to a meeting in his headquarters at Fort Omaha. The chief arrived with a number of women and children and seven Ponca leaders dressed in white men's clothing. General Crook arrived with seven officers dressed in military finery. Charles Morgan, the Omaha full-blood who spoke Ponca and English fluently, arrived to interpret, and Tibbles, the only civilian, came with his notebook. Lieutenant Carpenter, who had arrested the Ponca on the Omaha Reservation and marched them back to the fort, introduced the officers to the Indians. After they shook hands, the Ponca sat in a semi-circle on the general's floor, green Army blankets draped across their shoulders.

By 1879, Crook had long been regarded as the Army's most experienced Indian fighter, a distinction derived from more than twenty years of military campaigns against the western tribes. And for many of those years, he had held firmly to the popular belief that the enemy was a primitive roadblock in civilization's path, a hopeless relic of a distant past, people incapable of progressing until their culture and lifestyle were destroyed. But in recent years, he had grown weary of the broken treaties, the unprovoked massacres of women and children, the corruption in Washington, the moral bankruptcy of the reservation agents. And after more and more contact with the Apache and Lakota, with the Ute and Bannock, after seeing what had happened to Dull Knife and the Northern Cheyenne, after long discussions with his thoughtful and scholarly aide-de-camp John Bourke, who was a student of history and anthropology, the general began to alter his view. He began to see the Indian as a person whose beliefs and culture had sustained him for centuries, someone who could not be forced to adopt radically new values and traditions in a few short years. He began to believe that no amount of military firepower could solve the political, cultural, and legal problems the twenty-six Ponca camped outside the fort posed for the government that issued his orders. Yes, he was still a soldier first and foremost, but he was also becoming much bolder in trying to resolve the unsettling inner conflict between humanity and military duty.

After the greetings and handshakes, the general's aide-de-camp began writing in his diary. Bourke was a prolific chronicler of the many encounters with the Indian people and his voluminous diaries reflected personal observations, historical insights, and a good amount of specific detail. As the formal interviews began, he noted that the appearance of the Ponca chief differed from the others.

Standing Bear "was a noble looking Indian, tall and commanding in presence, dignified in manner and very elegantly dressed in the costume of his tribe. He wore a shirt made of blue flannel, having collar and cuffs of red cloth, ornamented with brass buttons; leggings of blue flannel, moccasins of deerskin, and over his shoulder was draped a beautiful blanket, one half red, the other half blue, with the line of entrance covered by a broad band of beadwork. His hair was parted in the middle, the dividing line marked with red paint, the hair itself gathered in two pieces, one hanging over each shoulder and braided with otter fur. The most striking feature in his attire was a necklace of claws of the grizzly bear, of which he appeared highly proud."

Going Home

The general asked what it was the Ponca wanted to say to him. Standing Bear rose to speak. He told the officers he was sad he could not read or write, that he hoped to send his surviving children to school so they would have a future. He recounted how they had been forced off their lands, been taken to the Warm Country, and how he had gone to see the Great Father and told him they were in a bad place, how they wanted his permission to return home where they could earn a living with their own hands. How they had stayed as long as they could, but the land was filled with death, and they wanted to live.

He asked the officers to take pity on them, to help them get back their land, to help him save the women and children. They had nowhere else to turn. "My brothers and friends—as I am saying, there is somebody clamping me down to the ground. I need help to get that man off of me, so I can stand up. I need help."

When he finished, the general turned to the chief. He said he sympathized with them, but there was little he could do. "I must obey my orders from Washington, where they know all these facts and still order them down." The best he could do, Crook told the chief, was to let them stay a few more days, let them and their horses rest up for the long trip south. Standing Bear asked for a little money to buy food, to pay for burial expenses along the way. "Half of my family are sick—half are not very strong. While we travel, the sick will die and the rest of us will think we'll die before we get there." Crook said he could do nothing, that any money would have to come from Washington. He promised they would have plenty of food at the fort until it was time to leave. He turned to the interpreter: "I know it's very hard and painful for them to go down and it's just as hard and painful for us to have to send them there." After three hours, the Ponca stood and shook hands with the officers.

About that same time, on the other side of town, the pastor of the Baptist Church in Omaha sent a telegram to an old friend in the nation's capital.

To Hon. Carl Schurz, Secretary of the Interior, Washington, D.C.:
Seven lodges of Ponca Indians, who had settled on Omaha

*reservation, and were commencing to work at farming, have, by
your order, been arrested to be taken south. I beseech you as a
friend to have this order revoked. Several churches and congrega-
tions have passed resolutions recommending that these Indians be
permitted to remain with the Omahas. Some of the Indians are too
sick to travel.*

It was signed by the Reverend E. H. E. Jameson and three other
Omaha clergy.

After the meeting, Standing Bear and the seven Ponca walked back
to their camp. He had begged the general to help him save the women
and children, but the general had his orders. He had begged the lieutenant who had come to arrest them to let him first go to the Niobrara
to bury his son, but he, too, had his orders. So in a few days, the sick
and the healthy, their horses, their wagons, the box containing the
bones of his son, the soldiers, would all turn south and begin the long
march back to the Warm Country.

Four miles away, Tibbles sat at his desk, busily transcribing his
notes from the speeches he had heard at the fort earlier that Monday
afternoon. When he finished, he telegraphed them to Chicago, St. Louis,
and to a number of newspapers along the East Coast. Then he began
writing a long story and an editorial for his paper. About 3:30 A.M., he
finished and went to bed.

On the morning of April 1, readers of the *Omaha Daily Herald*
awoke to find "Criminal Cruelty, The History of the Ponca Prisoners
Now at the Barracks," covering most of page four. In it, Tibbles recounted in detail his interviews with Standing Bear and Buffalo Chips,
and the meeting with General Crook. In an adjacent column, "The Last
Indian Outrage," he used his editorial as a pointed forum, pleading the
Ponca case and Indian reform to his readers. He asked them to examine
carefully the Ponca speeches and their remarks to the general.

"There are several things in these speeches which will command
universal attention. There can be found there a theory for solving the
Indian problem, differing in some of its details from anything hereto-

fore proposed. The Indians want land, the title of which shall never be questioned. *They also want courts established.* Now they have no one to appeal to but the agents when they are wronged. The agents have no authority to right any wrong, or punish offenders even if they were disposed to do so."

He asked his readers to consider the plight of the Ponca chief. "Standing Bear, four years ago, was worth several thousand dollars. To-day he is a beggar. Who has got his property? His horses, his cattle, his farming utensils, his farm, every thing he had is gone." He asked them to consider the plight of his small group. "Is it not a strange commentary upon this professedly religious and humanitarian policy of the Indian department, that we find in the circumstances which surround these prisoners? . . . Here is a band begging to be allowed to support themselves, and the government will not allow them to do it."

Tibbles kept it up, day after day, writing more articles, visiting local churches, imploring the Christian community and the citizens of Omaha to do a good deed, to send food and clothing to the Ponca, to organize, to right a wrong. Soon, his message began to spread. It went to local pastors and lay leaders, who formed the Omaha Ponca Relief Committee, chaired by the Reverend Robert Clarkson, Episcopal bishop of Nebraska. It went up the Missouri, to Niobrara, Sioux City, and Yankton, where the *Yankton Daily Press and Dakotaian,* which had lobbied to remove the Ponca two years earlier, now lobbied to return them to their ancestral homeland, vacant since the Lakota abandoned it almost a year earlier. It went to more and more ministers farther upriver and to senators, who sent letters, petitions, and telegrams to Washington, urging the makers of Indian policy to let the thirty sick and homesick Ponca stay on the old lands or stay with the Omaha, sentiments that neither the Commissioner of Indian Affairs nor the Secretary of the Interior responded to.

For two years, Standing Bear's plight had largely been a local story confined to the small western towns and villages along the waterways of eastern Nebraska and Dakota, but in the early spring of 1879, it crossed the Mississippi and headed east. It went to the pages of the

Chicago Tribune, where readers found a one-paragraph story on page five of their April 2 edition: "They only asked that Gen. Crook furnish the money to bury those of their number who must die on the way of fatigue and unaccustomed heat."

And then it arrived in New York. "Nothing more glaringly unjust and absurd can be found in our treatment of the Indians than the mismanagement of the Poncas. Under the direction of the Protestant Episcopal mission, these people had reached a degree of civilization and steady prosperity far surpassing that of most Western colonies of white men," the *New York Daily Tribune* said in an editorial. "They were emphatically a sober, industrious, God-fearing community. All that we demand of or hope for the Indians was answered in the successful progress of this tribe."

Before long, more and more stories began to find their way into the newspapers of Boston, Philadelphia, and Washington, and it wasn't long before a good many citizens up and down the East Coast began to read them.

Standing Bear and the Ponca knew nothing of the petitions and letters, the editorials and articles. For them, it had been a long month, one that began on foot during the last few days of their freedom flight north and ended as prisoners in an Army fort. In between, they had come within a few days' journey of returning the boy to the old burial grounds, had seen their friends and relatives, broken ground and planted wheat, tended to the sick, been arrested and marched to Omaha, told their story to a reporter, and pleaded with the highest-ranking officer west of the Mississippi to let them earn a living on the lands of their fathers. As a new month began, they knew as they huddled in their lodges outside the fort, that the decision had been made, that Washington would not waver on its long-established policy. They knew it was only a matter of time.

Tibbles also knew it, that no matter what the newspapers said, the general's orders would not be canceled, that any day now the Ponca would again be forced to turn their faces south. In earlier years, he had studied the law some and he had an idea, and so one afternoon, after finishing his editorial duties for the day, he went to a law library and scanned the room until he found what he was looking for. He took a copy of the U.S. Constitution off the shelf and sat down at a table and began to read carefully the Fourteenth Amendment.

The more he read, the more intrigued he became, particularly with the language in the first section of the eleven-year-old amendment: "All persons born or naturalized in the United States, and subject to the jurisdiction thereof, are citizens of the United States and of the State wherein they reside. No State shall make or enforce any law which shall abridge the privileges or immunities of citizens of the United States." He kept reading. ". . . nor shall any State deprive any person of life, liberty, or property, without due process of law; nor deny to any person within its jurisdiction the equal protection of the laws."

The intent of the Fourteenth Amendment to the Constitution, one of three amendments Congress sent to the states in the immediate aftermath of the Civil War, had been to guarantee equal civil and legal rights to the nation's recently freed black citizens. If Congress had its way, the right of every American citizen to due process and equal protection of the law would now apply to both federal and state governments. On July 28, 1868, after twenty-eight of the thirty-seven states had ratified the amendment, it became—on paper—a part of the supreme law of the land.

In the law library, the assistant editor read and reread the amendment, focusing more and more on the last two phrases of the first section. He began to wonder how far the promise of "equal protection" went, how far "due process" would go to protect life, liberty, and property. Did it go far enough to include Indians? Were they now entitled to the same civil liberties as black and white Americans? Had the government deprived Standing Bear of basic freedoms guaranteed by the law? Could the government legally remove him, someone born in the United States, from one place and prevent him from going to another?

The only way to find out, Tibbles knew, was to file a lawsuit, to bring these questions to a federal court, and to let a judge decide. He also knew it would cost money, probably a lot, money he didn't have.

But he had an idea and so he went to see a young Omaha lawyer who was an old friend.

At thirty-two, John Lee Webster had already emerged as a potent force inside and outside Omaha's legal circles. The well-respected lawyer was a solid constitutional scholar whose legal skills had generated a large practice during his ten years in the city. An avid patron of the arts, he was elected to the state legislature in 1873, and two years later he served as chairman of the State Constitutional Convention. As a teenager, he fought in the Civil War with an Ohio infantry unit, and had graduated from Ohio's Mount Union College, where Tibbles had also once studied.

After the editor laid out his idea, John Lee Webster said he would like to sleep on it. The next day the two men met in the lawyer's office. Webster said he, too, was intrigued by the idea—an important one that underscored basic principles of personal liberty, the inherent natural rights of citizens, and a broad range of constitutional issues, issues discussed at length by the nation's Founding Fathers. But he cautioned it would be a tough, complex case, a long shot given the peculiar relationship between Indians and government—a government that had always treated Indians as wards, as children whose governmental parents could do with them as they pleased, moving them about whenever they wanted, as long as it suited the parental interests. Still, he said, it would do no harm to try. And it was the right thing to do. "It seems to me that there ought to be power somewhere to stop this inhuman cruelty," Webster said, "and if it does not reside in the courts where shall we find it?"

Given the magnitude of the case, the intricate web of constitutional issues involved, and the groundbreaking attempt to clarify the status of a people suspended in legal limbo for a century, the lawyer told the editor they would need some help. They would need someone with political savvy and consummate courtroom skills. Someone with a commanding presence and impeccable credentials. Someone who could showcase a deft blend of legal firepower and oratorical flair.

Andrew Jackson Poppleton, born in Michigan in 1830, was smart, shrewd, stubborn, and proud, a wealthy power-broker whose ancestors had fought in the Revolutionary War. Upon receiving his law degree, Poppleton had headed to California. En route, he stopped over in Omaha in October 1854, was intrigued by the civilian government being organized in the new territory, decided to stay, and never left. In short order, he became the first lawyer to practice in Omaha, a member of the first territorial legislature, and eventually the first president of the Nebraska Bar Association. In 1858, he was elected Omaha's second mayor and five years later, when construction of the fledgling Union Pacific Railroad began, he became the company's general counsel, a position he would hold for the next twenty-five years.

The eminent lawyer had just returned from the East when the assistant editor of the local newspaper knocked on his door. The editor presented copies of the stories on Standing Bear and the Ponca published while Poppleton was away, and told him the plan he had discussed with his colleague. The next day, the editor returned to hear the verdict. "I believe you have a good case," Poppleton said. "It is true that these Indians have been held by the courts as 'wards of the nation' . . . A ward cannot make a contract, but it does not follow from that, that the guardian can imprison, starve, or practise [*sic*] inhuman cruelty upon the ward." He said he would be pleased to assist in the case—and he would do it for free. The editor left in an upbeat mood. In just a few days, he had assembled a formidable legal team.

Time was now the enemy. The editor knew the general could stall for only so long. Although he now had the city's two most prominent lawyers on board, he desperately needed a judge. He had a specific one in mind, but the judge had gone off on a bear hunt, and he wasn't sure how to track him down.

Tibbles frantically sent telegrams to all the places he thought the judge might pass through, waiting impatiently for some kind of response. When none arrived, he convinced a number of men to fan out on horseback, to roam the countryside where the judge might be, to try and get him a message that two lawyers needed him to hear their case. Two days later, one of the messengers got lucky and Judge Elmer Dundy agreed to return to his office in Lincoln, the state capital.

When the editor finally tracked him down, Elmer Scipio Dundy had been a federal judge for sixteen years. Born in Ohio, he arrived in Nebraska to practice law in 1857 and six years later was appointed a territorial judge by President Abraham Lincoln. In 1868, he became the first judge of the United States District Court in Nebraska. For years, Judge Dundy, who seldom expressed much compassion for the nation's original inhabitants, had personally held court in Nebraska, Kansas, Missouri, Wyoming, and South Dakota, and he often used his court travels to scout out potential hunting opportunities. He was a rugged man, a superb hunter, who counted Colonel William F. Cody among his closest friends and, as part of an active life, he ventured out into the wild at least once a year to look for bear.

After an exhaustive review of the issues, the lawyers arrived at a straightforward request: They wanted the United States government to prove it had the legal right to arrest and detain Standing Bear and the twenty-five Ponca under guard at Fort Omaha. They wanted the government to prove it could legally hold these prisoners against their will and prevent them from returning to their homeland. In the language of the lawyers, they wanted the judge to grant a writ of *habeas corpus,* a Latin phrase for "you have the body." If granted, the prisoners would be required to appear in court where the judge would determine whether they had been jailed unlawfully and whether they should be released. As far back as the Magna Carta in 1215, habeas corpus had been regarded as a fundamental hallmark of justice, as a legal tool designed to protect individual freedom, as a safeguard against arbitrary and unlawful arrests by the government. In the 103-year history of the United States, no writ of habeas corpus had ever been filed on behalf of an American Indian.

On April 4, in their formal application for a writ, Poppleton and Webster argued that General Crook had illegally imprisoned, detained, and confined Standing Bear and the Ponca, restraining them of their liberty. When they were arrested, the lawyers argued, their clients were living peacefully and lawfully on the Omaha Reservation, as guests of the Omaha, on lands the government had set aside for the Omaha. Their clients had advanced greatly on civilization's path, had broken ground and planted crops, were trying to support themselves through their own labor, and had not asked the government for any help or support. The lawyers said that, although still Ponca Indians, they had long since separated from the rest, had become independent and self-sufficient, and no longer considered themselves part of the tribe that remained in Indian Territory. They also had broken no laws, civil or military, and violated no treaties, the lawyers argued. Editor Tibbles and Lieutenant Carpenter witnessed the application for the writ, which was filed in Nebraska Federal Circuit Court as *Ma-chu-nah-zha v. George Crook.*

Four days later, Judge Dundy signed the application, granting the lawyers' request for a writ of habeas corpus, and it was served on General Crook that same day. On April 11, the military commander of the Department of the Platte responded in a sworn statement, telling the judge he had arrested the Ponca on orders from his superiors, General Sherman in Washington and Lieutenant General Sheridan in Chicago. He asked the judge to release him from the writ and return the Ponca to him so he could carry out his orders.

When the general's superiors in Washington got wind of Crook's legal order to produce twenty-six Ponca bodies in Omaha Federal Court, they launched a campaign to undermine the order and personally discredit Standing Bear. On April 10, Indian Commissioner Ezra Hayt had published a letter to Interior Secretary Carl Schurz, warning him of the potential havoc that a favorable ruling for the Ponca could wreak upon the system.

"If the reservation system is to be maintained, discontented and restless or mischievous Indians cannot be permitted to leave their reservation at will and go where they please," Hayt wrote. "If this were permitted the most necessary discipline of the reservations would soon be entirely broken up, all authority over the Indians would cease, and in a short time the Western country would swarm with roving and lawless bands of Indians, spreading a spirit of uneasiness and restlessness even among those Indians who are now at work and doing well."

Commissioner Hayt counted the Ponca among those who were

adjusting favorably to their new homes in the Indian Territory. They had been removed from their homeland for their own good, to save them from the Lakota, he said, and they now occupied the most enviable spot in the territory. He had visited them the previous fall and had personally seen dramatic improvements in their overall health and how well the government had supplied them with everything they needed to succeed. Of their ten chiefs, he noted, only one showed a bad spirit.

Standing Bear was "constantly grumbling, and held aloof from the other chiefs, and seemed full of discontent, which he took no pains to conceal, while the other Poncas were at work." While the other chiefs adjusted and went to work, Standing Bear escaped "and at the present time, as may be judged from current reports, endeavors to attract public sympathy by grossly misrepresenting the circumstances of the case." In his published letter to superiors, the commissioner summed up his view of the situation: "The removal of Northern Indians to the Indian Territory was probably not good policy, but it was done in pursuance of laws enacted before the present administration came into power."

When Standing Bear was read the letter, he could not believe what he heard. He said the commissioner had not told the truth. As proof, he went to a trunk in his lodge and got a roll of letters he had saved from recent years. A March 1876 letter from a former agent described him as a "reliable and trustworthy man, of industrious habits, and rare zeal in setting a good example to the Indians and inciting them to industrious and civilized habits." Another, from a U.S. Army lieutenant, said he was "civil, quiet, and well-behaved, a warm friend of the whites, and loyal to the government." A December 1877 letter from Commissioner Hayt himself noted the chief's influence "has been to preserve peace and harmony between the Ponca Indians and the United States, and as such is entitled to the confidence of all persons whom he may meet."

He admitted not all Ponca saw things as he did, that a rift had developed within the tribe between those who wanted to stay "in the blanket" and the progressives who wanted to adapt, to survive in the changing world, the ones, like him, who wanted to work for themselves, build their houses, send their children to school, own property, and become independent. "It may be that those lazy, bad Indians told the Commissioner that I had no influence," Standing Bear said. "They would do so if they had a chance. But if I could go down to the Territory, and tell all the tribe to follow me who wanted to work and send their children to school, nine out of every ten would come with me."

Not long afterwards, their friends and relatives tried to help. In the new way of doing things, twenty Omaha Indian leaders drafted and signed a petition on April 21, addressed, "To the friends of the Poncas now held as prisoners at Omaha barracks." The Omaha offered to share their land and equip the Ponca with whatever they needed until they could get back on their feet. "They are our brothers and our sisters, our uncles and our cousins, and although we are called savages we feel that sympathy for our persecuted brethren that should characterize Christians, and are willing to share what we possess with them if they can only be allowed to return and labor, improve and provide for themselves where they may live in peace, enjoy good health, and the opportunity of educating their children up to a higher state of civilization."

The petition, drafted by the Omaha Indian interpreter Charles Morgan, caught the eye of editors at the *New York Herald*. The newspaper commended the Omaha Indian leaders for their generosity of spirit, for offering land and farming tools to their friends, for offering them more than words and paper. "Church members talked and petitioned, but not an acre of land did they offer. It was reserved for a band of heathen redskins, who have hardly yet forgotten the war-whoop, to emphasize that sympathy which civilization and religion have talked about—and only talked about."

As April came to a close, Standing Bear and his splintered band of sickly Ponca had endured another complex month. They had expatriated themselves from the rest of the tribe, taken the well-traveled road back home, and accidentally wandered into a legal wilderness. From the beginning of their journey, the chief had wanted one thing above all others: to find a home for his son, a good home somewhere along the banks of the Running Water. Now, it was up to a federal judge to decide whether the road the father and son traveled would continue north, to the old burial ground—or back south, to the new one.

Grandma Rosetta has always liked this part of the story, one her people have told countless times at births and christenings, wakes and funerals, at powwows, dedications, school events, and in casual conversation. Seated in a living room not far from where the journey began more than a century and a quarter ago, she speaks forcefully, her voice shifting through a range of emotions as she recounts the story. Even now, though she has told it many times, it sounds as though it is only the first, that she somehow can't quite believe her own words. "I mean, they left here, not far from where I'm sitting, in the dead of winter. Today, how many people would do such a thing? Go north, on foot, six hundred miles in the dead of winter, to bury their child. He knew he was breaking the law to do this, but his promise to his dying boy was more important than any law." She pauses, temporarily lost in thought. "The old people believed a man was only as good as his word. Back then, a promise was a promise."

Back then, throughout the month of April 1879, and for a long time afterward, the assistant editor of the *Omaha Daily Herald* and the two prominent local attorneys would be grateful to the man who had tipped them off to the Ponca's plight, who initiated the idea of an American Indian suing an Army officer, to the one who had first suggested using a writ of habeas corpus as a legal tool to get the case before a federal judge.

They would all be indebted to the defendant—Brigadier General George Crook.

6

The Color of Blood

By the spring of 1879, the United States of America was well on its way to becoming a formidable presence on the world stage. Its divisive, bloody Civil War had ended fourteen years earlier, the crippling issue of slavery had technically been resolved, and Thomas Jefferson's vision of an American West filled with productive citizen-farmers was an everyday reality. On the East Coast, the captains of industry were energetically transforming the great cities into thriving centers of banking, business, trade, commerce, and manufacturing. Shipyards and fishing fleets bustled. Steel plants and coal mines boomed. Textile mills blossomed. Steamships laden with raw materials ceaselessly prowled a labyrinth of canals and waterways. Across the continent, a sprawling network of iron rails was beginning to bind the vast nation into an increasingly cohesive economy poised to harvest what seemed like an inexhaustible supply of minerals, timber, cattle, cotton, corn, and wheat. In some instances, the railroads had created communities overnight, communities often filled with ambitious, hungry immigrants and poor farmers staking their claim to a land and a dream they had never imagined.

All in all, America, now just a few months shy of its 103rd birthday, on the verge of flexing its considerable economic, political, and military muscle, was a country in which many of the citizens in its thirty-eight states shared a robust view of the future, a view colored by an unyielding optimism of who they were, where they were, and where they were headed.

That spring, the fledgling city on the west bank of the Missouri River also claimed a share of the nation's optimistic outlook. For years, a fair number of its thirty-thousand residents, many with a strong German heritage, had prospered trading with successive waves of emigrants heading west. Now, surrounded by hundreds of miles of some of the best corn-growing, cattle-grazing lands in the world, the Union Pacific Railroad in its backyard, the Mighty Missouri on its doorstep, Omaha was emerging as an important rail nexus, stockyard center, and shipping point for a multitude of goods headed to lucrative eastern markets. One packing plant alone already was slaughtering more than sixty-thousand hogs a year. The city, too, boasted some of the finest hotels between Chicago and Denver, its own police and fire departments, three daily newspapers—two in English and one in German—a modern Western Union office, the recently opened Creighton College, and a rich assortment of plays, concerts, and musicals. For much of the decade, it had also maintained a strong frontier flavor, a lawless edge that gave rise to no shortage of whiskey shops, gambling parlors, and brothels. Come election day, votes were commonly bought and sold for one dollar, so it was not unusual to see some of the same citizens moving briskly from one polling place to the next.

Along the way, the riverfront city had also been transformed into an important military outpost. Its Omaha Barracks had recently been renamed Fort Omaha after becoming the headquarters for the Department of the Platte, a region stretching from Nebraska to Montana, from Canada to Texas, a vast military territory under the command of

General Crook. Three miles south of the general's office, like a sentinel keeping watch on its wayward citizens, an imposing, three-story limestone building anchored the downtown corner of Fifteenth and Dodge streets, the home of the United States Courthouse.

As April gave way to May of 1879, two hundred Mormons passed through Omaha on their way to Utah, and famed Boston lecturer Joseph Cook arrived to promote a discussion on the "Ultimate America." Torrential rains sparked widespread flooding along the Missouri and scarlet fever raged throughout the city. Frank Kleffner caught a gray mare at the corner of Fifteenth and Farnham streets and Lou Wilson, looking for her husband one fine spring evening, smashed the windows of a neighborhood brothel, severely gashing one of her hands. A new pair of children's shoes went for a buck fifty, and a bottle of "Bill's Hair and Whisker Die"—black or brown—fetched fifty cents. The fire department was about to elect new officers for the year and the Grand Lodge of Colored People closed out its annual session with a marching band and rousing street parade.

In early May, careful readers of the *Omaha Daily Herald* also spotted another event about to unfold in their city. It was conveyed to them in one sentence on page four of a news-in-brief roundup column: "The arguments in the Ponca habeas corpus case are being heard today by Judge Dundy, who will probably take the matter under advisement for a day or two before rendering his decision."

That spring, far beyond the elegant Herndon House hotel and the bustling brothels, beyond the busy stockyard and stoic federal building, twenty-six Ponca men, women, and children milled about their lodges inside Fort Omaha, pondering their future in a nation poised to transform the world order for decades to come. Inside a trunk in one of the lodges lay the bones of a teenage boy, bones that remained more than a hundred miles from his ancestral homeland. Throughout the long days and weeks the Ponca had been held as prisoners in the fort, their presence had spawned a number of questions, questions that neither the people, their chief, nor anyone else could really answer. Did the chief have the right to walk away from his reservation to keep a promise? Could he sever himself from his tribe and start a new life if he wanted to? Could he and his people be integrated into the dominant culture, or would they continue to slowly die off on the margins? Did the government have the legal power to arrest and imprison him? Could the Army move his people whenever and wherever it wanted? Did the Indian—any Indian—have any legal rights a white man was bound to respect?

That spring, the Ponca wanted to try to find some answers, try to find out who they were in 1879 America, how they were to fit into the nation's vision of itself . . . and what the lives of their children's grandchildren might be like in a 1979 America.

Many of the questions confronting Standing Bear inside the fort three miles north of the city were ones that had confused and confounded the government for more than a century. Since 1776, its policies toward the native inhabitants had lurched from the forced removal of the 1830s and 1840s, to the treaty era of the 1850s and 1860s, to the reservation system of the 1870s. Francis Walker, commissioner of Indian Affairs from 1871 to 1873, had once attempted to define the underlying concepts of the reservation system. Under that system, he said, "it was expressly declared that the Indians should be made as comfortable on, and uncomfortable off, their reservations as it was within the power of the Government to make them: that such of them as went right should be protected and fed, and such as went wrong should be harassed and scourged without intermission."

But by decade's end, there were those both inside and outside the government who had come to see things differently. Valentine McGillycuddy, the Lakota agent on South Dakota's Pine Ridge Reservation, was among them. "What reason or inducement can be advanced why an Indian should go to work and earn his own living by the sweat of his brow," he asked, "when an indulgent Government furnishes him more than he wants to eat and clothes him for nothing?"

Historically, whatever the government's shifting policies toward the Indian had been, they had remained consistently piecemeal, makeshift, and desultory—policies designed primarily to settle immediate logistical issues while leaving the larger legal questions suspended in an out-of-sight, out-of-mind netherworld.

But now, as the nation's considerable economic, political, and military might began to congeal, a fifty-year-old father en route to bury his son along an ancient riverbed had unwittingly posed a modern legal challenge. He was about to force the government to answer some questions, to sharpen its constitutional focus on what had been a murky picture of a people who had been on the land for as long as anyone could remember.

That spring, the government was unwavering in its view of the legal landscape. It was certain Standing Bear had "gone wrong" by leaving his assigned reservation, by fleeing to another one without permission, by defying the system that had been installed by the Indian policy experts. So they had arrested him, detained him, and ordered the military to return him to Indian Territory. And they were equally certain that a judge would confirm that the military was well within its legal rights to punish Standing Bear, would uphold their policy, would keep the integrity of the reservation system intact. They were certain, too, of one other thing: that an American Indian had no legal standing in a federal courtroom. That he had no legal right to sue a U.S. Army general.

When Standing Bear looked out from atop a small hill outside his lodge near the fort, a hill he often climbed in the weeks after his arrest, he could see the city three miles to the south and the swollen river to the east, but there were a good many things he could not see and could not know. He couldn't see some of the forces that were gathering strength in some of the nation's most important cities. He couldn't see what some of the nation's most influential newspapers were saying about him. He couldn't see the flood of telegrams that some of the local ministers and preachers were sending on his behalf. And he didn't know that the citizens of Omaha's Jewish community had begun taking up collections for his lawyers.

From the top of the small hill where he often sought refuge, he could not see and not know that, in the two years he had gone from arrest and detention in one fort to arrest and detention in another, he had also gathered about him an unusual constellation of allies—not the least of whom was the U.S. Army's powerful commander of the Department of the Platte.

Unlike his superiors in the Interior Department and some within the military, General Crook's evolving philosophy on America's "Indian problem" had largely been forged from personal contact and intimate observation. As a result, he had come to better understand their predicament and to appreciate many of their values and cultural hallmarks. "The leading chiefs thoroughly understand the changed condition of affairs," Crook wrote in a long letter outlining many of his views. "They see that they can no longer depend upon game for their support, and are anxious to obtain cattle, seeds, and implements, and to have their children educated. They see the necessity of adopting the white man's ways and of conforming to the established order of things. But, I am sorry to say, they have, to a very great degree, lost confidence in our people and their promises. Indians are very much like white men in being unable to live upon air."

More and more, his sympathetic views placed him at odds with superiors and he increasingly found it difficult to privately follow orders without publicly acknowledging the internal conflict they created. The general believed he had found a better way, a solution beyond the Little Bighorn and the Indian Territory, and by the spring of 1879, he had become far more aggressive in promoting his views, in trying to restore the lost confidence of the Indian people.

It is what had prompted him to tip off the reporter after the arrest orders came down, and to suggest applying for a writ of habeas corpus when he was told to turn the Ponca faces south, and, a few years later, it would lead to a bitter confrontation with his immediate superior, Lieutenant General Sheridan. And it also triggered an angry response when he discovered what his government was now saying about Standing Bear and his people, words that appeared in an official court document above his signature.

At first, in his initial response to the application for the writ of habeas corpus, the government's lawyer had said that General Crook

136

was merely following orders when he arrested Standing Bear and the Ponca. But later, the lawyer amended his response—unbeknownst to Crook—to include additional allegations. Standing Bear, the lawyer argued, was a Ponca chief and his followers maintained tribal relations to the Ponca and owed their allegiance to the chief. Furthermore, the lawyer claimed, the Ponca "are not pursuing the habits and vocations of civilized life," and they had not been "illegally restrained of their liberty." Instead, they were on the Omaha Reservation illegally, where the government had the legal right to arrest them and return them to their reservation in Indian Territory "where they belong."

When Crook discovered what the government now said in the amended response, a document that bore his signature, he complained bitterly to Major Horace Burnham, the military judge advocate for the Department of the Platte. The general did not believe any of the statements in the amended return were true, yet his name appeared on it. He then took his complaint to the trial judge, arguing he could not allow his name to support alleged facts he did not agree with. The judge patiently explained his signature did not appear on the document as a private citizen, but simply as a government official, as a U.S. Army brigadier general. The legal distinction was lost on Crook and he continued to protest, formally and informally, to no avail. In the end, the judge allowed the paragraph to become part of the official court record.

The legal point—whether Standing Bear and the Ponca were government wards shackled to tribal allegiances or independent farmers capable of adopting white ways—was a crucial issue, one that the commander of the Department of the Platte understood as well as anyone.

April had come and gone with lawyers for both sides laying out their legal positions on what should become of the twenty-six Ponca men, women, and children clustered in their lodges three miles north of the imposing structure squatting on the corner of Fifteenth and Dodge streets. Now it was time for a federal judge to weigh their arguments and assess the merits, to try to sharpen the focus on the long-muddled picture, to decide whether the Constitution of the United

States afforded Indians any of the measures of protection and human rights it afforded the nation's white and black citizens.

At ten o'clock on the morning of May 1, 1879, U.S. District Court Judge Elmer Dundy's gavel smacked against a wooden bench and the trial of *Ma-chu-nah-zha v. George Crook* was officially underway.

The citizens had read about it for weeks in the local papers, and heard about it in many of their churches and discussed it in various law offices around town, and so on that Thursday morning the large court-room on the third floor of the Federal Building was unusually crowded. In the back and along the sides, newsmen and curious lawyers and several judges and some of the town's leading citizens milled about, jostling each other, jockeying for a better position in the boisterous room. On the wooden benches sat some of the local ladies and some of the church faithful, including the Episcopal bishop, Reverend Robert Clarkson, who, like everyone else, was craning his neck, trying to get a better view of the front of the courtroom. Closer to the front, they could see Yellow Horse and Buffalo Chips, two of the Ponca men who had walked away from the Warm Country, sitting quietly in tattered, worn-out clothes, and not far from them was the young Omaha Indian poet and teacher, Bright Eyes, and the newsman Tibbles. Near the front, they could see a young boy, the orphaned grandson of Standing Bear, squirming on the lap of the chief's wife, who was looking after him and calming him in the moments before the first witness was called. They could see that General Crook—who much preferred civilian dress, and who liked to stalk the prairie collecting butterflies and bird eggs while padding about in worn-out moccasins—had arrived on this unusually warm spring morning in the full dress of a brigadier general.

And when the crowd temporarily parted, when there was a fleeting glimpse all the way to the front, those clustered in the back and along the sides and on the benches could also see something that no one had seen before: an American Indian, dressed in traditional clothing, seated at the plaintiff's table in a United States courtroom.

Delayed by heavy spring rains and widespread flooding, the judge had just arrived from Lincoln the night before, but now he was settled at the bench and he asked the attorneys representing Standing Bear to call their first witness. Willie W. Hamilton, the son of the missionary on the Omaha Reservation, approached the stand. Hamilton, twenty-two, had lived on the reservation for twelve years, working at the agency store for the past six. He spoke both Omaha and Ponca fluently and had first met the prisoners when they arrived on Omaha Reservation land two months earlier. The younger of Standing Bear's two attorneys, John Lee Webster, began the questioning, asking the witness to describe the condition of the prisoners.

When the prisoners first arrived on the morning of March 4, Hamilton testified, they were in bad shape. Those who had them wore white man's clothes. They lived as families, as man and wife, with their children—two of whom were orphans.

What did they do after they arrived? Attorney Webster asked.

All the healthy ones began to break ground and sow crops, mostly wheat, the witness replied.

Did any of the prisoners put in a crop for themselves?

Buffalo Chips had put in four or five acres of wheat on land the Omaha gave him.

On that Sunday, the attorney asked, *were the prisoners resting on the Sabbath or working?*

The judge: "Is that necessary?"

The attorney: "The theory of this government is to Christianize these Indians, I believe."

The witness: "It is about the same as it is with white men, some do, and some do not."

When his opponent finished, Genio Lambertson had some questions for the witness on behalf of the government and his client, General Crook. Young and brash, Lambertson was trying his first case as the newly minted district attorney.

When the prisoners were on the Omaha Reservation, Lambertson asked, *who was their chief?*

Standing Bear was the head chief, the witness replied.

"Did they obey his orders?"

"Yes, sir."

The district attorney asked if they depended on the government for their wagons, clothes, and blankets.

Yes, for the most part, the witness said.

The young agency store clerk left the stand and Lieutenant Carpenter, the arresting officer, was sworn in as the second witness. Standing Bear's attorney again focused on dress and work habits.

When you arrested the prisoners, he asked, *were they wearing citizens' clothing?*

The lieutenant said the majority of the men were—only two wore blankets and leggings. And two of the sick Indians had recently said they wanted to go to work.

The general's lawyer approached, focusing again on loyalty to the chiefs.

"How many chiefs are there?" Lambertson asked.

The judge: "Why is that material?"

The district attorney: "To show that these Indians have their chiefs, to whom they profess allegiance."

With that, the trial recessed for lunch, resuming again at 2 P.M. When the plaintiffs announced the name of their third witness, the government lawyer jumped to his feet.

"Does this court think an Indian is a competent witness?" Lambertson asked.

"They are competent for every purpose in both civil and criminal courts," the judge replied. "The law makes no distinction on account of race, color, or previous condition."

Standing Bear approached the bench. He took the oath and the store clerk, Hamilton, was sworn in as interpreter. Webster asked the questions and, sentence by sentence, the store clerk translated the testimony from Ponca to English.

How had things been for them on their old reservation on the Niobrara? Webster asked.

"We lived well," Standing Bear said. "I had my own land, and raised enough so I could get along nicely. My children were going to school, we had a good school, and everything going nicely."

Were they becoming civilized up on the Niobrara?

"He says he wants to work, and become like a white man, and that he has tried his best."

How were things in the Warm Country?

"I couldn't plow, I couldn't sow any wheat, and we all got sick, and couldn't do anything. . . . Instead of our tribe becoming prosperous, they died off every day during the time. From the time I went down there until I left, 158 of us died."

The witness looked up at the judge.

"I thought to myself, God wants me to live, and I think if I come back to my old reservation he will let me live. I got as far as the Omahas, and they brought me down here," he said, his voice getting louder and stronger. "What I have done? I am brought here, but what have I done? I don't know."

Standing Bear got up from his chair and began to gesture, speaking louder to the faces staring back from the sides, the back, and the benches. "It seems as though I haven't a place in the world, no place to go, and no home to go to, but when I see your faces here, I think some of you are trying to help me, so that I can get a place sometime to live in, and when it comes my time to die, to die peacefully and happy."

The judge told the interpreter to tell the witness not to get too excited, to stay calm. Standing Bear sat back down. His lawyer turned to the interpreter.

"Ask him how many of his children died in the Indian Territory before he came away?"

"He says two died down there. He says his son could talk English and write, and was a great help to him . . . and whenever he thinks of it, it makes him feel bad."

Does he still consider himself the chief of his people?

"He says he didn't consider himself a chief . . . He says he felt himself to be as poor as the rest of them."

The general's lawyer approached the witness. He told the interpreter to ask if he was the chief of those Ponca now in the north or any of those in the Territory?

"He says, I was not the head man; I don't consider myself any better than they are."

The district attorney wanted to know if the government furnished them with wagons and farming tools.

"He says they got some wagons and some mowing machines."

Did they escape from the Territory in government-issued wagons?

"Two were government-issued. The third—a light spring wagon—he bought himself," was the response.

The district attorney wanted to know why he left the Indian Territory.

"He says he wanted to go on his own land, that had always been his own land . . . that his son when he died made him promise if ever he went back there that he would take his bones there and bury him, and that he has got his bones in a box, and that if ever he goes there he will bury his bones there; that there is where he wants to live the rest of his life, and that there is where he wants to be buried."

Does he want to go back to the Niobrara and live as he did before?

"He says he might go there and work until he was blind, but that would not change his color; that he would be an Indian in color, but he wants to go and work and become a citizen."

When Standing Bear finished, his lawyers rested their case. The government offered no witnesses and no testimony, and though it had been a long day, the judge instructed the lawyers to begin their closing arguments. Webster, who hadn't felt well all day, started to summarize the important points on behalf of Standing Bear and the Ponca, but he soon informed the judge he was too sick to continue and so the closings were postponed until ten the next morning.

As the first day's testimony ended, as the boisterous throng began to file out of the courthouse, it was clear to legal observers that the complexities of the case had winnowed down to one essential issue: Had the Ponca prisoners genuinely expatriated themselves from their tribal past and become firmly lodged on civilization's path? If so, then they were entitled to the protection of the Fourteenth Amendment and the government had no business trying to deprive them of life, liberty, and property. If not, then they were government wards who had illegally left their reservation and it was the military's duty to return them to the Indian Territory.

Promptly at ten the next morning, the younger lawyer, Webster, still a bit under the weather, began to lay out his case in support of the Indian prisoners. First of all, he told the judge, the Omaha legally owned their reservation and, as such, had every right to share the land with their Ponca friends and relatives. Standing Bear and the Ponca did not want the government's help. They simply wanted their own land and the chance to work it and become self-supporting. They cannot, he stressed, be moved "at the whim and pleasure of the commissioner at Washington" who does not have "the power to move the Indians when and where he pleases." In fact, the government's behavior in this case, he told the judge, openly defies the philosophy of the nation's third President, who, in a letter to an Indian chief in 1803, had said, "these lands can never go from you but when you wish to sell." Thomas Jefferson also was emphatic in believing Indian nations were "entirely independent and the government could in no way interfere with their internal relations." So how could the government now interfere with business between the Omaha and Ponca? Although these tribes are often called barbarous, the Omaha and Ponca "are not savages or wanderers. They cultivate the soil, live in houses, and support themselves."

For three and a half hours, Webster roamed far and wide across the oratorical landscape, alternately quoting William Cullen Bryant, Alexis de Tocqueville, and Frederick Douglass to underscore his legal arguments. After a rugged winter march of sixty days, he told the court, the prisoners had finally arrived at the home of the "savage" Omaha. And why had they endured such a harsh journey? Because they had been dumped in a place where malaria was "floating like a cloud over the land," where, in less than two years, their numbers had dropped from 780 to 580—a greater mortality rate than that of Union soldiers during the Civil War, greater than the death rate at the infamous Andersonville prison.

But, mostly, Webster began to bear down on the issue that had now taken center stage. If Standing Bear and the Ponca had broken away from the rest of the tribe, he argued, if they had declared their independence and commitment to a new way of life, then they had come out from under the government's yoke. Then they had the right to return to the lands they owned, or to share the Omaha land, and the government had no legal right to restrain, detain, or return them. After all, wasn't that the point of the Fourteenth Amendment—to promote and protect individual rights and liberties? That the Indian prisoners qualified for its protection, he told the judge, there could be no doubt. As proof, he cited an 1870 U.S. Senate report specifically stating that when tribal relations are dissolved, the Fourteenth Amendment applies. And when the amendment applies, it made "an Indian who was born in this country and who did not owe allegiance to any other form of government, a citizen beyond all dispute."

To drive home his point, Webster quoted directly from the amendment: All persons born or naturalized in the United States are citizens of the United States and cannot be deprived of life, liberty, or property without due process of law. And so if these prisoners, born on American soil, were not citizens, then what were they? "Are they wild animals, deer to be chased by every hound?"

In the end, he said, it came down to a matter of fundamental civil rights, of basic human liberties, and the prisoners were now asking for the court's help. It was like the slave Douglass had once said: "A man belongs to himself. His hands are his own, his feet are his own, his body is his own, and they will remain his until you storm the citadel of heaven and wrest from the bosom of God man's title deed to himself."

Webster spoke until three o'clock. After he finished, the young District Attorney Lambertson approached the bench on behalf of the defendant, General Crook. He began with an appreciative tribute to his opponents, Webster and A. J. Poppleton, thanking them for "their generosity in coming to the assistance of these poor people, prisoners and friendless in a strange land." And then, for the next three hours, Lambertson laid out the case for the government of the United States, offering a variety of reasons and legal arguments underscoring why Standing Bear and the Ponca ended up in the barracks at Fort Omaha, and why they should be returned to their reservation in Indian Territory. The 1871 federal law forbidding any more treaties with Indian tribes, he told the judge, absolved the government from needing Ponca consent to move them from their Niobrara homeland to the Territory. He also suggested U.S. laws did not apply to Indian tribes. To be included, Indians had to be either foreign subjects or citizens—and the Ponca were neither. Nor were these tribes independent nations. They were dependent communities, government wards relying upon the United States for their survival. Nowhere in the law of the land, he said, could he find any legal precedent allowing an Indian to file suit in a federal court. And he recounted the history of Indian atrocities against innocent white citizens, implying they were a people too savage to be given legal rights.

But mostly, again and again, his arguments circled back to one central theme, the foundation of his case: The Indian—as far as the law was concerned—was neither a citizen nor a person, and so he could not bring a suit of any kind against the government of the United States. As a result, the court had grievously erred in granting Standing Bear a hearing for a writ of habeas corpus and then awarding him the legal opportunity to sue an Army general. Lambertson maintained this was a legal right available only to American citizens. And since Standing Bear was not a citizen, the court had no right to issue the writ. Furthermore, he argued, the Ponca had never abandoned their traditional ways. They retained tribal ties, an allegiance to their chief, and depended on the government for their survival. So, clearly, they were not entitled to Fourteenth Amendment protection.

To support his main argument—that only American citizens had access to U.S. courts—the district attorney relied a good deal on a decision the nation's highest court had reached twenty-two years earlier, a case involving a black man who had also wanted his freedom.

Dred Scott, born a slave in Virginia around 1800, had bounced around as the property of several white masters, traveling from the slave states of Virginia, Alabama, and Missouri, to the free state of Illinois and the free federal territory of Wisconsin. Back in St. Louis in 1843, after his master's widow hired him out to an Army captain, Scott decided he wanted a different way of life. So he offered the widow three hundred dollars for his and his wife's freedom. When she refused, he eventually asked the courts, with the help of antislavery lawyers, to set him free—a test case his lawyers and supporters hoped would lead to the freedom of all slaves.

In 1857, after a decade of appeals and court reversals, his case finally landed in the United States Supreme Court. In a 7–2 vote on March 6, the high court settled the matter: Anyone of African ancestry—slaves and those set free by their masters—could never become a U.S. citizen and therefore they could not sue in federal court. Since Scott was black, he was not a citizen and so he could not sue for his freedom—or anything else—in federal court. Slaves were the private property of their owners, the majority ruled, and the court could not deprive owners of their property. To do so would violate the Fifth Amendment guarantee against the government seizing property from an owner "without due process of the law."

So, according to the court, Scott would remain a slave. The sons of his first master had been his friends since childhood, and they helped pay Scott's legal bills throughout the long court fight. Not long after the Supreme Court decision, Scott and his wife were returned to his boyhood friends, who bought them and then set them free. About a year later, Dred Scott died of tuberculosis.

Although each justice had written a separate opinion in the case, Chief Justice Roger B. Taney issued the court's majority opinion. A loyal advocate of slavery, he said a Negro was not entitled to the legal rights of a U.S. citizen and cited the right to sue in federal court as an example. Furthermore, Taney concluded, Negroes had "no rights which any white man was bound to respect."

In the spring of 1879, on the third floor of the federal courthouse,

District Attorney Lambertson did not want the present court to forget its past. In this case, he said in his concluding remarks, Judge Taney's decision remained the guiding legal principle upon which a decision must now be based: So if a Negro did not have access to federal court, he told the judge, then surely an Indian didn't either. When the district attorney finished at six o'clock, the judge ordered a dinner recess. The last summary would begin in an hour.

All along, the dean of the state's legal community had been scheduled to have the final say, and so on the warm, early May evening after the dinner break, he made his way to the front of the courtroom. For the next three hours, Andrew Jackson Poppleton fused history and philosophy, religion and politics, humanity, literature, and the law—isolating each of the district attorney's arguments with a focused rebuttal.

No Ponca consent needed?

The district attorney, he told the court, had cited the 1871 resolution banning further treaties as the government's justification for removing the Ponca without their permission. But he neglected to mention that the law was not retroactive. In other words, the language of the original treaty still applied—the government had needed Ponca consent.

U.S. laws don't extend to Indian tribes?

Then why, Poppleton asked, had the government entered into numerous treaties with the Indian people—treaties ratified by Congress obligating the government to honor Indian lands, protect them, and provide food, clothing, and shelter. The government, he told the judge, can't have it both ways. "When a great nation of forty millions of people, wielding the purse and the sword, and possessing all the arts of civilization, breaks faith with the feeble remnants of humanity which all its life has had the sunlight of civilization excluded from its view, it is simply infamous."

The Indian—as neither citizen nor foreign subject—has no rights?

If the government no longer sees them as tribes or Indian nations, he asked, then what are they? What is their status? "Are we to say that the Ethiopian, the Malay, the Chinaman, the Frenchman, and every nationality upon the globe without regard to race, color or creed, may come here and become a part of this great government, while the primitive possessors of this soil . . . are alone barred from the right to become citizens?"

He did not believe, he said, that this government—his government—would do such a thing. "I have been accustomed to believe that I lived under a beneficent government. I have believed it to be my duty to thank God I was born under the shield and protection of this North America Republic—which has solved so many problems and which in God's good time we hope will solve so many more—but is it possible that this great government, standing here dealing with this feeble remnant of a once powerful nation, claims the right to place them in a condition which is to them worse than slaves, without a syllable of law; without a syllable of contract or treaty? I don't believe, if your honor please, that the courts will allow this; that they will agree to the proposition that these people are wild beasts; that they have no status in the courts. If it be true that these Indians have no souls to save, the churches had better leave them alone; had better not try to induce them to lead a civilized life if they have no rights, not even the right to that salvation which has been proclaimed as free to all."

He wondered aloud about the term "savages": "Because we cannot civilize these Indians in a single generation we conclude that we cannot civilize them at all. . . . Because these Indians in 200 years have not reached the degree of civilization which it required us 2,000 years to attain, we lift up our hands in holy horror and call them savages."

And were they really dependent government wards?

He told the court the prisoners had established families and communities throughout their Niobrara homeland. They had become skilled farmers and peaceful neighbors who went to church and sent their children to school. And just as they were well on the way down civilization's path, he said, the government illegally pulled them from lands they legally owned and shipped them to strange, barren ones where they died in droves. Now, they had severed their tribal ties and ancient allegiances and once again wanted to take up a civilized life. "I am lacking in the power to show to this court what, to me," Poppleton said, "is as

148

clear as the daylight—that is, to show that if these Indians are honestly desirous of adopting the ways of civilization and becoming civilized men; of pursuing the habits and industries characteristic of the civilization of the present age, there is no power, human or divine, that has a right to interpose a barrier between them and the goal to which they seek to march."

Poppleton had spoken for close to three hours, and as he began to wind down, after he had confronted each of the government's arguments, he slowly began to drive a legal wedge between the slave of yesterday and the Indian who sat before them. *Dred Scott,* he said, was strictly a citizenship issue. The only question the case resolved was that since Scott was not a citizen of Missouri, he could not sue in federal court. It had also confirmed, the lawyer noted, that a slave at that time in American history had no civil rights. But in his haste to justify slavery, Chief Justice Taney had strayed far from the legal question at hand and now—twenty-two years later—his ruling was out of date. In the spring of 1879, there were no slaves. The Fourteenth Amendment had seen to that. Hence this case now before the court was not specifically about citizenship at all. It was simply about *who* had a legal right to a writ of habeus corpus—a straightforward request compelling the government to justify why it had arrested and detained the prisoners. And the law on this particular point, he told the judge, was quite clear. It said nothing about being a citizen. It said only that *"any person or party"* had the legal right to apply for a writ.

So there was really but one question, and one question only, before the court: Was Standing Bear a person? To deny his legal right to the writ, he said, the court would have to conclude that he and the other Ponca prisoners were not people. They were not human beings.

"And who will undertake that?" Poppleton asked. "Why, I think the most touching thing I have heard in courts of justice or elsewhere for years was the story this old man told on the stand yesterday of the son who had gone with him to the Indian Territory, whose education he had care for; whom he had nurtured through the years of boyhood and sent to school in the belief that that boy would be a link between him and that civilization to which he aspired; that he would protect him from the wiles of agents; that there would be one person on the wide earth, the issue of his own loins, who would stand between him and the whites, whom he knew from experience were trying to overreach him—he said to that boy as his eyes were closing in death in a foreign country that he would take his bones to his old home on the Running Water, and bury him there, where he was born."

The lawyer paused and turned, glancing at Standing Bear.

"That man not a human being? Who of us all would have done it? Look around this city and State and find, if you can, the man who has gathered up the ashes of his dead, wandered for sixty days through a strange country without guide or compass, aided by the sun and stars only, that the bones of that kindred may be buried in the land of their birth. No! It is a libel upon religion; it is a libel upon missionaries who sacrifice so much and risk their lives in order to take to these Indians that gospel which Christ proclaimed to all the wide earth, to say that these are not human beings."

It was well after nine o'clock, almost twelve hours since the day's session began. The three lawyers had spoken for more than nine hours and the large crowd of prominent citizens, of clergy and church faithful, judges and lawyers and newsmen, the general's large staff decked in military uniforms and their wives, milled about after Poppleton finished his closing argument, heading for the door.

Before the crowd began to file out, the judge made an announcement. Although the trial now had officially ended and the legal proceedings were finished, one last speaker, he said, had asked permission to address the court. He supposed it was the first time in the nation's history such a request had been made, but he had decided to grant it and he had earlier informed all the lawyers of his intention to do so. The crowd settled back down and turned its attention to the front of the courtroom.

They saw him rising slowly from his seat, and they could see the eagle feather in the braided hair wrapped in otter fur, the bold blue shirt trimmed in red cloth, the blue flannel leggings and deerskin moccasins, the red and blue blanket, the Thomas Jefferson medallion, the necklace of bear claws. When he got to the front, he stopped and faced the audience, and extended his right hand, holding it still for a long time. After a while, it is said, he turned to the bench and began to speak in a low voice, his words conveyed to the judge and the large crowd by Bright Eyes.

"That hand is not the color of yours, but if I pierce it, I shall feel pain. If you pierce your hand, you also feel pain. The blood that will flow from mine will be of the same color as yours. I am a man. The same God made us both."

Then he turned and faced the audience, pausing for a moment, staring in silence out a courtroom window, describing after a time what he saw when he looked outside.

"I seem to stand on the bank of a river. My wife and little girl are beside me. In front the river is wide and impassable." He sees there are steep cliffs all around, the waters rapidly rising. In desperation, he scans the cliffs and finally spots a steep, rocky path to safety. "I turn to my wife and child with a shout that we are saved. We will return to the Swift Running Water that pours down between the green islands. There are the graves of my fathers."

So they hurriedly climb the path, getting closer and closer to safety, the waters rushing in behind them. "But a man bars the passage . . . If he says that I cannot pass, I cannot. The long struggle will have been in vain. My wife and child and I must return and sink beneath the flood. We are weak and faint and sick. I cannot fight." He stopped and turned, facing the judge, speaking softly.

"You are that man."

In the crowded courtroom, no one spoke or moved for several moments. After a while, a few women could be heard crying in the back and some of the people up closer could see that the frontier judge had temporarily lost his composure, and that the general, too, was leaning forward on the table, his hands covering his face. Soon, some people began to clap and a number of others started cheering, and then the general got up from his chair and went over and shook Standing Bear's hand, and before long, a number of others did the same.

"I Am a Man"

The bailiffs asked for order and when it finally grew quiet again, the judge said he would take the case under advisement and issue his decision in a few days. Then he adjourned the court shortly after ten o'clock on a warm spring evening on the second of May, 1879.

In his office in the building that dominated the corner of Fifteenth and Dodge streets, one floor below the large courtroom, the judge would have much to ponder in the days ahead. He was aware that he was now in a position to bring some clarity to the long-muddled picture of exactly where the American Indian stood upon the nation's legal landscape. He also knew that the location had eluded several generations of his judicial colleagues and that neither the country's legislative nor its executive branch had been much help. And he knew, too, that he would be harshly criticized—from anxious white settlers and a powerful military on one side to newspapers, clergy, and a burgeoning East Coast Indian Reform movement on the other—no matter which way he ruled. Still, he knew the legal issues that had landed on his desk were long overdue, and he intended to take his time in sorting through the important questions they raised.

Were these Indian prisoners, as the young district attorney maintained, still loyal to their tribe and chief? Were they dependent government wards who had illegally fled their assigned reservation and must now be returned—as the law required—to the Indian Territory? Were they neither citizens nor foreign subjects in the eyes of the law and therefore ineligible to file a suit of any kind against the government? Were these Indians then, by definition, not entitled to the same constitutional protection, civil rights, and legal privileges enjoyed by all other American citizens?

Or were they, as the dean of the state's legal profession contended, a group of people who had broken from their past and genuinely sought a civilized future for themselves and their children? Indians who farmed, went to church, sent their children to school, and, much like Dred Scott had once done, were now asking the court to set them free. Indians whom the government had no legal right to arrest and detain and return to the Territory. Indians who were people—human beings within the meaning of the law—who had a legal right to sue the government, and were entitled to the full protection and provisions of the Fourteenth Amendment.

So, sitting in his office in the federal courthouse, the judge knew the case had its share of complex questions and broad legal issues to sort through—not the least of which was a meticulous examination of the relevancy of the Fourteenth Amendment. Eleven years earlier, when Congress passed the landmark legislation, debate by and large had focused on slaves becoming free men and women, citizens who would now join the ranks of those born or naturalized in the United States. At one point, the congressional debate shifted to whether Indians who had abandoned tribal life, were taxed and had set off on a domestic course should also be considered citizens. By a thirty to ten vote, however, the Senate killed an amendment that would have included citizenship rights for those Indians.

But what did that now mean for the twenty-six Ponca prisoners holed up in Fort Omaha during the spring of 1879? Did the government still have the legal right to tell them when to move? Where to live? How to live? And what if they didn't want to? What if they wanted to find a better way? And if the government tried to stop them, had they been illegally deprived of life, liberty, and property? In the early part of May, it was not unusual to see the lights burning late into the night in the office on the second floor of the large building on the corner of Fifteenth and Dodge.

On the morning of May 12, 1879, ten days after hearing about the rising flood waters and the path to safety, about the color of blood, Judge Elmer Dundy delivered his decision in a lengthy written opinion to the Indian prisoners, the Army general, and their lawyers.

"During the fifteen years in which I have been engaged in administering the laws of my country," he began, "I have never been called upon to hear or decide a case that appealed so strongly to my sympathy as the one now under consideration. On the one side we have a few of the remnants of a once numerous and powerful, but now weak, insignificant, unlettered, and generally despised race. On the other, we have the representative of one of the most powerful, most enlightened, and most christianized nations of modern times. On the one side we have the representatives of this wasted race coming into this national tribunal of ours asking for justice and liberty to enable them to adopt our boasted civilization and to pursue the arts of peace, which have made us great and happy as a nation.

"On the other side," he continued, "we have this magnificent, if not magnanimous, government, resisting this application with the determination of sending these people back to the country which is to them less desirable than perpetual imprisonment in their own native land. But I think it is creditable to the heart and mind of the brave and distinguished officer who is made respondent herein, to say that he has no sort of sympathy in the business in which he is forced by his position to bear a part so conspicuous."

If sympathy were the only issue before the court, the judge said, the prisoners would have been freed the moment closing arguments ended. But in a nation where law determines liberty, sympathy alone cannot guide the courts. Instead, fundamental legal principles must decide this case. And if it cannot be determined that the prisoners are entitled to constitutional protection, they must be returned to Indian Territory, which they left without government consent.

The judge then broke down each of the government's legal arguments and addressed them one by one.

First of all, the government had argued, there was the problem of jurisdiction. Put simply, the court had overstepped its legal boundaries in allowing this case to see the light of day. The judge, in other words, had no legal right to compel the government to justify its arrest of the Indian prisoners because an Indian has no legal right to sue in federal court. Furthermore, since no Indian had ever been allowed to sue for a federal writ of habeas corpus, there was no legal precedent to let the case proceed.

In his written opinion, Judge Dundy labeled this argument a "non sequitur." Conceding he didn't know of a similar case, Dundy said it was nevertheless illogical to assume that just because no Indian had ever sought a writ of habeas corpus before that he could never seek one. The court also had jurisdiction in this specific case, the judge noted, because Standing Bear and the Ponca had been restrained of their liberty in violation of an earlier treaty provision. When that occurs, it is the federal courts—and only the federal courts—that can determine if the prisoners' constitutional rights have been violated. It would be "a sad commentary on the justice and impartiality of our laws, to hold that Indians, though natives of our own country, cannot test the validity of an alleged illegal imprisonment," the judge wrote.

Dundy next addressed the question of who could legally apply for the writ. Throughout the trial, the government had steadfastly argued that only citizens could do so. And since Indians were not citizens, they could not sue and thus the court had grievously erred in granting Standing Bear and the Ponca that legal privilege.

But the law, Judge Dundy said, clearly states "persons" or "parties" can do this—it says nothing about citizens or citizenship being a requirement. And the most natural and reasonable way to define a "person," the judge wrote, is simply to consult a dictionary. "Webster describes a person as 'a living soul; a self conscious being; a moral agent; especially a living human being; a man, woman or child; an individual of the human race.'" This, he said, "is comprehensive enough, it would seem, to include even an Indian."

Having resolved the question of jurisdiction, the judge then turned to the trial's key issue: Did Standing Bear and the Ponca have the right to expatriate themselves from the tribe, sever their tribal allegiance, and pursue a more independent and civilized life? To answer that question, the judge began by reviewing the events and forces that had set in motion the Ponca's long flight north from the Warm Country.

"The love of home and native land was strong enough in the minds of these people to induce them to brave every peril to return and live and die where they had been reared. The bones of the dead son of Standing Bear were not to repose in the land they hoped to be leaving forever, but were carefully preserved and protected, and formed a part of what was to them a melancholy procession homeward. Such instances of parental affection, and such love of home and native land may be *heathen* in origin, but it seems to me that they are not unlike *christian* in principle."

This, the judge noted, demonstrated Standing Bear and the Ponca had done all they could to terminate their tribal allegiance and underscored their desire to become independent farmers intent on adopting the ways of civilization. So did the Ponca prisoners detained at Fort Omaha have a legal right to expatriate themselves? Although there had been decades of heated discussions on the right of expatriation, those arguments had been silenced for eleven years now, the judge said. They were silenced on July 27, 1868, when a congressional act declared "the right of expatriation is a natural and inherent right of all people, indisputable to the enjoyment of the rights of life, liberty, and the pursuit of happiness." It was a short step then for the judge to render his decision: An Indian "possesses the clear and God-given right to withdraw from his tribe and forever live away from it, as though it had no further existence."

Finally, there was the matter of whether the government had the legal right to remove Standing Bear and the Ponca from the Omaha Reservation, and send them back to Indian Territory. A careful reading of the law, Dundy wrote, shows no such power exists. The government could not arbitrarily round up Indians who had severed their tribal ties and simply move them whenever and wherever it wanted. He did note the government could legally remove the Ponca from the Omaha Reservation if they were deemed "detrimental to the peace and welfare" of the reservation. But in such cases, the law required they must be turned over to civilian—not military—authorities. And that had not happened in the Ponca case. The judge said he had looked, and looked carefully, but had found no congressional act or treaty provision that gave the government the power to send the Ponca "back to the Indian Territory to remain and die in that country against their will."

Judge Dundy wrapped up his lengthy written opinion with a five-point summary that concisely pulled together the essential decisions he had reached. First, he concluded, "an *Indian* is a PERSON within the meaning of the laws of the United States, and has therefore the right to sue out a writ of habeas corpus in a federal court." Second, General Crook had illegally detained the Ponca prisoners. Third, the military has no legal authority to forcibly remove the Ponca to Indian Territory. Fourth, "Indians possess the inherent right of expatriation as well as the more fortunate white race, and have the inalienable right to 'life, liberty, and the pursuit of happiness . . . '" And fifth, since they have been illegally detained in violation of their constitutional rights, the Ponca "must be discharged from custody, and it is so ordered."

For ten long days and nights, the judge who had been lured in from the wilderness had sat in his office below the courtroom, poring over federal statutes and constitutional amendments, case law and congressional acts, testimony and trial records, trying to chart a course through the legal swamp of U.S.-Indian relations. For more than a century, those relations had been largely overwhelmed by successive waves of broken promises, broken treaties, land grabs, greed, graft, corruption, cultural ignorance, incompetence, indifference, and military might. For much of the past decade, it had gotten to the point where government programs and private agencies were often aligned in contradictory orbits, where some federal agents and Army officers increasingly were ordered to implement policies they abhorred. But on the afternoon of May 12, 1879, something else began to emerge from the legal swamp, something beyond the unfocused, uncharted landscape—the first inkling that there might be a better way.

With a stroke of his pen, Judge Dundy had done something unprecedented: He had not only granted the hearing, but had declared for the first time in the nation's history that an Indian was a person within the meaning of U.S. law. That the country's native inhabitants were a people who, if they obeyed the law, now had legal rights whites were bound to respect. People who, having dissolved their tribal allegiance, now had the protection of the Fourteenth Amendment, and were as entitled to life, liberty, and the pursuit of happiness as white citizens. People who were something more than cattle—powerless dependents the government could round up at will and herd to whatever part of the country suited its interests. People who now had the right of expatriation and who, in time of peace, could not be arbitrarily moved about the country without their consent. And if the government violated their constitutional rights, they could now sue the government in federal court.

Many years later, reflecting on his long legal career, Andrew Jackson Poppleton wrote about what had occurred in Judge Dundy's courtroom in the spring of 1879. "The question of whether the writ would lie on behalf of a tribal Indian and also whether the United States had any lawful power by its soldiery to remove him were wholly new and of vast importance . . . I delivered my argument upon that case in the evening in the large Federal Building on the corner of Dodge and Fifteenth Streets. There were present in addition to the court and its officers, an audience taxing the fine capacity of the room, including General Crook and other officers under his command, and many ladies. I have spoken to larger audiences, but I think never to one more intelligent and sympathetic, and in looking back I cannot now recall any two hours' work of my life with which I feel better satisfied."

The lawyer for the Union Pacific Railroad also remembered something else about the case. "Let me say here that it is within my personal knowledge that General Crook was the first person to suggest the remedy of habeas corpus," Poppleton wrote six years after the general's death. "I believe him to have been the first person who conceived of the idea that the great writ would lie at the suit of a tribal Indian. This, in my judgment, is not the least of his titles to the affection and gratitude of his country."

It wasn't long before news of the landmark decision began to spread far beyond the intersection of Fifteenth and Dodge streets. Readers of the *Omaha Daily Herald* awoke Tuesday morning, May 13, to find "Standing Bear's Victory—An Indian has Some Rights

Which the Courts Will Protect" in their local paper. In an article that covered several pages, the newsman Tibbles had reprinted the entire text of the judge's opinion. That same day, the *Chicago Tribune* alerted its readers to Standing Bear's triumph—"the only case of the kind ever brought in behalf of Indians in a Federal court." A few days later, the *New York Daily Tribune* told its readers: "Out in Omaha, at least, the idea has come to the surface at last, that an Indian is a man with human rights . . . The terms of the decision by Judge Dundy read oddly enough in a free country. The second century of the Republic is a late date to announce that any body of men born heirs to the soil, intelligent, moral, hard-working Christians, have the inalienable right to 'life, liberty, and the pursuit of happiness.'" And *The New York Times,* in a lengthy editorial, told its readers that Judge Dundy's unprecedented decision allowed Standing Bear and the other prisoners to come and go as they pleased, the same as any other U.S. citizen. "The Poncas by this time understand that the Indian is just as good as a white man, as long as he behaves himself."

Out West, however, the reaction was far less charitable. There, many editors throughout the mountains and plains lashed out at sympathetic Easterners for having solved their Indian problem by shipping native tribes across the Mississippi long ago. "The people in the East who have never been brought into immediate contact with the Indians in their savage state may feel a philanthropic exultation over this new interpretation of law, but to us it is a serious calamity," the *Denver Tribune* said. After paying the judge his due for a sincere and fearless decision, the newspaper then urged the Supreme Court to overturn it. If not, the paper predicted, the Great Plains will be soon be overrun by "a new race of tramps" bent upon stealing livestock, raiding farms, and murdering innocent whites. The *Rocky Mountain News* labeled the decision a "heavy blow to the present Indian system," one that would be dangerous for both Indians and whites alike. If the government is stripped of its power to control their movements, "the Indians will become a body of tramps moving without restraint wherever they please," creating a kind of open season on them from frontier settlers.

James M. Lawrence, meanwhile, apparently had a less than charitable view of the court case as well. The Ponca's former agent was fined one hundred dollars for using the U.S. mail to send an offensive, "smutty" postcard to the judge. But few were less charitable than the general of the U.S. Army. A week after the decision, William Tecumseh Sherman offered his verdict in a telegram to the Secretary of War. "Inasmuch as Judge Dundy has released from custody the Ponca Indians who escaped from their agency, where they were fed and maintained by the Indian Bureau, I think it would be fair to allow him in his charity to feed and clothe them. They are, in fact, paupers turned loose on the community by him, and he should assume the task and expense of their maintenance. If the Ponca prefer to rely on him, I suppose the Army can well allow him to assume that function."

One week after the judge's decision, the orders from Sherman's boss, Secretary of War G. W. McCrary, had made their way down the military chain to General Crook: Standing Bear and the other twenty-five Ponca men, women, and children could leave the Fort Omaha barracks behind. They were now free, free to go, shielded from the Army's grasp by the Fourteenth Amendment to the Constitution. Although the judge's decision had said nothing about the citizenship rights of Indians, it had begun to address the fundamental issue of exactly how the government should treat its native people—an issue that had been gathering momentum since the end of the Civil War. In the short term, Dundy's ruling had caught the wave of energy created by East Coast reformers and would trigger far-reaching changes in federal Indian policy. In some ways, it had also begun to explore and chart the headwaters of a much larger issue: The right of blacks, women, Indians, and other minorities to vote, to own property, to live where they wanted, to engage in the full democracy—an assortment of burgeoning human rights concerns that would continue to fester and haunt the country for much of the next century, and beyond.

When word of the judge's decision first reached White Eagle and the rest of the Sacred Head People in Indian Territory, they could not believe what they heard. They could not believe that one of their own—

a Ponca, an Indian—had walked into the white man's court, taken on an Army general, told his story to a roomful of powerful white citizens, and asked a white judge to set his people free—and won. It was a story the people in the Warm Country could not believe for a long time afterwards.

Even now, more than a century and a quarter later, it is a story the people have never forgotten, one they continue to think about, to talk about, and to celebrate, a story they have passed down from one Ponca generation to the next. Most summer days, sixty-three-year-old Deborah Robinette can be found in her Native arts-and-crafts shop along Highway 12 in the village of Niobrara, Nebraska. Sometimes, when she sees the children in her shop or at the only gas station down the highway a few blocks or across the street in the local cafe, she thinks back to the events that unfolded in the limestone courthouse in the spring of 1879. Sometimes, the light-skinned children go over to the dark-skinned ones and they're told they're too white to be Indian. Then they go over to the white children and they're told they're too dark to be white. "So some of these children develop an identity problem— and they start to ask, 'Well, who am I, then?' They don't really know," she says. "But Standing Bear gave them an answer for that. Because of him, they can say: 'I'm somebody, too. I'm a person. I'm a human being just like everyone else.' He was the first one who gave us a right to say that. It's the most powerful legacy we have. And it's one I want my little great-grandson to know all about."

It was now past the middle of the Month When Summer Begins and Standing Bear was in his lodge at the fort, packing up his things, when the newspaperman came to say good-bye. He said there were a few things he didn't want others to hear, so Standing Bear motioned for the interpreter and the three of them walked to the small hill overlooking the city where he had often gone during the fifty-four days they had been prisoners at the fort. He thanked the reporter for all he'd done, that if not for him, and the kindness of the soldiers and the medicine from the Army doctor, that he would be back in the Warm Country and many of his people in their graves. He told the newsman if he was ever down on his luck, he should not forget them. "While there is one Ponca alive you will never be without a friend."

When he finished, they walked back to the lodge and he opened a trunk and took out three gifts. He gave the newsman a pair of beaded buckskin leggings and asked if he wouldn't mind delivering the others to the two lawyers. The newsman thanked him and suggested maybe he should present them himself.

So the next day, Standing Bear and Bright Eyes got in his light spring wagon and rode to the home of the younger lawyer. He shook hands with the ladies first, and then the lawyer, and told him he had a beautiful home, and he thanked him for all he'd done for his people. Then he took out a tomahawk with his name engraved on it, one that signified his rank in the tribe, and laid it on the floor. "I have no more use for it," he told John L. Webster. "I have found a better way."

Afterwards, he got back in the wagon and drove to the corner of Fifteenth and Harney streets, to a boarding house where the older lawyer had recently moved after a fire destroyed his Capitol Hill home. He told the older lawyer he would be heading north soon, but he wanted to say good-bye first, and he wanted to give him something before they left. In his hand was a headdress that was maybe two hundred years old, maybe more—no one really knew for sure. It was the most sacred object in the tribe, one his father said had come to the people generations ago. It was worn by the head chief during solemn occasions, had been worn by the chief when he signed their first treaty with the government in 1817, and he wanted the older lawyer to have it because he had no other way to pay him. "I thank you for what you have done," he told Andrew Jackson Poppleton. "I want to get my land back. That is what I long for all the time. I wish to live there and be buried with my fathers."

On the morning of May 19, 1879—two years to the day after they had been forcibly marched across the swollen Niobrara, prisoners whose faces pointed south to the Warm Country—he got his family and his three orphaned grandchildren comfortably settled. Then he carefully put the trunk with the bones in it in the back of the light spring wagon, and pulled out of Fort Omaha, setting the horses on a course north by northwest.

7

A Ponca in Times Square

They were almost there, close enough that they could see the high chalk bluffs, the place where they had buried their dead for generations, the land where almost exactly two years earlier the soldiers had turned their faces south and marched them to a different country.

Telling no one, Standing Bear had left quickly, had slipped away and made a beeline to the old homeland, and now he and his small group were camped on the south bank of the Running Water. On the Northern Great Plains, it had been another tumultuous spring. For weeks, torrential rains had pummeled the region, swamping rivers and washing out bridges. Two days before they were released, a large meteor had plunged to earth not far from the barracks. On May 19, the day they walked out of the fort as free men and women, the worst storm of the season struck Omaha, preventing passenger trains from crossing the Missouri River Bridge. The Niobrara, too, was running full and swift and so they stayed in camp that night, waiting until dawn to try to cross the dangerously swollen river.

It hadn't been dark long when they heard horse hooves pounding across the distant prairie and then up along the valley where they had pitched their tents. About ten o'clock that night, the rider charged into camp and Standing Bear soon could see that it was the newsman from Omaha.

When Thomas Henry Tibbles discovered the Ponca had abruptly left the fort, that Standing Bear had made haste for the Niobrara, he rushed to the Omaha Reservation, where he knew the father of Bright Eyes kept two fast horses. He and a young Omaha Indian boy grabbed the ponies and took off, riding hard, covering 120 miles in eighteen hours.

That night, the newsman patiently explained the dilemma to Standing Bear: He and his people could not cross the Niobrara, could not return to their river homeland. Yes, the judge had freed them, that was true. But, legally, their old land still belonged to the Lakota, even though the Lakota had abandoned it almost a year earlier. If the Ponca crossed over, they would be arrested as trespassers. They also could not move in with their Omaha friends and relatives. The judge had let stand a law allowing the Army to arrest anyone on reservation land without government permission. And given the military's mood in the wake of the decision, it was unlikely they'd cut the Ponca much slack. Nor could they return to the Indian Territory, a place where they had severed tribal ties and sacrificed so much to escape.

Then where are we to live? Standing Bear asked.

The newsman suggested they pull back from the river, that they set up a camp near the Omaha, at a safe distance from the reservation boundaries. So the next morning, Standing Bear and the Ponca, but a few miles from the end of a journey that had begun in a blizzard five months earlier, glumly packed up and headed southeast, eventually setting up a new camp near Decatur, Nebraska, not far from the Omaha Reservation.

In their new camp, Standing Bear could no longer see the bluffs, and the river was once again a long way off. Walking idly around those first few days, he could feel the frustration and the sorrow whenever he looked at the trunk in the corner of his lodge. In just a few short weeks, he had gone from a prisoner in a fort to a free Indian with legal rights to a prisoner in his own homeland, a man without a country. He and the others had spent a great deal of time and effort and energy, had endured a good deal of hardship, to try to get out from under the government's thumb, to chart a course where they could fend for themselves and live as free and independent farmers, responsible for their own families and livelihood. Now, as spring turned to summer on the Northern Plains, he found himself in a forlorn camp at the edge of Decatur—landless, homeless, jobless, and penniless, a leader with twenty-nine others to care for, many of them women, children, and orphans, many of them sick.

Before long, he got the healthy men in camp to earn money chopping wood for the townfolk and working at a mill, and he encouraged his people to attend church on Sundays. Standing Bear and his family were often seen at the local church services and that summer he was invited to speak at a district Sunday school convention, his remarks translated to the crowd by a number of Omaha Indian English-speakers.

But as had often been the case in the Warm Country and during the long journey north and throughout much of the past decade, a familiar enemy soon began to stalk them. The planting season had long since passed and so hunger was a constant problem. During the summer and for months afterwards, they were kept afloat by their friends on the Omaha Ponca Relief Committee—the coalition of local clergy and parishioners led by Omaha Bishop Robert Clarkson.

That summer, besides providing food and clothing to the destitute Ponca, the committee was also engaged in several other issues that had spun out of Judge Elmer Dundy's ruling, issues that soon began to track closely along legal and political lines.

About a week after the ruling, the government lawyer filed papers in federal court appealing the decision. As a result, Standing Bear's lawyers believed the time was ripe to take the case all the way to the

Supreme Court, to push the issue of Indian citizenship and legal rights to the federal level, to try to settle the vexing Indian question once and for all. While the lawyers researched legal strategies, the newsman and local clergy began a series of long, late-night brainstorming sessions, sessions that also included the commander of the Department of the Platte. They were all looking for a way to achieve the group's second goal: getting the 96,000-acre Niobrara Reservation back in Ponca hands.

They knew they had some momentum now and they wanted to capitalize on it, keep it going. They also knew the Omaha could be the next tribe relocated to the Indian Territory, and they knew, too, that another twenty-five starving Ponca had recently arrived from the south and wanted to live and farm on the old lands. So they kept brainstorming, kept talking, looking for a way to "free every Indian in the country from ever again dreading that the whims of anyone in Washington" could dictate how and where they lived. In the end, Standing Bear's legal victory, they were convinced, could become the opening shot in an intense campaign to try to reform Indian policy from the top down. To pull that off, they believed their best chance was through the courts and Congress. But first, they needed to heighten public awareness on the issues and to obtain some cold, hard cash to finance their ambitious plan.

After days of kicking around various ideas, they settled on a strategy: The newsman would temporarily swap his pen and paper for a railroad ticket and a lectern.

The prospect of an East Coast speaking tour seemed like a good idea. For weeks, the plight of the Ponca had played out on the national stage and a tour would help keep the public lights burning. And the newsman seemed like a logical choice. Idealistic, bombastic, relentlessly energetic, Thomas Tibbles was part crusader and part showman, a restless, passionate, obsessive character who seemed to spring from one of the dime-store novels becoming popular throughout the country. Tibbles was happiest when he saw a windmill to tilt at or a dragon to slay, and it was even better if he could cloak himself in the hero's clothing. Although it was sometimes difficult to separate fact from fiction with the newsman, it was also true that when he locked onto a cause, it took a formidable force to dislodge him. Five years earlier, he had gone east and passed the hat for farmers stripped of their livelihood by grasshoppers, and by the summer of 1879 no one could seriously question his sincerity and devotion to the Ponca. So now he would head east again—educating, enlightening, haranguing, arousing, and fund-raising on behalf of thirty men, women, and children struggling to survive on the Great Plains.

Resigning his post as assistant editor of the *Omaha Daily Herald,* he immediately set about collecting a sheaf of documents that would help bolster his remarks and credibility to East Coast audiences. By the time he bought a train ticket to Chicago, he was armed with numerous news clippings on the Ponca, testimonials from Bishop Clarkson and other local clergy, as well as endorsements from the mayor of Omaha and the governor of Nebraska. And he had something else—a twelve-page, personal letter from the highest-ranking Army officer west of the Mississippi.

Dated June 19, 1879, George Crook's unusually blunt letter confirmed that the general could no longer traffic in the shadow world of duty versus conscience. The letter was intended for public consumption and would soon find its way into the nation's newspapers and a good number of the newsman's speeches. In the letter, the general reviewed his twenty-five-year career as an observer of both Indian culture and government policy, alternately offering praise for honest, dedicated, able men, and harsh criticism of the nation's unreliable dealings with its native people.

"I will say, without hesitation," Crook wrote Tibbles, "that our Indians have adhered more closely to the spirit of treaty stipulations than the white man or the white man's government has ever done." That said, the general noted the Indian was now well aware of the changing times and needed help to adapt to them. During this crucial stage, if the government can find a way to advance their human rights, to protect their property, they will—by and by—become a part of the dominant culture, he predicted. "Between the advocates of the theory that an Indian is incapable of good and the supporters of the antipodal idea that he will never do wrong, the red man is in danger of annihilation—of starving to death in the center of a country which is feeding the world with its exuberant harvest; or of being killed trying to defend rights which the Negro and Mongolian are allowed to enjoy." Now, he wrote, "when his horses and cattle are big enough to be of service, they are driven off in herds by white renegades; when his wheat and corn and vegetables are almost ready for market his Reservation is changed and, sometimes, as in the case of the Poncas, he is compelled to abandon everything." But "keep white thieves from plundering him, let him see that Peace means Progress, that he has a market for every pound of beef, every hide and every sack of grain, and, my word for it, he will make rapid advances."

The newsman was happy to have the general's pronouncements in his satchel when he boarded the train in Omaha.

Tibbles arrived in Chicago in late June. On the last day of the month, he appeared on stage with several others at an evening rally in Farwell Hall. The chairman of the event opened the rally by saying "the question of civilizing and Christianizing the Indians had been, from the time of Columbus on down, one of the important questions to be met here in the New World." Given a hero's introduction, Tibbles stepped forward and told the large crowd about the many crimes the "Indian Ring" had committed. He told them how Standing Bear and the other chiefs had abandoned their inspection of the Indian Territory, wandering barefoot in the wilderness with empty pockets, empty stomachs, and bleeding feet. He told them how the Ponca had withered and died off in the Warm Country, losing more than half the tribe and entire families. With the impassioned flair of a former preacher, he told them "there was nothing in all Russia as villainous as all this." In remarks frequently interrupted by applause, he closed by recounting Judge Dundy's decision and how they now wanted to press on to the Supreme Court and how they would need money to pay the legal bills.

Before the evening ended, Colonel C. G. Hammond, a U.S. Indian Inspector, rose from his seat on stage and offered fifty dollars. Others
soon followed and then some more and by the time the rally ended, the
newsman had six hundred dollars that he passed on to the treasurer of
the Omaha Ponca Relief Committee. The next morning, the event and
the newsman's speech received extensive coverage in the *Chicago
Tribune.*

Boston was next and Tibbles, bolstered by the strong Chicago
showing, arrived in the heart of the humanitarian-reformist movement
full of confidence and energy. But he quickly discovered many of the
prominent citizens he had hoped to meet were out of town and his spirits sagged. A letter from his wife encouraging him to keep fighting
bucked up his resolve and soon he had an audience with the editor of
the *Boston Daily Advertiser,* who pledged his help. Not long after, Ed-
ward Everett Hale, the popular Unitarian minister, reformer, and soon-
to-be chaplain of the U.S. Senate, broke the ice with a passionate
editorial championing the newsman's efforts on behalf of the Ponca.

On July 30, Tibbles rode the editorial momentum to a meeting of a
group called the Society for Propagating the Gospel Among the Indians
and Others of North America. Citing Standing Bear and the Ponca as
examples, he told the society that government treatment of the Indian
was now worse than ever. But testing the waters of Indian citizenship in
federal court required money. He said he'd like to raise four thousand
dollars by September 1. During the meeting, members elected a number
of leading citizens to serve on a recently created Ponca Indian Committee. The group eventually included the Reverend Hale, the mayor of
Boston, a wealthy publisher, a businessman, and the speaker of the Massachusetts House of Representatives. The committee's goal was to pub-
licize the Ponca cause and to raise money to help finance it. To that end,
committee members scheduled a public rally for the following week.

At noon on August 5, a large crowd gathered at Boston's Tremont
Temple. The Nebraska newsman sat on a corner of the stage watching
the guests arrive. "Poets, historians, scientists, lecturers—in they
walked until I got thoroughly frightened." On the other side of the

stage sat the rally's keynote speaker—the famed sixty-seven-year-old one-time abolitionist Wendell Phillips. Boston Mayor Frederick Octavius Prince gave the opening remarks and it wasn't long before the newsman heard his name called. "By the time I got to my feet I was trembling so badly I could hardly walk. For fully a moment I stood where I had been told to stand—silent, the world a blank. My shaking hand could not hold my manuscript and my bunch of proofs. Luckily the thud with which these fell brought back my senses." Speaking without notes, the newsman assaulted what he labeled a corrupt, evil system that had stolen Indian land, money, and civil rights from day one. A better way, he suggested, was to allot Indian land to the individual, not the tribe, and give them full protection of the courts. To sustained applause, the newsman wrapped up his thoughts by quoting Judge Dundy: "Any human being that God ever made can come into my court."

Phillips closed the public rally with a long, fiery speech that began by contrasting federal Indian policy with that of a neighbor's. In Canada, he said, the government had very few problems because Canadian Indians were under the protection of the law. Greed, he said, was largely to blame for America's Indian problem and it would not be resolved until U.S. courts protected their property and their rights.

After the rally ended, the elderly abolitionist and the middle-aged newsman went out to dinner. At a small Boston restaurant, Phillips encouraged Tibbles to keep fighting. In his day, he had fought for the Negro, and now it was the newsman's turn to keep spreading the word, to keep making as many waves as he could on behalf of the Indian. He also warned him not to be misled by Boston's enthusiastic reception. It would be a long, difficult road, and he would be ridiculed and attacked by formidable foes. Noting the newsman's head of thick black hair, Phillips told him it "will be gray before the first law is passed that does away with the present system."

The old abolitionist's warning proved prophetic. By early August, the tour, its publicity, and the relentless broadsides against federal Indian policy had taken their toll within the offices of the Interior Department. Soon, the government was forced to defend itself against the harsh public criticism of its policies, setting off a long war of words that escalated the heated debate over Indian reform. Both sides were digging in their heels, using the national press to reflect their respective positions. And, on both sides, the truth was often in short supply. The newsman, readers learned, was either a fearless crusader with a big heart or a shrewd huckster out to line his pockets. The government had either done everything in its power to help the Ponca adjust to a new life or had callously fleeced them of land, life, and human rights—it all depended on which paper was telling the story.

An August 3 *New York Times* article accused Tibbles of playing fast and loose with the facts, and discouraged Bostonians from donating to his cause. Instead, they could "serve the Poncas just as well without turning over to that gentleman $4,000, and without giving him authority to use the society's name to collect from the public." Across town, the *New York Daily Tribune* referred to the newsman as "the heroic Editor of Omaha, who forced Justice, in the shape of Judge Dundy, a few months ago, to take off her bandage and deal fairly with Standing Bear." The paper urged readers to financially support his dogged effort to expand Indian legal rights. "This is a move in the right direction. Bring the red man under the protection of the courts and give him the ballot, and the problem is solved."

By August's end, the charges and countercharges forced Interior Secretary Schurz to write a long, open letter to the public. In it, he recounted the Ponca removal history, said the government had bent over backwards to help them, and largely blamed the previous administration for most of the problems. "No effort has been spared by the Executive branch of the Government to rectify all the wrongs that the Poncas have suffered, so far as those wrongs can be rectified," he wrote. Standing Bear, he said, was a morose, sullen, and indolent man and "about the time the Spring work began at the agency he ran away to the North." The secretary also published a letter he received from Colonel A. B. Meacham, a self-described lifelong friend of the Indian who edited the *Council Fire,* a monthly journal devoted to Indian issues. Meacham had recently returned from an inspection of the Ponca Reservation in the Indian Territory. "I found them in an excellent country, under the management of an active, earnest, competent agent," he wrote the Interior Secretary. "Nearly half of the 82 new houses built by the Government for the Indians around the border of the prairie stand in view, while near each one a small farm was being made . . . I saw no idle, vagabond Indians. I saw no sickly, discontented Indians. I heard no serious complaint about the country or the Government."

Two weeks later, the earnest, competent agent filed his second annual report on the condition of the Ponca. Echoing many of the colonel's observations, Agent William Whiteman reported the Ponca were now acclimated and well on their way to a healthy recovery. Although twenty-six Ponca had died that year and another sixty-six had fled north, there were also sixteen births. The tribe now numbered 530 and occupied the best land in all of the Territory. They were all working hard, had all the farming implements and livestock they needed, and had been given all of their annuities. He had built more than seventy homes for them, fine log houses with floors, doors, windows, and roofs. Before closing, he also lashed out at those in Judge Dundy's courtroom and the national press who had harshly criticized government treatment of the Ponca. Those claims, he said, were made "either in ignorance of the facts or else purposely and maliciously fabricated to subserve personal ends, for certainly there is nothing in the facts to warrant such a statement." Commissioner of Indian Affairs Ezra Hayt backed up his man in the field. "In brief," the commissioner said, "everything possible has been done to promote their comfort and civilization."

But there were a few things the agent omitted from his upbeat report. He neglected to mention that of the more than seventy new homes, only two were habitable. He didn't mention there were huge gaps between the logs, no bedsteads, tables, or chairs, and no stovepipes for heating. That, as a result, when it snowed five inches that winter and then a sleet storm froze on top of the snow, the Ponca were forced to live in unheated tents on the river bottom—eighteen months after their arrival in the Territory. Nor did the agent mention he'd forced the Ponca to sign receipts for cattle, wagons, and dishes, among other things, that they never received—tax dollars that had gone somewhere else.

The following winter, Whiteman's boss also made a personal inspection of the Ponca Reservation. After he saw the unfinished homes, saw their tents on the river bottom, saw the receipts for all the goods that never arrived, after he had interviewed many of them, Indian Inspector William J. Pollock, an Illinois lawyer, fired Agent Whiteman on the spot.

Six hundred miles away, while Standing Bear and his newly freed band were trying to survive on the Northern Plains, their Omaha lawyers contacted several local surveyors. After consulting with the lawyers, the surveyors began to study a detailed map of the Great Sioux Reservation, a sprawling area that included the old Ponca homeland. After a time, they discovered that several islands in the Niobrara had been excluded from Lakota ownership and so they sent word to the small, makeshift village in Decatur. Not long afterwards, Standing Bear and the Ponca broke camp, and once again moved north by northwest until they reached the river. They eventually found shelter in a willow thicket on one of the larger islands, land owned by a private citizen in a nearby village.

When Standing Bear now looked out from their new camp in the willows on the large island, when he looked far upstream from the Nebraska side, he saw a homeland that in his lifetime had shrunk from one-hundred miles along either side of the Niobrara to 96,000 acres near its mouth to a single island in the middle of the river. But when he looked downstream, toward where the Niobrara emptied into the Missouri, he could also see something else—he could see the tall, green hills and the imposing chalk bluffs with their commanding view of the confluence. He was close enough now that he could see the spiritual heart of his people's ancestral lands. For as long as anyone could remember, the Ponca had buried their dead high in the hills and bluffs overlooking the rivers. In the old days, if it was winter and the ground was frozen, the dead would be placed on a scaffold until a grave could be dug in the spring. Often, gifts were placed by the grave and sometimes a favorite horse would be tied down nearby. The dead were dressed in their best clothes, which were often marked with special designs or styles that signified the specific clan to which they belonged. In this way, they would gain safe passage to the spirit world and be easily recognized by their own people when they arrived.

That summer, in the Moon When Hot Weather Begins, Standing Bear and his family left the island and followed the river a short journey north, stopping where it empties into the Missouri. Then they pushed a few miles west until they reached a towering bluff perched high above the old Fish Smell Village. For generations, the people had wanted their dead to be high enough in the hills and bluffs so that they could always see the water, and the bluff, the one the people call *Máazì,* offered a commanding view of the river valley that had come to define them. After they arrived, they found a good spot with a good view of the river and they dug a fresh grave in the soil of their homeland. Honoring him with the full ceremonies of the tribe, the father laid Bear Shield's bones to rest, and said good-bye to his son.

Their many allies were convinced there had to be a better way, a way to get them off the island and back on the land of their ancestors, to a place where they could farm and feed their families, build homes and schools, give their children—like those of all the others—a shot at the American Dream.

So as summer turned to fall, the Omaha Ponca Relief Committee held more meetings and more brainstorming sessions, trying to figure out what to do next to help their friends. They had sent Bright Eyes and Joseph La Flesche down to the Territory, and the father and daughter had returned with their own report—about the dismal housing, the lack of food and farming equipment, the crooked agent, the many families who had turned their faces north. "The agent's residence was handsomely built and finished off and somehow looked strangely out of place among the tents and graves," Bright Eyes told the committee members. The members knew, too, the Ponca cause had now taken off in the public arena. They had kept close tabs on the newsman's trip east, had read many of the stories in some of the nation's most influential newspapers, and seen the names of the many prominent citizens who had spoken out on behalf of Standing Bear and his people. And they had seen some money begin to come in to help their cause.

By the time the newsman returned to Omaha on September 6, 1879, the committee had decided on its next step: a full-blown East Coast speaking tour. This one would be more formal, better organized, and include far more cities. At each stop, it would focus on four things: the initial inspection tour and long walk home by the chiefs in 1877, the forced removal south that spring, the deaths and deplorable conditions in the Warm Country, and the freedom flight north. In the end, they believed, it was their best shot at achieving their two-pronged goal: expanding Indian civil rights in the courts and restoring the Ponca homeland to its rightful owners. And, besides Tibbles, committee members decided, the ambitious fall tour would include Standing Bear and Bright Eyes.

The newsman objected to a trio of speakers. It would be an expensive trip, he argued, and to cut costs they should exclude Bright Eyes. She, herself, didn't want to go anyway and her father wanted nothing to do with it. But when a bill to remove the Omaha to the Indian Territory began making the rounds in Congress, the father had a change of heart. His daughter could go, he said—but only if her nineteen-year-old brother, Woodworker, went along. The latter proved to be a wise decision.

One-quarter French and three-quarters Omaha, Bright Eyes had lived in the East, knew the white ways and customs, and spoke English and Ponca fluently. She also knew a good deal about the Ponca from personal observation, from letters and conversations with her uncle, White Swan, a Ponca chief, and because the two cultures had a lot in common. And it didn't hurt that she was articulate, modest, dignified, and beautiful.

Yet in other ways, it didn't seem like Bright Eyes and Tibbles were a good match. At twenty-five, she was fourteen years younger than the newsman, and they were opposites in most respects. Shy, quiet, and reserved, she was terrified of large crowds and public speaking. At the Elizabeth Institute, the girls' school she had attended in New Jersey, she developed a passion for literature and writing and her last essay before graduation had been published in *The New York Times*. All in all, she much preferred getting lost in her books, her poetry, and her artist's sketch pad or discussing the value of a good education with her younger sister, Susan, who, in ten years, would graduate at the head of her medical school class in Philadelphia, becoming the first female Indian doctor in the nation.

But the committee needed Standing Bear's message to come through and only a good interpreter could make it happen. Besides, she had seen first-hand the problems in the Territory and she wanted to help the Ponca and her own people, too. So, in the end, Bright Eyes agreed to become, in effect, the first Indian woman to enter the public speaking arena.

That settled, the newsman began to organize the tour through the many contacts he had developed during the summer. He got a contract with the head of a Boston lecture bureau and commitments from an assortment of influential politicians, editors, citizens, and artists.

In late September, Bishop Clarkson invited Standing Bear and Bright Eyes to speak at a local Omaha church. When her name was called, she stood alone and motionless before a large crowd that began cheering, clapping, and waving handkerchiefs at the small, delicate figure trembling on stage. Finally, she gripped the side of the pulpit and began to speak about the loss of her friend Prairie Flower, the chief's daughter, and about the many complexities of the new civilization she was trying to understand. "The Christian ladies of Milford, Nebraska, come to the Indian camp, pray for the dying girl, and give her a Christian burial . . . Part of the white people murder my girl companion and another part tenderly bury her, while her old father stands over her grave and says: 'My heart breaks.'" After her plain, soft-spoken remarks, a few women began to cry and some men began to shout and a few others swore aloud. Bright Eyes stared back from the stage and began to rock back and forth, clutching the pulpit for support, then abruptly stopped speaking. Soon, several women came up, took her arms, and led her away.

Her first public appearance had been a rocky one, but it had also sent an electrifying spark through the crowd.

In mid-October, the chief, the poet, her teenage brother, and the newsman boarded a train in Omaha and headed east. For some time, the group had discussed how each should dress when they arrived in the big cities. It was agreed that most of the time they would appear in what the government called "citizens clothes"—white clothing. But when addressing an audience, Standing Bear believed he could better deliver his message if he appeared in the best clothes of his people, similar to what General Crook had done during the trial. Woodworker, meanwhile, would wear civilian clothing, which was his custom, and Bright Eyes would dress in a manner reflecting what she was—a modern woman.

On Sunday evening, October 19, 1879, the foursome made their first appearance of the fall speaking tour. Standing Bear walked across the stage at Chicago's Second Presbyterian Church in moccasins, deerskin leggings, blanket, and bear claw necklace, an eagle feather in his straight, black hair. Bright Eyes stood beside him in a plain dark dress with a white lace scarf at the throat, interpreting his remarks. He told the one thousand parishioners he frequently thinks of God and that he reveres the Bible, which he credited for making the white people strong. His people, he told the parishioners, were weak and powerless, and they needed the kindness and generosity of the faithful. "I have been told that Jesus the son of God says for us to help one another when in trouble," he said, "and I hope all of you Christian people will help me, as I am in trouble." By the time the event ended, the faithful had contributed several hundred dollars.

Standing Bear had spent much of the summer and early fall in a tent on a river island and, until Omaha, had seen little more of "civilization" than the dugouts, sod houses, and pine shacks of white settlers. And although Chicago could be overwhelming, he never seemed ill at ease or in danger of losing his way. An acquaintance once asked how he managed that. "When I sat down at a table for the first time," he replied, "I watched what the others did and kept just a little behind, so I would make no mistake about the white ways."

One night in Chicago, the group arrived at the elegant Palmer House for dinner with a number of prominent citizens. With its large rooms, a barbershop floor tiled in silver dollars, and a range of sumptuous cuisine, it was among the nation's finest. After everyone ordered, the newsman quietly tipped the black waiter a quarter to ensure Standing Bear's plate always had a fresh supply of roast beef, well done. Throughout the meal, the waiter stood off to one side and as soon as one piece of roast beef disappeared, a new one appeared. Among his people, it was considered rude not to eat the food put before you, so Standing Bear kept eating. After a while, he gently nudged the newsman, who had been lost in conversation. "There was a look of distress on his face that showed he was in serious trouble," recalled Tibbles, who quickly called off another serving.

Their Chicago leg finished, the group boarded a train in late October and headed farther east. The first stop had gone well and as Standing Bear picked up some of the language and customs, he began making a play on words every now and then that kept the group laughing. After a brief stop in Pittsburgh, in good shape and fine form, they boarded a car on the Boston and Albany Railroad line, and pushed farther east.

They arrived in Boston on Wednesday morning, October 29, and checked into the Tremont House. After breakfast, Mayor Prince held a private reception in their honor in the hotel parlor. The mayor told Bright Eyes to tell Standing Bear that he and his people should be patient, that they should do nothing rash, because the injustices were well known and a serious effort to expand their legal rights was well underway. As he closed his remarks to the one-hundred invited guests, Standing Bear indicated he would like to speak. "This morning, when I see you all, although I have felt sad all along, I feel no longer sad," he told the guests. "It seems that I have come to a place I can call home."

The city was abuzz with news of the group's arrival, heralded on the front page of the local newspaper. "Standing Bear," the *Boston Daily Advertiser* noted, "realizes in noble appearance the Indian of Cooper's tales, of whom it has so often been said that he never could have existed." Besides the small, private reception, a much larger public one was scheduled for that evening. The tour seemed to be unfolding so smoothly, with such enthusiasm and interest, the group could scarcely believe it. "That afternoon of October 29 we laughed at everything, especially Standing Bear's many puns," Tibbles recalled.

About five o'clock, the head of the Boston lecture bureau found the newsman in the hotel lobby. He approached slowly, ashen-faced, hands trembling, struggling to speak. "I have some very bad news." In his hand were two three-day-old telegrams routed from Chicago to Pittsburgh to Boston.

One was for Tibbles: His wife of eighteen years, mother of their two young daughters, had died suddenly of peritonitis. She was buried that morning.

The other was for Standing Bear: His brother the soldier chief, the one he had shared a prison cell with when they refused to march their people south, had died in Indian Territory. Unarmed, surrounded by a dozen soldiers, he'd been shot in the face.

Big Snake, according to the agent and the official Army report, was killed in self-defense while "resisting arrest." The day after Judge Dundy's ruling, he and a few others went to visit the nearby Cheyenne, who had offered some ponies to replace all the dead Ponca ones. Agent Whiteman had denied them permission to leave, but Big Snake left anyway. After he arrived, the agent asked the military commander at the Cheyenne agency to arrest Big Snake and jail him "until the tribe has recovered from the demoralizing effects of the decision recently made by the United States District Court in Nebraska."

Jailed for two and a half months, Big Snake returned to the Ponca

Reservation in early August. A few months later, the agent reported he was a "sullen" and "morose" troublemaker who frequently challenged his authority and had recently threatened to kill him. He asked his superiors to imprison him "and there confine him for the remainder of his natural life." General Sherman obliged. When the arrest orders arrived in late October, Big Snake was in the agent's office surrounded by ten soldiers. According to Agent Whiteman, Big Snake said he "would rather die" than be taken back to prison. When they tried to grab him, he put up a fierce struggle. The corporal who finally shot him in the head said he fired only after the soldier chief pulled a knife. "Big Snake was a very bad, insolent, and dangerous Indian," Agent Whiteman reported. "I regret that he should be killed in this manner, but am of the opinion that the tribe will be more tractable now that he is dead."

It would be a long time before Standing Bear discovered the truth about his brother's death. Joseph Esaw, a full-blooded Pawnee who worked as a government interpreter on the Ponca Reservation, was in the agent's office when the soldiers came. Some months later, under oath during a congressional inquiry, Esaw described what he saw in the agent's office that day:

> *Big Snake had filled his pipe, and was just about to smoke, when this army officer told me to tell Big Snake that he had come for him. I told Big Snake. He did not even lift his head to look at the army officer; he only sat there and smoked, and did not say anything for quite a while. Then the officer told me to ask Big Snake if he would go with him. Big Snake said that he would like to know what he had done; he said he had been arrested and kept in that fort for a long time, and had but just got back from it. The officer told Big Snake that he did not know, himself, what he was wanted for; but he had been sent for, and he must go . . . Big Snake shook his head and said that he had committed no crime at all, and that he did not want to go to be put in jail without cause; that he was not going . . . The agent gave the officer permission to tell Big Snake the reason why he had come to arrest Big Snake. The officer told Big Snake that he had come to arrest*

him because he had threatened to kill the agent and two other per-
sons beside the agent. Big Snake turned to the agent and told him
that he was mistaken . . . that he had no enemies; if he did, he would
carry a knife or some weapon with him; and he showed them his
belt, and asked them to look and see if there was any knife or
weapon there . . . Then Big Snake told the agent that he was the one
that had got him arrested before when he had not committed any
crime, and that he was not going to be arrested by him any more . . .
He said that he would rather die right there than to be arrested
again . . . Then the officer called in the soldiers. Then the officer
went up and caught hold of Big Snake by the arm and told him to get
right up and go. Big Snake said that he did not want to go . . . Then
the officer told one of the soldiers to take up the blankets, and he
called two others of the soldiers to bring the handcuffs, and put them
on Big Snake. As they were about to put the handcuffs on him, Big
Snake did that [forcibly opening his arms outward], and flung them
off. Then they caught hold of him by the arms, and he threw them off
again. Then the officer called all the soldiers to come and help. Then
six soldiers caught hold of Big Snake three by each arm, and tried to
put the handcuffs on him, but they could not hold him; he would just
throw them right off . . . Then all tried again to pull him down, but
he just stayed right there in his chair and threw them off as fast as
they came. Then all the soldiers came in and got on him all together.
They were too many for him, so he got up out of his chair and tried
to throw them off. Then one of the soldiers struck him with a gun,
struck him in the face with the butt-end of the gun. Then the soldier
that had the gun struck Big Snake with the barrel of the gun in the
face and knocked the skin off from his forehead. Then, the third time,
he took the gun and just shot him through the head . . . The gun was
close to him; only about [four inches] . . . Big Snake had got up,
then, and was standing with his back against the wall. As he was
shot through the head the bullet passed through the wall and nearly
struck an Indian that was standing outside . . . It hit him in the left
temple, and came out through the cheek, on the right side of his

face . . . I told the soldiers that he had not any weapon, and the soldiers saw that he did not . . . I examined his body, but I found no weapon on him at all . . . They brought the coffin in where the body lay; but his relations came after him and put him in a wagon and took him home, and did not lay him in the coffin.

Indian Inspector William Pollock, a former deputy clerk of the Illinois Supreme Court, also investigated the shooting. During the same congressional inquiry, he was asked his opinion. "At the time of the killing, there were ten or twelve soldiers present in the office; Big Snake was alone and unarmed. I cannot see the necessity of killing an unarmed man, confined in a room and surrounded by eighteen or twenty men, a dozen or more of whom were armed soldiers. It looked to me, to put it in plain English, like a cowardly, willful murder." No arrests were made, no charges ever filed.

In the late-afternoon light of the Boston hotel lobby, Tibbles stared blankly at the telegrams. He felt light-headed, felt like he might get sick to his stomach, and so he hurried back to his room and closed the door. After a time, the door slowly opened. The newsman was lying facedown on the bed. The chief knew the newsman's wife had been put in the ground, his nine- and eleven-year-old daughters were with Bishop Clarkson in Omaha, and the father was in a hotel room 1,400 miles away. And he knew the large public reception began in an hour. Standing Bear walked over and knelt down. He put a hand on the newsman's head and began to speak in Ponca. When Woodworker came in, he asked the boy to tell him the words—they had come too far, sacrificed too much, buried too many dead. They couldn't quit now.

Horticultural Hall was packed when they arrived. The Boston Indian Committee members were sad, sympathetic, but said each would need to take the stage and say at least a few words. The newsman said he could not do it. Standing Bear said he must. He had not given up after the deaths of his children, and now his brother, and the newsman couldn't either. "I know how sore your heart is," the chief told him. But he had to say something "for those who suffer and die with no one to pity. If you can do that, it will make your burdens lighter, not heavier."

Mayor Prince spoke first, telling the large throng that when the government was forced to pick between the Lakota and the Ponca, it had sided with the strong over the weak. And then it had gone to court and argued that the weak had no legal rights. But Judge Dundy had said the weak do have certain rights. Now they needed more donations to carry the fight to the Supreme Court, to have the nation's highest court confirm and expand the judge's ruling on behalf of the Ponca and all Indians.

After brief remarks from the chief and the newsman, the mayor introduced the young poet. She spoke slowly and carefully, in precise English, her voice rising and falling to make her points. There was a time not long ago, she said, when she had given up hope, had lost all faith in the future of her people. "I felt as though if there were a God he must have created us for the sole purpose of torturing us," Bright Eyes told the crowd. "I think if it had not been for the memory of the noble Christian women with whom I lived at one time, I should have become an utter disbeliever in God and humanity." It was nights like this, she said, that kept her away from the edge. "I come to you with gladness in my heart and to try and thank you, for here, after a hundred years of oppression, my people have for the first time found public sympathy, and as soon as the truth of their story was known help was given them."

For many in the heart of the nation's humanitarian and reformist movement, the news of Big Snake's death, and the circumstances surrounding it, seemed to confirm their suspicions, to bear out what their visitors from the West had been saying all along about the government's treatment of its native people. Before long, news coverage of their visit expanded, the already considerable civic interest increased, the public crowds grew larger. And the donations began to come in. Although it had limited funds, the Society for Propagating the Gospel Among Indians voted to give $425 to the Ponca cause in early November, and soon hundreds more began to flow in. All the while, the guest lists and invitations kept piling up.

Throughout the early days of the tour, their hosts kept the group too busy to dwell for long on personal loss. They visited the Massachusetts State House and were greeted by Governor Thomas Talbot. They went to East Boston, touring the docks and a large Cunard luxury liner. That evening, they took tea with *Boston Daily Advertiser* editor Delano Goddard during a private reception at his home. The next day, they spoke at the Harvard Congregational Church in Brookline in the morning and at the Clarendon-Street Baptist Church that evening.

On November 3, they joined the Reverend Cook on stage at the Old South Church for the 131st talk in the Boston Monday Lectureship series. The famed church was full by the time Cook opened his noon talk.

"Call the roll of the ghosts which float through this building as thickly as leaves in Vallombrosa—John Adams, John Hancock, Joseph Warren, George Whitefield, George Washington," he began. "I venture to say that there is not one of these historic souls that does not sympathize with this Indian chieftain. For his demand is precisely what theirs was—that a laborer should be allowed to dispose of the results of his own work. One hundred and five years ago this house was packed to suffocation, and the steps of this platform were covered by British officials, who threatened death to the young men who should celebrate the patriotism of those who didn't like the Boston massacre." The American Revolution, he told the cheering crowd, was based on a simple premise—no taxation without representation. So why should those who now benefit from the fruits of that Revolution not want to help others attain the same freedoms? Nodding to the young woman seated to his left, he said he had been struck by something she recently said: "An Indian does not want to cultivate a piece of land, fence it in, build him a house, furnish and stock his farm, and just as he is ready to enjoy the fruits of it, to have it taken from him, and he and his family sent to a southern clime to die." If the government had inadvertently awarded a large tract of Union Pacific Railroad land to the Lakota, the Reverend

Cook wondered, how long would it have taken the courts to correct that "blunder?" The Ponca, he said, need their land back—plain and simple—and the Indians need legal protection.

When the reverend finished, Standing Bear walked to the pulpit at the front of the Old South Church. With Bright Eyes at his side, he turned and faced the large throng. "My brother has been killed. He was trying to do just as I did—to break away from that land . . . It is hard for me to speak today and I cannot say much more, but I am glad to have been able to tell you some of the truth. I feel sad, but I think of my family. They are all alone on the prairies in a tent . . . That is all."

Throughout their stay, wherever they went, they were treated like foreign heads of state—every visit, every move, every word chronicled in the daily papers. In the mornings, Bright Eyes would often read aloud to Standing Bear—stories about the "noble chief," the "Indian princess," the "dignified warrior," the "Indian maiden," the "three fine species of the aboriginal race" who were in Boston. The year after she was born, one of the local poets, Henry Wadsworth Longfellow, had written *The Song of Hiawatha,* an epic tale about native life by the shores of a great lake, about a Victorian Indian hero of the forest and his loyal Indian wife. Back then, most of the stories were about "redskins," "heathens," and "barbarous savages." But as the nineteenth century wound down, as more and more tribes were swept from the land and a gridwork of farms and ranches took hold, no one seemed to know who they really were anymore or where they fit into the national consciousness. They could be loved or loathed, romanticized or reviled, patronized or promoted—depending on the storyteller and the motive. Although Standing Bear and Bright Eyes had gone east to assert their freedom, to declare their independence from the old way of doing things, to build a future, they often felt shackled by the past—by the simplicity, the sentimentality, and the shopworn stereotypes. It was something that had bothered them for a while, had confused them, and sometimes they weren't sure what to do or how to react. As the weeks went by, they encountered a lot of ghosts on both sides of the red and white road, a road they frequently found difficult to travel without a misstep. The issue of Indian identity had never been an easy one—then or now.

These days, Janet Saiz spends her days in Albuquerque, New Mexico, taking care of three grandchildren so her son can concentrate on finishing law school and begin a career specializing in Indian and environmental law. Her mother, Clara, was born along the Niobrara in 1910 and shipped off six years later to an Indian boarding school in Genoa, Nebraska, where the process of assimilation—of cutting hair, dressing in white clothing, banning native languages, and reading the Bible—was in full swing. The sixty-eight-year-old Saiz, who raised her children and then got a bachelor's degree in history from the University of Wisconsin, has never forgotten something her mother told her a long time ago.

For years, her mother said, Standing Bear had struggled with how to strike a balance between learning the new ways and holding on to the old ones. He told the Northern Ponca that the only way they could survive as a people was to go to school and learn English, and to try to learn as many of the white ways as possible. But at the same time, they also needed to know and remember the Ponca ways, to hold on to as much of their own tradition and culture as they could. "If they lost that," her mother said he always told them, "then they wouldn't survive either—no matter how well educated they were or how successful a farmer they became. If they did the one thing to survive, but not the other—then what was the point? What did it mean to survive? Who were they? If they lost their identity as a people, none of the rest mattered."

One night in the fall of 1879, about a week after Standing Bear arrived in Boston, they were all invited to the Cambridge home of wealthy publisher Henry Houghton. Traffic jams delayed their arrival and forced one of the evening's guests to stare impatiently out the window. As the western visitors finally made their way up the long front walk, the eastern poet stood in the doorway, eagerly awaiting Bright Eyes.

When she stepped through the door, Henry Wadsworth Longfellow stepped forward, clasped her hand and, looking intently in her eyes, exclaimed: "*This* is Minnehaha!" Still holding her hand, he led her through the crowded home to a quiet corner, where they sat and talked for a long time.

As the days went by, as each Boston event generated more and more news coverage, the Ponca cause also gained more and more momentum, eventually spilling outside the churches and public halls and into the private sector.

One day in late November, as Thanksgiving neared, almost five-hundred Boston businessmen arrived at the Merchants' Exchange, among the largest such gatherings in city history. The businessmen stood for more than an hour, listening as a succession of speakers detailed the injustices and encouraged their support. The new battle, they were told, had moved from the western lands to the eastern courts. To carry on the legal fight that had begun in Judge Dundy's courtroom, they planned to file three more lawsuits and they would need a good amount of money to get it done. It was a just cause, the speakers said, and it was now up to the citizens of Boston to lend a hand. "Twenty-five years ago," noted John Long, the new governor of Massachusetts, "this whole country was rocked through its length and breadth by the question of whether a black man had any rights which a white man was bound to respect— a question upon which the destinies of the country turned. And now a similar question, without raising hardly more than a ripple in the public mind, is presented in regard to the red man."

The newsman briefly recounted the plight of the Ponca and their legal rights and Standing Bear urged them to do all they could to restore his people to their homeland. Bright Eyes closed with a long speech about the world she saw around her, the white world and the red world, and how one—if it chose to—could help save the other.

"I have come to you to appeal for your sympathy and help for my people," she told the businessmen. "They are immortal beings, for whom Christ died. They asked me to appeal to the churches, because they had heard that they were composed of God's people, and to the judges because they righted all wrongs. It is a little thing, a simple thing, which my people ask of a nation whose watchword is liberty; but it is endless in its consequences. They ask for their liberty, and law is liberty."

Before returning to work that day, the businessmen adopted four resolutions aimed at protecting Ponca land and legal rights. They also asked their new governor to appoint a five-member committee to look into the Indian issues and report their findings in print. The Boston Indian Committee, as it came to be known, included the state's former governor, the mayor of Boston, and a wealthy businessman. It would initiate the first serious investigation into the Indian claims, methodically reconstructing what had gone wrong with the removal and recommending what the government's obligations were—not only to the Ponca, but to all its native people.

Throughout their stay, the small group of visitors from the Great Plains moved freely throughout Boston. They attended the requisite town hall meetings, made the required public appearances, gave their speeches, and dutifully showed up at the teas and dinners held in their honor. In between, they occasionally saw and heard some things that were not a part of the speaking tour, things they would remember for a long time.

One Saturday evening, a few weeks after his brother's death, Standing Bear and the others walked into the Berkeley Street Church. It was a chilly night in mid-November and the huge crowd inside had squeezed into every available space in the old Boston church. They said he seemed sad that night, that the face of the homeless chief gave it away as he took a seat near the front and looked up at the stage, watching the evening performance about to begin. He had seen one of their kind on the plains every now and then and in Omaha and that time at dinner in Chicago, but never anything like this, and so he sat and watched as the Reverend William Wright introduced the all-black Fisk University Jubilee Singers and explained a little bit about the different sound they created.

The singers were headed for a European tour, but they had wanted to do something for the western visitors before leaving and soon the church began to fill with the sound of their melancholy spirituals. After each song, the applause would come in waves, one encore following another, and he sat transfixed, watching emancipated slaves singing African gospel in a Christian church for the benefit of the Ponca. Moments before the last selection, they asked him and Bright Eyes to join them on stage and when they had, they began to sing the final song. He couldn't understand the words, but he could hear the voices turning soft and tender and he could feel "Home, Sweet Home" was a haunting song, and he could see in the eyes and faces of the others that they had all heard something special on a rainy November night in the old Boston church.

When the month ended, one thing seemed certain: The Boston leg of the tour had been a rousing success, far exceeding the expectations of both hosts and guests. In a few short weeks, they had captivated the city's interest, enlisted the support of publishers, preachers, prominent artists, powerful politicians, and wealthy businessmen, created a committee to investigate their claims and generated a robust, first-of-its-kind national debate on Indian civil rights. And when it was over, the four-thousand-dollar goal to carry the fight to the country's highest courts already had been reached, so it was bumped to ten thousand dollars.

In early December, the newsman, the chief, the poet, and her brother bid good-bye to the citizens of Boston, boarded a train and, armed with a good deal of money and momentum, headed two hundred miles south.

Early on the morning of December 5, 1879, the middle-aged chief of a small Northern Plains tribe arrived in a city unlike anything he had ever imagined. Its size, energy, and pace, the sheer number of people and buildings, was overwhelming.

He and the others checked into the Fifth Avenue Hotel and a few days later they walked into a lavish home at 999 Fifth Avenue, the guests of Josiah Fiske, a well-connected, well-to-do businessman, who hosted a reception that evening in their honor. Standing Bear wore ordinary civilian clothes and throughout the evening he seemed reserved, a little hesitant in the company of the wealthy merchants, doctors, lawyers, and university presidents, dressed in their fine clothes, sipping drinks in expensive glasses, speaking a language he did not understand in a city a long way from an island in the Running Water.

On December 12, the group made its first public appearance in New York, sharing a stage with Peter Cooper and other prominent citizens at Steinway Hall. Professor Roswell Hitchcock was among the first to speak. On Indian matters, he said, the nation's pendulum had swung maddeningly back and forth—between romantic forest dweller and bloodthirsty savage. But the truth, he noted, is never at the extreme. The Indian, too, is human. "Take away the accident of savage costume," he told the cheering crowd, "dress us just alike, and there might not be much difference between Manhattan and Omaha."

At their last public appearance in Boston, more than two-thousand people had to be turned away from Faneuil Hall. But two hundred miles south, the crowds were not as large, although a thousand New Yorkers turned out that night at Steinway Hall to hear what the man in the linen shirt, vest, rough sack coat, black pants, and long black hair had to say. As Bright Eyes interpreted, he spoke easily and confidently, alternately wheeling around to face the other speakers, then back to the crowd, gesturing, waving his hand, tapping a forefinger on his palm to drive home the story of their removal, the long walk back, the decision of the judge, why they had come east, and how New Yorkers could help. "I have been away from my home a long time," he told them, "and I am waiting to hear what you will do for us. Good night."

The next morning, Bright Eyes could have read that Standing Bear, with his long, black hair and turned-down collar, looked like "an athletic savage—if such a term may be applied to a very docile Indian—clad after the conventional style of the pale-faces."

For a long time, the chief's manner of dress had been an issue, one that increasingly bothered Standing Bear. So one day during their New

York stay, he told Tibbles he was going to cut his hair and pack up his chief's clothing for good. The newsman tried to dissuade him, arguing it would be endlessly analyzed in the press and detract from the cause that had brought them east. He didn't care—he was going off in search of a barbershop. In a panic, the newsman asked an acquaintance, Helen Hunt Jackson, a writer who had traveled with them for several weeks, to intercede.

Jackson took Bright Eyes with her to see the chief in his hotel room. About ten minutes later, the writer found the newsman and told him Standing Bear had reluctantly promised to stay away from the barbershop. But the chief later made it clear he had agreed to do so only for a short while longer.

A New England essayist, Jackson had picked up the tour in Boston, where she had become obsessed with Standing Bear, Bright Eyes, and the Ponca cause. And they, in turn, were quite taken with her intensity, passion, and devotion to their plight. Before long, Jackson began to embrace the Indian cause with much the same fervor as the newsman. In the long term, after years of frenzied research, she would write *A Century of Dishonor,* a searing blueprint of the troubled history of Indian-government relations. In the short term, she engaged in a spirited debate with Interior Secretary Schurz on the issue, a public and private duel that began when parts of his annual report on the state of America's Indians—most notably, the Ponca—found their way into the nation's newspapers. In his report, Schurz maintained the government had done all it could to redress wrongs done to the Ponca. The injustices, he insisted, occurred on the watch of another administration. On his watch, the tribe was now in good hands, all their needs were met, and they were prospering in the Territory.

Jackson's research indicated otherwise. In mid-December, in a letter to the *New York Daily Tribune,* she posed ten pointed questions to the American public—questions designed to illuminate government mistreatment of the Indian, including the loss of the Ponca homeland. The Interior Secretary responded by granting an interview to a *Tribune* reporter to defend the government policy. Jackson then began writing the secretary privately, challenging his assertions in personal letters. And so it went, each of them punching and counterpunching, but giving no ground. After months of the back-and-forth exchange, the secretary suggested a specific solution: breaking up Indian land from tribal ownership to individual ownership. It was the same solution championed by the newsman, and soon it would be a cause taken up by many others.

Standing Bear knew little about the letters that appeared in the papers with his name in them, but he knew about Schurz. He didn't like him and he didn't trust him. The famed cartoonist Thomas Nast had met the group shortly after they arrived in New York and one day Standing Bear passed a newsstand and saw a large Nast cartoon of the Interior Secretary. He couldn't negotiate the price, so he gave the newsboy a quarter, grabbed the paper, and went back to the hotel. He asked the hotel barber for a scissors, patiently cut out the cartoon, then went looking for the newsman. When he found him, he asked him to put it in his scrapbook and the newsman obliged. Every now and then, Standing Bear would ask for the scrapbook and flip to the Nast cartoon, stare at it awhile, and chuckle to himself.

By late December, Standing Bear had a lot to think about, a lot to sort out in reflecting upon the events of the last twelve months. About this time a year earlier, he had knelt on the floor of a damp lodge along a river bottom in the Warm Country and watched the eyes of his son close for the last time. In the winter, he had walked more than five hundred miles through the snow and cold and wound up a prisoner in an Army fort, and then a plaintiff suing the government that had arrested him. In the spring, he had walked out of federal court a free man with nowhere to go and by summer he had settled on an island in the middle of a river that had long defined his people. That fall, he had boarded a train and slept in fashionable hotels, dined at expensive restaurants, sipped tea from fine china in elegant mansions, heard the melancholy chorus of freed slaves in an historic church, been examined, fawned over, and interviewed by famed poets, politicians, preachers, editors, university presidents, doctors, lawyers, bankers, and businessmen.

And now, he was on another island, in a hotel near Times Square, the crossroads of the world.

8

Righting a Wrong

It was a different kind of cold, this hard chill of the East, and he couldn't seem to get used to it.

He had been born in the north country, had spent most of sixty winters on the open prairie, and when he would walk up the hard steps and down the long avenues, the snow didn't look right anymore and the wind swirling around the corners and sweeping off the brick facades of the tall buildings didn't feel right. Nothing really did. It had been more than twelve weeks, more than eighty days of going from hotel reception to public hall to church stage to train station without feeling the cottonwood leaves or the foxtail, the buffalo grass or the riverbank, and it got to him. And whenever he thought of the women and children, the old people and the sick ones foraging for wood and looking for food in the willow thicket of their island home, it got even worse.

But he had come for them. It was a different kind of struggle, he told himself, a fight for all the ones still living in tents on the river bottoms in the south and on the island in the north and though it was a chill he often found unbearable, it had been worth it. The people of the East were good people. He had come with a message, to ask for help, and many thousands had heard it and many thousands more had read about it. For him and all the people like him, there had never been anything quite like it—the donations from strangers, story after story in the big city papers, a pointed national debate on citizenship, civil rights, constitutional protection. He could feel the energy and the momentum and after two difficult, punishing decades, a new one was now about to begin, one that seemed to offer a good deal more hope and promise than any in a long time.

On the fifth day of the New Year, a directive from the United States Secretary of the Interior became official: The government would not challenge Judge Dundy's ruling in favor of Standing Bear. Schurz had advised the attorney general to withdraw the appeal and so it was dismissed on January 5. The Interior Secretary had come to believe an appeal was too risky. Instead of reversing Dundy's decision, he feared a federal court, maybe even the Supreme Court, might actually expand Indian civil rights, giving them more legal clout to challenge government authority. And that could throw everything—the reservation system, military control, department policy, and the entire Indian Territory philosophy—into an unmanageable state of chaos. It could also seriously undermine his claim that the Ponca removal was justified and that they were now receiving proper care and treatment. So he decided damage control was the prudent course of action. Doing nothing to stir things up any further would help restrain and limit the problem. As long as Indians were not declared citizens, he reasoned, they were not likely to disrupt the status quo.

Before long, the government's decision to withdraw its appeal crippled the effort of the humanitarians and reformers to achieve one of their two primary goals: getting the issue of Indian citizenship squarely in the hands of the Supreme Court. It also curtailed their fund-raising efforts. Asking for money to pay lawyers whose legal wings had now been clipped was a hard sell. But the two Omaha attorneys decided to carry on anyway. Appeal or no appeal, they wanted to try to get other federal judges to build on the human rights foundation Judge Dundy had laid. And they offered to do it for free.

Standing Bear had never really understood all of the complex legal issues, all of the talking in the other language, the rules and procedures, all the paperwork. That was for the men in suits with their thick beards and thick books to worry about. More and more, he thought only of the second goal, of going home, of getting his people across the Running Water and back in the shadow of the high chalk bluffs. That much he understood clearly—in a way none of the others ever could. From the beginning, it was all he had ever wanted. And in the early weeks of the New Year, it was where he and the others began to focus all of their energy and attention.

In the wake of Judge Dundy's ruling, the Omaha attorneys filed four lawsuits in federal court—two in Nebraska and two in Dakota Territory—each aimed at establishing the Ponca as legal owners of their old reservation. For Standing Bear and his people, for the lawyers, the humanitarians, the reformers, and the clergy, it seemed the nation's judicial branch had now gotten far ahead of the other two.

More than a century earlier, the Founding Fathers of the new nation had envisioned a bold republic knit together with a delicate system of checks and balances, a republic in which informed citizens would have a powerful stake in the three branches of government that represented them. In turn, the legislative, executive, and judicial branches would oversee each other, making sure one did not overwhelm the other. By working together, the three branches would uphold the Constitution, protect the rights of the people, and respond to their concerns. That was the theory behind this new republic.

In the last eight months, in Omaha, Chicago, Pittsburgh, Boston, New York, and Philadelphia, Standing Bear and his allies had seen citizens respond to the newspaper stories and the judge's ruling and to all the public talks detailing what had happened to him and his people. In Boston, a city that had once rebelled against a foreign government for injustices against its people, he had seen first-hand how the concerns of informed citizens had spawned a committee to examine the plight of the Ponca. And after a lengthy investigation, the Boston Indian Committee had issued a final written report. In it, committee members recommended the government honor the original Ponca title to the Niobrara reservation and return the old homeland to Standing Bear and his people. The committee of five citizens also demanded that the legislative branch of the government now weigh in on the issue, that the United States Congress take a long, hard look at the whole Ponca affair.

The senior senator from Massachusetts, a cofounder of the state's Republican Party who had closely followed the activities of the western visitors during their Boston stay, was well acquainted with the committee members. A Yale graduate and lawyer who had once done a brief stint as a journalist, Henry Laurens Dawes had already served eighteen years in the House of Representatives and six years in the Senate. Ten years earlier, he had campaigned vigorously against the treaty system, arguing that the annuities and circumscribed reservations would hopelessly shackle tribes to their distant past. Instead, he proposed breaking up tribal land into individually owned plots, an ownership arrangement he believed would greatly accelerate the assimilation of Indian people into the dominant culture.

In 1880, the New Year wasn't far along before Dawes became the legislative liaison to Boston's citizen-reformers and humanitarians. And by the time the Forty-sixth Congressional Session began, he was part of a Senate Select Committee officially charged with investigating "the circumstances of the removal of the Ponca Indians from their reservation" and whether it should be legally restored to them. For the next several months, Dawes and four other senators would research treaties, gather documents, and interview witnesses. When all was said and done, they would issue a final report and forward their recommendations to the full Senate. So as the mid-winter days began to unfold in the nation's capital, the legislative branch began to catch up. By then, a relentless, informed citizen-essayist from New England and a knowledgeable, powerful senator had joined forces to take on the executive branch of the government on behalf of an aging chief and his small band of homeless people.

While Dawes and his colleagues geared up for the Senate investigation, the tour group kept up a frantic pace, bouncing around a corridor of Northeast cities throughout January and early February. They made several more public appearances in New York, speaking twice at Chickering Hall. They went to receptions and spoke at public rallies in Philadelphia and attended a gathering to promote the Ponca cause at a large church in Carlisle, Pennsylvania. On February 10, weary and homesick, they arrived in Washington. The next day, the Senate Select Committee called its first witness. Senator Dawes began the questioning.

When you and your group fled the reservation, he asked, *where did you intend to go?*

"Where should we start to go to except our own land, to our old home? We didn't think of doing anything else; we thought only of that, all the time."

For the better part of two days, Standing Bear answered questions about the appearance of the strange white man in their village, going to the stockade with Big Snake, the forced march south, life in the Warm Country, the death of his son, the long flight north.

When he finished, his interpreter took the stand and Senator Dawes began anew.

Do you know why the Ponca are here?

"Yes, sir," Bright Eyes replied.

Why is Standing Bear here?

"He came East to speak to the people, and tell what had been done to his tribe by white men, so that the lands belonging to the Poncas shall be restored."

Do you know anything about this matter yourself?

"Yes, sir; I think I do."

Five years earlier, she had been unable to get a response from the Commissioner of Indian Affairs about a job teaching schoolkids on the Omaha Reservation. On Valentine's Day 1880, after finishing her session with the five senators, Bright Eyes walked into the White House to see the President of the United States. She arrived with Senator Dawes and his wife and she spoke with President Hayes and his wife, and before the evening ended she heard the chief of the nation's executive branch remark how much the Ponca misfortunes disturbed him.

While the Senate inquiry continued throughout the late winter and early spring, Standing Bear, Bright Eyes, and Tibbles kept up their hectic pace, shuttling back and forth between the congressional hearings and engagements in other cities. They went back to Philadelphia, then to Washington, down to Baltimore, and back again to the capital. By early April, fatigue and exhaustion had taken their toll. They could go no more.

Early one morning during the final days of the tour, Standing Bear left the group in their hotel and walked briskly to a nearby shop. When he rejoined them later for breakfast, he had short hair and a suit similar to what the others were wearing. The waiter approached and, as he had always done, turned to the newsman and asked, "What will the chief have?" Before the newsman could reply, Standing Bear said: "Bifsteak."

Not long afterwards, they all caught the next train west, crossing back over the Mississippi and the Missouri until they reached Omaha. When they arrived, the city they had left seven months earlier was in the midst of a blinding, suffocating dust storm.

He didn't care. It was early spring on the Northern Plains and soon he left Omaha, heading north by northwest.

While Standing Bear made his way to the Niobrara, the investigation along the Potomac picked up steam. Off and on for four months, the five senators called witness after witness, asking question after question about the treaties between the Ponca and the government, the circumstances that had led to their removal, the planning and preparation for their relocation in the Indian Territory, the details of Standing Bear's departure and Big Snake's death, the present conditions on their reservation, and whether the government was obligated to redress a wrong. By late May, the committee had interviewed chiefs from the north, chiefs from the south, former inspectors, agents, interpreters, white settlers, clerks and clergy, bishops and missionaries, blacksmiths, newsmen, Army officers, the Secretary of the Interior, and the strange white man from the East who had suddenly appeared in the Ponca village more than three winters ago.

During questioning that consumed several days, E. C. Kemble vigorously challenged all of the Ponca claims. The former Indian inspector testified he had done everything by the book, that he had patiently explained everything to them, that they had understood everything he said, and that they had given their full consent to leave their homeland and relocate to the Territory. And at no time, he told the senators, had he ever abandoned the chiefs and forced them to walk home.

"I desire to contradict, if I may be permitted to do so," he told the senators, "the testimony which has been given out, all over this country by Mr. Tibbles, I understand, by Standing Bear, and by others, that I was asked for money, for passes, or for any safeguard or permit to travel, and that I refused it. Not one word was said to me about anything of the sort." In the end, he said, the chiefs had simply fled on their own, walking off like spoiled children and setting a bad example for the others.

Before ending, he asked the committee for permission to insert his personal opinion into the official record. "As I look upon it now," he told the senators, "I think a great wrong was done them in taking them to the Indian Territory; not because the Indian Territory is less desirable as a country, in my estimation, or in their estimation, but because I think they should have been protected in their possession of the lands that were given them."

On May 31, 1880, the Senate Select Committee published the results of its exhaustive four-month investigation in a 534-page report. Beginning with the Fort Laramie Treaty of 1868, a committee majority found ample evidence of chronic government mistreatment of the Ponca and their findings were publicly aired out in what was often blunt language. The Ponca had lost their Niobrara homeland to the Lakota because of a government "blunder," yet no one in government could tell the committee "whether it was a blunder in policy or a mistake in boundaries." To make matters worse, the Ponca were the legal owners of the land and were not warned, or told for years afterwards, that their land now belonged to someone else—in this case, their age-old enemies. They also were never informed of the government's decision to march them south, discovering it only after the strange white man appeared in their village. "With this most important matter in the hands of a person totally unfitted for the work devolved upon him, accompanied by indifference and lack of knowledge upon the part of his superiors, what follows is not only not surprising, but entirely inevitable," Dawes wrote in his report for the majority. Nor could the committee find any evidence the Ponca had ever consented to the removal. "This failure has involved the government in a transaction which can find no justification. It has led the government to violate in dealing with one of the most peaceable, orderly, and well-disposed of all the tribes of Indians, in the most flagrant manner, their rights of property, to disregard their appeals to the honor and justice of the United States, and the dictates of humanity."

All in all, the committee majority concluded, the treatment of the Ponca "on the part of the United States was without justification, and was a great wrong to this peaceable tribe of Indians and demands at the hands of the United States speedy and full redress."

For the committee majority, that redress meant one thing—the one thing Standing Bear had wanted from the beginning. Senator Dawes posed it in the form of a question: "If the Poncas have been deprived without right of their reservation, by the Government of the United States, and taken against their will from their old home in Dakota to the Indian Territory, and are there against and without right by the strong arm of the government, why should they not be restored to their old home, under the same conditions, as near as possible, which existed at the time of the removal?"

Before the committee wrapped up its inquiry, the Interior Secretary had appeared as one of its last witnesses. By then, Dawes had pored over hundreds of pages of treaty rights, government correspondence, military telegrams, and witness testimony, becoming a self-taught expert on the Ponca and a formidable legislative champion of their cause. Under relentless questioning from the Massachusetts senator, Secretary Schurz shifted most of the blame for the disastrous Ponca removal to his subordinates. He testified he had been kept largely in the dark by the Commissioner of Indian Affairs and flat-out lied to by his eyes and ears on the ground, Inspector Kemble. "I am free to confess, however, that had I understood Indian affairs as well then as I do now," he told the committee, "I should have opposed the removal."

Nevertheless, the Interior Secretary strenuously objected, as he had many times before, to the pivotal question Dawes now posed. The government, he argued, could not open that door, could not let one tribe go north and order the others to stay in the south. It would breed too much uneasiness and discontent among the other tribes. In his report, Senator Dawes offered a pointed rebuttal: "If any other tribe there has suffered like treatment with the Poncas, restitution cannot be made too soon."

All along, the committee had conducted its investigation in partnership with a Senate bill aimed at restoring the Ponca homeland. The proposed bill would provide fifty thousand dollars to return the Ponca to their lands and restore their dilapidated homes. So it was the committee's job to investigate all aspects of the Ponca removal and, after sifting through the evidence, to recommend whether the bill should live or die. For a majority of committee members who had endured hundreds of hours of testimony, the decision was not a difficult one. "If the government expects to exterminate this tribe," Dawes concluded, "it has but to continue the policy of the past few years. The committee can see no valid objection, therefore, to that means of redress which comes nearest to putting these Indians in precisely the condition they were in when E. C. Kemble undertook, without authority of law, to force them from their homes into the Indian Territory."

Two weeks after the report came out, the Forty-sixth Congress adjourned for the summer. Senate debate on the proposal to restore land and homes to the Ponca would have to wait until the legislative branch reconvened in the fall.

As a result, a good many things remained suspended in limbo throughout the summer. The long speaking tour had unleashed an energetic response from East Coast citizens, who had in turn ignited a formal investigation by their elected representatives. Four lawsuits challenging the ownership of the northern reservation were tied up in court. A lingering debate between private citizens and public officials over Indian citizenship and human rights remained unresolved. A specific plan to spend fifty thousand dollars to return the Ponca to their homeland was up in the air. And the Ponca people, meanwhile, hovered between two divided camps—a large one in the Indian Territory and a small one in the middle of the Niobrara River.

Standing Bear was unaware of the congressional summer recess, the fate of the committee recommendation, the sluggish rhythm of legislative life, and he didn't give it much thought. After the grueling tour in the strange cities, he was back on the river, closer to the land of his fathers than he'd been in a long while. After he settled in with his family in their camp on the island, he was surprised to see how much they had accomplished in recent months. That spring, while he was away, they had slipped off the island and sowed a number of crops in the fertile river valley, just like the old days. Their friends in Omaha had supplied them with plows, harnesses, pitchforks, axes, grindstones, and eight lumber wagons, and although they remained in their island village, the abandoned valley across the river now blossomed with an enviable corn crop.

He was also surprised at the reaction of his white neighbors. They were kind and generous, welcoming him back as an old friend. They remembered the time the Lakota had made off with one man's horses and how White Eagle had sent the Ponca out after them, and even though two of his own men were killed, they came back with all of the stolen horses and returned them to the owner. They told Standing Bear they were glad to see him, that they hoped he would get his lands back, and the time would come when they would be neighbors once again.

Unlike Standing Bear, those who had initiated the legal fight to reclaim the Ponca homeland were getting restless. They knew the judicial and legislative wheels turned slowly and they didn't want to see the energy fade, their momentum stall, ground up by the sluggish bureaucratic machinery. They wanted to keep pushing, to try to unite both camps, to move the southern people north, to get all of the Ponca back on the lands near the confluence of the Niobrara and the Missouri.

So in the early summer days of 1880, while the senators were leaving Washington, while Standing Bear got caught up with family and old friends on the river island, they came up with a plan: The Omaha Ponca Relief Committee would send someone south to get out the word. Someone to tell the southern people they had been illegally removed from their northern home, that they were being illegally held in the Warm Country. Someone to tell them the treaties and the courts and the white settlers were on their side. That they could turn their faces north and come back home now—if they wanted to.

Thomas Tibbles left Omaha on June 14, and arrived in the Indian Territory late the following day. For the next two weeks, the newsman and an interpreter tried to reach as many of the southern people as they could, urging them to do as Standing Bear had done, to slip away in small groups during the night, to keep moving until they rejoined the others in the north. He told them the Territory had no state courts to protect them, so they would have to cross into Kansas. If they were arrested there, the Omaha committee would help fight for their freedom before a judge. The committee would also provide food, money, and shelter during their journey north and after they arrived in the Niobrara country. It was only a matter of time, he told them, before the government returned their former lands and all the tribe could be reunited on them.

Although he always claimed otherwise, it was said by many that the newsman often moved about the Ponca camp dressed in the clothing of an Indian woman, that he disguised himself in this way to conceal his movements from government agents. The new Ponca agent, William Whiting, knew something about spying. He had spent part of the Civil War as a secret agent infiltrating the ranks of the Knights of the Golden Circle, a clandestine order of Southern sympathizers living in the North who opposed the war and the power of the federal government. As the new agent, Whiting became furious when he first saw hungry Indian women cutting down the agency's pecan trees to harvest the nuts, killing off the future crop. To preserve the pecans, he said he would shoot the next woman he saw cutting down one of his trees.

Toward the end of the month, Tibbles decided to visit the nearby Nez Perce Reservation to interview Chief Joseph for a newspaper story. Agent Whiting got wind of his whereabouts. On June 30, the newsman's visit to the Territory abruptly ended when government police escorted him to the Kansas state line.

After the newsman left, many of the Southern Ponca were confused and many others afraid. They knew that, since the early spring, more than one hundred of the southern people had already drifted off to join Standing Bear's group in the north. But the large group that stayed behind that summer didn't know what to do. They didn't understand words like jurisdiction and Fourteenth Amendment and habeas corpus, and they didn't know what would happen if they tried to steal away from the Warm Country in the dead of night like the newsman suggested. They knew what had happened to Big Snake when he tried to leave without permission—shot down, unarmed, in the agent's office—and that image had stayed with them for a long time. They also knew that things were getting better now in the Warm Country. The land was good and more seed and farming tools had arrived. More of the sturdy wooden homes were finished, there was more food and lately, there had been more births than deaths. And they knew something else—they were weary, exhausted, tired of moving, tired of everything that had happened in the last three years. More and more, many believed it was a good thing to stay where they were.

Standing Bear's people felt even more strongly about staying put in the north country. Throughout the spring and summer, they had done exactly what they had wanted to do for years: On their own, without government handouts or restrictions, they had transformed some of the nearby Niobrara Valley into a robust 250-acre field of corn. In late September, a delegation of local clergy and private citizens from New York visited the valley, marveling at its beauty, the rich, fertile bottomlands, at how Standing Bear's people had energetically put plow to soil to feed themselves. By then, the Lakota had long since moved out of the old Ponca homeland and no white settlers had moved in. So in the autumn of 1880, their former 96,000-acre reservation stood empty and uninhabited. It made no sense to the eastern visitors and to those who lived there. The local paper, the *Niobrara Pioneer,* favored giving the Ponca citizenship and the head of each family 160 acres to support himself, his wife, and their children. The days of the reservation, the paper argued, were finished. "If some arrangement could be made by which the remainder of the lands could be opened to settlement, and the proceeds of such sales given to the Poncas, it would be entirely satisfactory."

As fall turned to winter that year, while the northern people lived off a good harvest in their island river village, Standing Bear was unaware of the many forces that were beginning to converge along the Potomac, forces that he, the newsman, the young Omaha Indian poet, the judge and the general and all the clergy, reformers, lawyers, politicians, private citizens, editors, and publishers had set in motion. For months, they had done their job, illuminating and championing the Ponca cause, and now it was left to the country's legislators and its chief executive to decide what should be done with the splintered remnants of the Sacred Head People.

The nineteenth president of the United States was a Harvard Law School graduate who had a thriving Cincinnati law practice in the years before the Civil War. Wounded during the war, he rose to brevet major general and was still in the Army when a powerful group of Cincinnati Republicans nominated him for the House of Representatives. Although he accepted, Rutherford Hayes refused to campaign, saying "an officer fit for duty who at this crisis would abandon his post to electioneer . . . ought to be scalped." Nevertheless, Hayes won easily and served two years in Congress and then three terms as governor of Ohio. By 1876, he had become an attractive Republican candidate and squared off against New York Governor Samuel Tilden for the presidency. Although Mark Twain and a glittering array of Republican leaders all took to the campaign trail on his behalf, Hayes believed he had little chance to win. On election night, the early returns confirmed his hunch and so he went to bed. When he awoke the next morning, he discovered he and Tilden were engaged in the closest, most contentious presidential election, up to that point, in American history. As near as anyone could determine, Democrat Tilden had almost 300,000 more popular votes than Republican Hayes. The presidency would turn, however, on the fiercely contested electoral votes in three Southern states: South Carolina, Louisiana, and Florida. Hayes needed to win all three—or the Democratic governor of New York would move into the White House.

For months, chaos and confusion reigned. Finally, in January 1877, Congress created an Electoral Commission to referee the dispute. On an eight to seven vote, the commission of eight Republicans and seven Democrats awarded all three contested states to the Republican candidate. And so, not long after, Hayes arrived at 1600 Pennsylvania Avenue on the strength of a 185–184 Electoral College vote margin over his Democratic opponent.

The new president quickly established a reputation for integrity, truthfulness, candor, and hard work. He based appointments on merit, not political cronyism, and filled his Cabinet with honorable men who shared his penchant for discipline, dignity, and modest reform. And much to the liking of the Woman's Christian Temperance Union, he gave his wife, Lucy Webb Hayes, the green light to make the White House off-limits to all wine and liquor consumption.

He had also made it clear from the beginning that he intended to serve but one term. As his presidency began to wind down in the autumn of 1880, before retiring to his beloved Ohio, Hayes was determined to tie up some loose ends—one of which involved a small tribe of displaced Indians on the Great Plains. He had largely inherited the Ponca situation and it had vexed him and his administration for nearly four years. He no longer trusted the reports of the field agents and their superiors in Washington and he had become frustrated enough with his own Interior Secretary that he considered firing him.

Righting a Wrong

In a letter earlier that fall, the principal chief of the Ponca had told Secretary Schurz his people were now inclined to stay put in the Territory. Conditions had improved enough, White Eagle wrote on October 25, that the majority of the tribe would agree to remain if they were compensated for the loss of the old lands and were left alone on the new ones. Yet the President had also heard from others that such sentiments were coerced and exaggerated, that they were face-saving gestures on the part of Washington bureaucrats looking for a quick fix to the nagging problem in the waning months of his presidency.

By December 1880, Hayes was awash in conflicting accounts of what the Ponca really wanted, who spoke for them, how accurate the interpretations were, and what the federal government could and should do on their behalf. Tired of the back-and-forth bickering and the inconsistent accounts, feeling the pressure from informed citizens and an aggressive legislative branch, he wanted to cut through the politics and get to the truth. And so, more and more, he began to listen to the two senators from Massachusetts, men he trusted, men who knew a good deal about the Ponca situation, men who urged him to use the power of his office to right a wrong that had festered for years.

A week before Christmas, Hayes appointed a commission of four men to visit the Indian Territory and, if necessary, to also meet with Standing Bear and his smaller group in the north country. Hayes ordered the four white men to talk to the Indian leaders in both groups, gather facts, and "determine the question as to what justice and humanity require should be done by the Government of the United States." The President's friend and fellow Ohioan, Brigadier General George Crook, would lead the commission. It would also include Brigadier General Nelson Miles, William Stickney, an Indian Commission board member from Washington, D.C., and Walter Allen, a *Boston Daily Advertiser* reporter and Boston Indian Committee member. When they finished the investigation, they were to report their conclusions and recommendations to the nation's chief executive. The year was almost over and in less than three months Hayes would be leaving the White

House. He knew there was a lot to be done, and little time to do it, before he became a gentleman farmer in Ohio.

On January 5, 1881, the four white men arrived by rail car at the Ponca Agency in Indian Territory, determined to find out first-hand the wishes of those living in the south and the government's obligation to meet them. At ten o'clock that morning, about 250 Ponca men, women, and children—and all of their headmen—and several interpreters were waiting for them in the agency schoolhouse. Their leading chiefs, White Eagle and Standing Buffalo, told the commissioners the people wanted to stay on the 101,894 acres set aside for them in the Territory and build permanent homes there. They said they would give up all claims to the old reservation if they were compensated for those lands and for the loss of personal property and injuries suffered during the removal. The commissioners then asked for all those who agreed with the interpretation to stand. Everyone in the room stood up.

General Crook had a question. Not long ago, he noted, they were all opposed to staying in the south. What had changed their mind?

There were many reasons, White Eagle replied. They hadn't enough ponies to slip away in the night, as the newsman had suggested, and they were afraid of what might happen if they did—of being arrested and jailed like Standing Bear. They were afraid of taking a bullet in the head like Big Snake. They had also become acclimated and the fresh graves were not piling up like before. They were living in decent homes now and the land was beginning to blossom from their labor. And in the south, they didn't have to fight the floods, the droughts, the hordes of grasshoppers and blackbirds anymore. But mostly they were tired and worn out from the last four years. They wanted to settle down.

"We are just like putting a stone in the ground," Standing Buffalo said. "It is solid; it is fixed there. So we consider we are fixed here. We have come to this determination, and we propose to abide by it."

Finally, White Eagle told the commission, he and the other headmen had recently returned from Washington where they signed an agreement to stay put in exchange for compensation and a firm title to their new lands. "I have put my hand to the pen," the chief said, "and when an Indian has put his hand to the pen, he considers that he has done a precious thing." Before adjourning, the commissioners wanted to know one last thing: Would they like to have Standing Bear and his northern people rejoin them in the south?

"I want them," White Eagle said. "They are my own people and I have been hoping they would come." But, as he had said before, "they walk according to their own hearts."

The next day, the four white men boarded a train and headed north, arriving near the confluence of the Niobrara and the Missouri on January 10. The temperature was fourteen below zero and snow lay in five-foot drifts. That evening, several members of the commission's group took a sleigh across the frozen Running Water to a large island in the middle of the river. When they arrived at the Ponca village, they saw that the 115 northern people were now divided into twenty-eight families living in tipis and log houses. They saw their ponies, wagons, cattle, hogs, and hay, and they saw all the wood stacked in neat piles. They saw, too, that the Ponca had already cultivated more than one hundred acres of corn, storing it in granaries on their island home. In the cold and the snow, they watched as the Ponca headmen distributed a fresh supply of blankets from their Omaha friends to the women and children in the village. With the exception of a little assistance from their Omaha and Boston friends, the visitors noted that the northern people had survived remarkably well "independent of outside help."

Around noon the next day, Standing Bear arrived at the hotel where the commissioners were staying in the small village of Niobrara across the river. To his surprise, two of the southern chiefs had also made the journey north and when he saw the two old men in the hotel, old friends he had not seen in a long time, he stepped forward and hugged them warmly. Outside, it was another frigid day, the snow drifting across the village streets and piling up against the door of the Academy of Music. Inside, dozens of curious local citizens sat in the middle of the room. The two chiefs of the southern people sat against one wall of the academy, across the way from where about twenty of the northern people sat, including Standing Bear's younger wife—a "tall, stout, comely and well-formed" woman about thirty-five "with a good face and presenting a neat appearance."

When her husband stood up shortly after two o'clock and looked at the four men seated at the front of the room, he saw that a good deal had changed in the last two years, more than he could have ever imagined when he fled the Warm Country that frozen January day with the body of his son in the back of their wagon. He saw now that one of the four men was George Crook, the same Army general he had sued in federal court, the one who had ordered his arrest, the one whom he had gotten to know as a prisoner at Fort Omaha. He saw there was another brigadier general at the table, Nelson Miles, a Civil War hero who had chased Chief Joseph on his 1,700-mile freedom flight across the American West, finally catching him thirty miles short of the Canadian border. He also saw William Stickney, a private citizen from the nation's capital, a devout Christian who had traveled extensively in foreign lands, particularly the Holy Land. And he saw, too, Walter Allen, one of the East Coast humanitarians, a smart, energetic Boston reporter who had developed a strong sympathy for the Ponca.

Soon, he heard the four white men say they had come at the request of the Great Father—not to ask the Ponca to sell their land, or choose a new home, or order them to go to a strange country—but to find ways to right a wrong, to correct an injustice, to figure out how the Ponca might reclaim their old homeland. He heard the commission chairman, the general he had defeated in court, tell him they came as friends and they would now try, as best they could, to do what was in the best interests of him and his people. At all times, he should speak openly and freely, tell them the truth.

When the general finished, Standing Bear began to walk the room, moving slowly among the people in his civilian clothes, the interpreter conveying his words to the commissioners. "I do not think we have made this day," he told the four white men, "but I think that God has caused it, and my heart is glad to see you all here." He said there were now about 195 Ponca living in the northern lands and after a couple of rough years, with a little help from their Omaha friends, they had adjusted, had planted and harvested crops in the rich soil of their river valley homeland. This last year, they finally felt it again, the thing they had all felt before, but never in the south. "My friends, now I've no troubles at all. I work for my living and I get food."

Are your people self-supporting? General Miles wondered.

"They are working; trying to make their own living, and they get their food from their own industry."

How many acres were cultivated this last year?

"I think two hundred acres."

Do you receive any government assistance?

"No sir; nothing from the government; our Christian friends have given us five or six plows."

Can you raise good crops in this country?

"Yes, we raised a great deal last season."

The general then said he wanted a word with Smoke Maker, the oldest Ponca in the room.

Have you been able to raise good crops here since you were a boy?

"I was a boy the time Lewis and Clark went up the river. I can recollect that when I was a boy we worked the ground with buffalo shoulder-blades, and raised good crops always."

Standing Bear began to pace more rapidly, walking up and down the room, up toward the table, back toward his people, his voice rising and falling. "My friends, whatever I tell you to say, I hope that you will carry back to our Great Father and give him an exact account of it. I hope you will tell him that I am living back on my old land, that I am doing well there, and that I am working for myself . . . I admire your dwellings very much. My friends, I want to live in just such a house as you live in—a house that is bright and full of light. If I live in such a house, then I will cultivate the land and will make an effort for myself. Now I have learned a number of things from you. I have known them for some time. I speak of raising cows that will give milk to the family—for the children, and of raising hogs and poultry . . . and I don't wish anyone to get beyond me, to get the better of me or to take me away from my own lands."

When the white men asked about the southern people wanting to sell the northern lands, about wanting compensation for their share of the old homeland, his voice grew louder. He was on his own land now and he would never give it back. "Since I got from the Territory up to this time I have not wished to give even a part of it to the Great Father. Though he were to give me a million dollars I would not give him the land . . . My children have been exterminated; my brother has been killed and . . . I will strive to get that which is good and that alone . . . But they can't scare me, drive me into a bad hole yet."

Is everyone here satisfied with this land? General Miles asked.

All of the Ponca inside the Academy of Music replied at once: "Yes."

Is there anyone here who wishes to return to the Indian Territory?

The interpreter surveyed the crowd, then turned to the front: "No; not one."

After the conference ended, after the four white men packed their belongings and boarded a train heading east, a number of things seemed clear to them: Tired of moving, their health and homes and crops stabilized, the Southern Ponca wanted to stay put. They also wanted title to their new lands and compensation for the loss of their old ones. The Northern Ponca were just as resolute. Productive and self-supporting, Standing Bear and his people wanted nothing to do with selling off any of the Niobrara homeland or rejoining their relatives in the Warm Country.

Not long after arriving in Washington, the four white men sent their findings and recommendations in a sixty-three-page report to the President. The Ponca, they concluded, had been unjustly removed from a homeland they legally owned, triggering severe hardships, and a serious loss of life, property, and possessions. Their removal was "also without lawful authority, inasmuch as the law requiring the consent of the Indians as a condition precedent to their removal was overlooked or wholly disregarded." The Standing Bear Ponca in the north, the commissioners noted, have a deep, entrenched attachment to their lands and are on friendly terms with all the neighboring tribes, including the Lakota, as well as their white neighbors. "They pray that they may not again be disturbed, and ask for a teacher to aid and instruct them in the arts of industry, and for a missionary to teach them the principles of morality and religion."

To resolve the dilemma of two groups wanting to remain on separate lands—both demanding compensation, title, and legal protection—the commission recommended that each Ponca man, woman, and child be given one year to select 160 acres in either place, north or south. After selecting a new home, the Ponca would be given a patent to their land that would not be taxable for thirty years. The commissioners also recommended the government continue its annual appropriations of $53,000 to the tribe for five more years and immediately grant an additional $25,000 for farming tools, livestock, and seed—$5,000 of which would be set aside for Standing Bear and the northern people. The Crook Commission further suggested the government award up to $5,000 to the Northern Ponca for a new school and another $5,000 to build new homes in the old lands. Finally, the four white men respectfully suggested, it was time the government extended legal protection not only to the Ponca, but to all Indians.

When the commission report landed on his desk on January 25, 1881, the nineteenth President of the United States kept one eye focused on the detailed recommendations and another on the calendar. In less than six weeks there would be a new occupant of the White House and so he knew he would have to move quickly. On February 2, President Hayes accepted the commission's findings and forwarded them to the Senate Select Committee.

In a lengthy message accompanying the report, the president also made clear how he viewed the matter from the executive office. "The public attention has frequently been called to the injustice and wrong which the Ponca tribe of Indians has suffered at the hands of the Government of the United States," the President wrote to Congress. A year earlier, he noted, a Senate committee had thoroughly investigated those injustices and concluded the government had a solemn duty to correct them. To make his point, he quoted from the Dawes Committee report: "We should be more prompt and anxious because they are weak and we are strong . . . we should be liberal to the verge of lavishness in the expenditure of our money to improve their condition, so that they and all others may know that, although like all nations and all men, we may do wrong, we are willing to make ample reparation." But a Senate bill pegged to the Dawes investigation got bottled up in a congressional committee and nothing ever came of it and so there was no reparation.

Now, the President wrote, a second investigation has arrived at the same conclusions as the Dawes Committee—and "their recommendations point out conclusively the true measures of redress, which the Government of the United States ought now to adopt." It is clear, he told Congress, that the Ponca in the south wish to stay where they are and that Standing Bear and his fragment of the tribe prefer to remain in the north. In view of those facts, Congress can solve the Ponca problem and restore the government's good name by doing the right thing—by embracing the commission's recommendations.

Down to his final month in office, Hayes then offered a blueprint for what the nation's Indian policy should be as the century wound down—a vision that differed markedly from the one in place when the century began. In the future, he wrote, Indian children should be educated and trained for jobs that enable them to be self-supporting citizens with legal rights living in civilized communities. Their lands should be allotted to individual owners, legally protected, and they should be paid fairly for any surplus lands with the money safely invested for their benefit. Once these have been achieved, he said, Indians should be made citizens and given all the legal rights and responsibilities of citizenship.

"In short nothing should be left undone to show to the Indians that the Government of the United States regards their rights as equally sacred with those of its citizens," Hayes wrote. "The time has come when the policy should be to place the Indians as rapidly as practicable on the same footing with the other permanent inhabitants of our country." He concluded his four-page statement to Congress by saying the blame for the Ponca problem stopped at the White House door. "As the Chief Executive at the time when the wrong was consummated, I am deeply sensible that enough of the responsibility for that wrong justly attaches to me to make it my particular duty and earnest desire to do all I can to give to these injured people that measure of redress which is required alike by justice and humanity."

About a month later, in the waning hours of his presidency, the Forty-sixth Congress passed a bill appropriating $165,000 to the Ponca. The Southern Ponca would receive $50,000 to buy 101,894 acres from the Cherokee for a permanent reservation in the Warm Country. They would also get $10,000 for cattle and horses and $10,000 to be divided among the southern people. Standing Bear's people would receive $5,000 to build new homes, $5,000 for a new school, and $10,000 to be split among the northern tribe. The government would also set aside another $70,000 in a permanent trust fund, with a 5 percent annual interest generated by the fund to be divided equally among all the Ponca.

When Congress passed the Ponca bill on March 3, 1881, it marked the end of a tumultuous four-year relationship between the government and Standing Bear's people. The question of what should become of a father who had wanted to bury his son on their traditional homeland, of what his legal rights were and the government's responsibility in protecting them, had been ceaselessly debated in the nation's newspapers, among its citizens, in the White House, in the federal courts, and in the halls of Congress. Unintentionally at first, Standing Bear had ultimately forced all three branches of government to confront a series of difficult questions and provide some answers at a time when many of those issues had languished for years in confusion, ignorance, and apathy.

As a result, the policies had now begun to inch forward, catching up to the reality of the American West and those who had lived there for as long as anyone could remember. In the early spring of 1881, the notion of forced removal, of confining northern tribes to the Warm Country, had given way to settling tribes in their traditional homeland and making them individual stakeholders as a potential prelude to citizenship.

Standing Bear had initiated that possibility, had opened the door to possibilities that seemed improbable when the strange white man from the East had burst into their northern village four years earlier. And although the government chose not to apply it broadly, Judge Dundy's decision had revealed perhaps the most unlikely possibility of all: It was now possible for an Indian to get justice in a white man's court.

Among the Northern Ponca of today, the legal door that Standing Bear pried open more than a century ago remains a cultural and historical touchstone. From his trailer near their powwow grounds, Larry Wright Sr. has a clear, clean view of the old homeland. A member of the Birdhead Clan, Wright manages the small tribal buffalo herd and not far from an earthen lodge the people recently built, he can climb a hillside cemetery where the names of the old chiefs are fading on the headstones and look out at the herd, at the waves of Junegrass, switchgrass, and foxtail, at the green, rolling countryside and fertile valley, to where the Niobrara empties into the Missouri. At fifty-eight, he has the skin and hair color of the traditional people and a strong sense of what Standing Bear's ordeal has long meant to him. "To me, that's where the Civil Rights fight began. And he was the first Civil Rights warrior this country ever had. What he did was not only important for us—it was important for everyone."

Back then, throughout a long and contentious four years, the nation's leaders had received a kind of crash course on Indian history, culture, and policy—perhaps none more so than Carl Schurz. The Interior Secretary had been on the job but six weeks when the Ponca removal began, and for the next four years it would torment and challenge his position as the government's chief architect of Indian policy. Strong-willed, high-minded, vigorously independent, Schurz struggled mightily to balance the government's official position with his own personal convictions. On the one hand, he stubbornly clung to the belief that the Ponca removal had occurred on someone else's watch, that they had fairly prospered in the Indian Territory and been treated favorably by the government.

On the other hand, he fired a derelict Indian Commissioner, cleaned out a nest of incompetent bureaucrats, and forced agents to be more responsive to Indian needs. For much of his tenure, he fought an aggressive battle in the nation's newspapers, dueling with Helen Hunt Jackson, defending his policies in the New York papers and taking on editors up and down the East Coast who berated his treatment of Standing Bear and the Ponca. The day after Congress approved the Ponca relief bill, Schurz resigned and took a job as managing editor of the *New York Evening Post.*

The relief bill that the President had insisted upon had gone a long way in righting a number of wrongs. It provided White Eagle and all the Southern Ponca with the means to acquire a large tract of land along the Salt Fork River and to furnish it with cattle, horses, and oxen. But for Standing Bear and the northern people, there was a hitch: Where were they to build their new homes? A new schoolhouse for the children? Farms to raise their crops?

Their old homeland, as far as government legal records went, still belonged to the Lakota.

9

On the Land of the Fathers

It stands alone in the piercing summer light, a gnarled sentinel staring impassively across the river, past the sweep of meandering channels, wooded islands, silhouetted sandbars, and oxbow lakes, looking out at the high chalk bluffs on the other side.

For more than a century and a quarter, it has fought to sink its roots deep into the banks of a riverbend, not far from where the Running Water ends its 535-mile journey across the Northern Great Plains, not far from where the village of the Sacred Head People once stood. Its girth measures twenty-three feet and although lightning, wind, blizzards, and age have now worn away many of its branches, fresh ones have sprung up around the blackened stumps, creating a jagged jumble of withered leaves and fresh ones, weathered bark and new bark. Thick and stout, it has open views on three sides, clear windows looking out across the verdant alluvial plain to the sloping green hills, hills dusted with the bones of bear and buffalo, deer and elk, horses and cattle, Mormons and Lakota, Germans and Ponca.

In the early spring of 1890, not far from where the cottonwood tree was taking root, Standing Bear could not believe what had come down the valley. He could not believe the words that he and his people were now hearing from their agent, words about what the whites intended to do with the Ponca homeland, words that trapped him between two opposing forces. They were going to force him to choose one way over the other. If he finally wanted legal claim to his land, a clear legal title, he would have to give up much of what he had fought so long and hard for. But how could he choose between his land and his people—they were one, they were the same.

It is what he had long feared. Year after year, he had done everything in his power to prevent it and now it was happening anyway and there was nothing he could do. So that spring, Standing Bear and a small group of his people saddled good horses and, once again, they turned their faces south.

Sudden as it seemed, their flight had been set in motion almost a decade earlier. Although the Ponca Relief Bill of 1881 resolved many problems for the government and the Ponca, it had not resolved exactly where Standing Bear and his people could legally plant their crops, build their new homes, and send their children to school, where a new life could take root. So the government decided, as it often did in moments of crises, to bring the leading chiefs and headmen to Washington for a council on the matter.

Because the Lakota remained legal owners of the ancestral Ponca homeland, the government invited a delegation of Lakota chiefs to Washington in the summer of 1881. Throughout the nineteenth century, it was unusual for Indian leaders to journey halfway across the continent to discuss giving away their land to traditional enemies. Years earlier Spotted Tail, the Brulé chief, had agreed to do so, but his offer had fallen on deaf ears. At the time, the government's approach to the Indian problem was too narrow and inflexible to accommodate such an offer. The solution to the problem, it believed back then, was to forcibly remove northern tribes to Indian Territory.

But by the late summer of 1881, Standing Bear's plight had obliged all three branches of government to radically rethink the nation's policy toward its original inhabitants. In a few short years, his case had not only generated intense newspaper coverage and fostered a continuing national debate, but it had also prompted control of the Indian problem to increasingly pass from military to civilian hands. Along the way, it had gradually forced the architects of Indian policy to alter their view of the native population, to shift the debate from a conquered, confined, and dependent people of the past to an assimilated, constitutionally protected, self-reliant citizen of the future. And at the heart of this new vision was the concept of individual Indians privately owning their own land.

When Lakota leaders gathered in the Indian Office in early August 1881, a powerful Oglala chief headed the group. Red Cloud had made many trips to Washington, where the government widely viewed him as the preeminent leader of all seven sub-tribes of the Lakota, and he dominated the discussion from beginning to end. In an unusually generous mood, Red Cloud and the Brulé representative, White Thunder, agreed to give up a small part of their sprawling reserve to Standing Bear and about 175 of his Northern Ponca who remained free but homeless. After all, the Lakota legally occupied the western half of what would become South Dakota, far more land than they needed, while the Ponca had none. In an unprecedented gesture, the Lakota also informed both the Indian Commissioner and the new Interior Secretary of something else: They would agree to do this without demanding anything in return.

By the time the meeting ended, Lakota leaders had put the pen to an agreement awarding 640 acres of the old Niobrara homeland to the head of each Northern Ponca family and to all unmarried men twenty-one and older. Under the agreement, other unmarried Ponca men and women were eligible for eighty acres. The land was to be tax-free for twenty years and not subject to lease. All in all, the agreement ended up transferring 25,000 acres to the Ponca, substantially less than the 96,000-acre reservation that had been conveyed to them by solemn treaty sixteen years earlier. Still, for the first time in years, Standing Bear and his people were on the verge of being able to carve out a new life on lands they legally owned, lands they had lived on for as long as anyone could remember.

Although individual ownership was outlined in the agreement with the Lakota, it was still just an idea, one without the force of law. So, as the 1880s began to unfold, there was a good deal of congressional effort and energy devoted to championing the idea as the one surefire way to eventually integrate America's native people into the nation's political, cultural, and social mainstream. On Capitol Hill, Senator Dawes was again the dominant voice, riding herd in congressional hallways on an idea he had long advocated. The newsman Tibbles also was an active supporter, proposing it as the best safeguard against uprooting any more tribes from their homelands. So, too, was former Interior Secretary Schurz, who saw it as a vindication of his progressive ideas. And General Crook believed as well in the overall philosophy. Title to their own lands and legal protection, he thought, offered Indians the best hope for themselves, their children, and eventual citizenship.

The advocates of awarding individual allotments to the Indian people were often well intentioned, and they passionately believed in their cause. But there were also others who believed something else: that the sparsely populated, underdeveloped reservations were a waste of valuable land—land that more ambitious, productive white settlers could put to better use. Meanwhile, no one knew for sure what Standing Bear and his people believed because no one ever asked.

The concept of private ownership, of an individual holding a piece of paper declaring he alone owned a specific section of land with precise borders, was a difficult one for Indian people to comprehend. For centuries, they had lived on lands whose boundaries were fluid, lands the tribe often claimed as its own, but not in a legal sense, and not as individuals. For generations, the need of the individual had always been subordinate to the needs of the tribe. They had hunted buffalo, raised corn, picked chokecherries, harvested wild turnips, gathered wood, shared pastures, and pooled resources for protection against enemies—all for the common good, for the collective benefit of the whole, not the individual. It is how they had survived. And when the reservation system came about, it was the tribe that owned the reservation lands, never the individual members.

Indian reluctance to breaking up tribally owned land into individual plots had confused and confounded successive waves of Washington bureaucrats. To them, not wanting to own your own land, your own home, your own crops, your own stock made no sense. Among Indians, a frustrated Senator Henry Dawes had once remarked, "There is no selfishness, which is at the bottom of civilization."

After years of debate, unbeknownst to Standing Bear, the Northern Ponca, the Lakota, and the rest of the nation's Indian people, the wishes of the senator, the newsman, the former Interior Secretary, and the Army general became law. On February 8, 1887, under the terms of what became known as the Dawes Act, each Indian family head was now to receive 160 acres—land the family would privately own and the government would hold in trust for twenty-five years. During this time, the policymakers believed, individual native families would learn the true value of private ownership, how to nurture and take care of their own land, how to make a profit from it. In effect, it would force them to become self-sufficient farmers and ranchers, motivated by the principles of a competitive, free-market economy. Ultimately, a taste for money and possessions would take hold, allowing many to achieve the same status as the white farmers and ranchers who increasingly had begun to crowd their lands. Meanwhile, any surplus land—reservation land left over after all the individual plots had been awarded—could be sold to whites. The sale proceeds would go into a government account with the interest used to finance a general education fund for the Indians.

Now, only one legal obstacle stood in the way of returning the

Ponca homeland to its people. Disposition of the Ponca lands depended on the Lakota agreeing to break up the vast Great Sioux Reservation—43,000 square miles, which included the Ponca homeland, set aside exclusively for the Lakota by the Fort Laramie Treaty of 1868. During the ensuing twenty years, the railroad, ranching, oil, and mining industries began to covet the vast, underpopulated reservation and by the last half of the 1880s, they increasingly pressured Congress to carve up the valuable land. The land boomers and industrial magnates wanted to set aside smaller and smaller tracts for the Lakota and sell off the large surplus to white homesteaders and businesses. Squeezed by the powerful business interests, the government eventually proposed breaking up the Great Sioux Reservation into six smaller ones, reducing Lakota land holdings from 21,593,128 acres to 12,845,521 acres. The 8.7 million surplus acres would then be sold on the open market for $1.50 an acre.

But, led by Red Cloud and other headmen, the Lakota steadfastly refused to go along with the plan. After months of fruitless debate, the government finally turned to the one man the Lakota trusted, an aging Army general whom Washington hoped could convince them it was now in their best interest to sell off some land in exchange for the security of long-term annuities and critical food supplies. Throughout their long discussions with George Crook, food repeatedly surfaced as the one key issue. The Lakota firmly believed their food rations would be dramatically cut as soon as they signed away their lands, and it took all of Crook's considerable diplomatic skills to assure them otherwise. Finally, after weeks of heated discussion, after Crook's pledge that their food rations were safe, the general left camp with the number of signatures Congress needed to approve the Lakota land sale. On March 2, 1889, the Sioux Act officially broke up the large tract of Lakota land into six smaller reservations.

Two weeks after Crook left with the necessary signatures, much to his dismay and disgust, the government slashed the Lakota beef rations by one million pounds and threw open the surplus lands to white settlers. Not long after, the Lakota's aging, half-blind chief spoke for many of his countrymen: "They made us many promises, more than I can remember," said Red Cloud, "but they never kept but one; they promised to take our land and they took it."

Throughout the 1880s, Standing Bear and his people, unaware of the loud voices arguing in Washington, had been busy transforming the fertile Niobrara bottomlands into lush fields of corn, squash, wheat, and beans, as the Sacred Head People had always done.

While neighboring tribes often starved, their crops devastated by inexperienced farmers, inadequate rainfall, poor soil, and hungry grasshoppers, the Ponca flourished. When Standing Bear looked out across their lands in the early years of the 1880s, he saw his people fanned out once again across a broad, fertile valley wedged between the Niobrara and Ponca Creek, a valley filled with rich, bottomland soil and just enough undulating hills for excellent drainage. Up and down the valley, he saw thriving farms flush with corn, wheat, beans, and livestock. He saw new homes being built, a new school, freshly fenced pastures, and his people often working the land in civilian clothes. To supplement their income, they began selling cords of wood to white settlers in the nearby village of Niobrara for two to three dollars. By 1883, they had become completely independent of government rations. Two years later, their harvest was so bountiful they fed themselves, sold a considerable surplus to neighboring whites, and still had a significant amount left over. Forced to store the excess grain in their homes, Standing Bear asked their agent either to build them houses to put their grain in or to build new houses for them to live in.

When he looked out upon his people in those years, he also saw something else, something most of the others did not. He saw that his fragmented tribe was a small one and the low numbers worried him, made him think they could be vulnerable to losing their land in the years ahead. So he began to actively recruit mixed-bloods into the tribe, trying to bolster the Northern Ponca numbers to reach a reservation-size tribe, trying to give them more protection against outsiders who he knew would one day covet their lands. And through-out the decade, the number of Northern Ponca steadily increased.

In 1887, the year the Dawes Act began carving reservations into in-dividual plots, they numbered 210. That year, they used 2,500 rods of fencing to create pastures for their 145 head of cattle. Five new homes went up, two-story frame homes measuring twelve feet by twenty-four feet. They had a successful day school and another bumper crop, again selling their surplus to help feed the white ranchers and their families in town. Throughout the decade, their many white neighbors and the in-fusion of mixed-bloods helped propel the Northern Ponca into the mainstream and acclimate them to the lifestyles and rhythms of the dominant culture much more rapidly than their southern relatives. They were, their agent noted, "making commendable progress as farm-ers and stockmen." Left alone, they had succeeded far beyond their agents' expectations. No one had told them how to farm or where to farm, how to live or where to live, which plot belonged to whom, and what crops should be planted on it. They had figured it out for them-selves and they had prospered as a result.

In February 1887, Standing Bear did not know about the passage of the new federal law named after the Massachusetts senator he had of-ten met during the East Coast speaking tour, the law that would break up reservations into individual plots. But there were a good many things he did know. For one thing, he knew that the legal status of his homeland had been floating in limbo for almost twenty years—ever since the government "blunder" had given it away to the Lakota in the Fort Laramie Treaty of 1868. He knew a Senate committee, one he had testified before, had long since recommended awarding the Ponca legal ownership of their old lands. He also knew a civilian commission chaired by his friend, the Army general, had urged the same. He knew, too, that the nation's former chief executive had agreed and forwarded the recommendation to Congress. And he knew that Congress had passed a bill making it law.

Yet, the Ponca could produce no paper showing they were the legal owners. By the winter of 1887, it seemed he had been waiting a long time for the Great Father to honor the treaties, the Senate reports, the civilian recommendations, and the law. He had known for a long time that when the government wanted his land, they were quick to seize it—by treaty, force, or blunder. But when they agreed to give it back, it was often a long wait. So two more winters passed, two more years after the Dawes Act became law, and still no one had told him about the legal status of the Ponca homeland.

Now, in the early spring of 1889, word of the breakup of the Great Sioux Reservation had come down the valley and he feared that their lands, too, would become a checkerboard—two Indian-owned plots next to three white-owned plots adjacent to one Indian plot beside four white plots. Standing Bear believed the Ponca were legally entitled to their full 96,000-acre reservation. He believed every level of the federal government had said as much for years. But because their numbers were so small, he knew that when the last paper was signed and the last surveyor left, most of their tribal land base would vanish.

"There has been a good deal of restlessness during the year, arising chiefly from the prospective opening of the reservation," the Ponca Agency teacher reported in the summer of 1889. "Very few favor the movement with any degree of heartiness." None more so than Standing Bear, who had done all he could to resist and protest breaking up the tribal base and selling off the surplus.

During the past thirteen years, he had returned three times to a homeland that had been taken from him, enduring blizzards, floods, death, and disease to make the journey. Now, finally, he and his people were to have a legal claim in that homeland. But only to pieces of it, as individuals. The tribe would have nothing. Disgusted, dispirited, and distraught, Standing Bear and about sixty Northern Ponca decided to flee their Niobrara homeland.

The chief, Indian Agent James E. Helms told superiors, "is a shrewd, cunning savage, one who, if his intellect was directed in a channel to benefit his people, could do much good; but as he now is he is the only one of the Ponca band in Nebraska who persists in the old savage way."

"I Am a Man"

Standing Bear arrived in Indian Territory in April 1890, and it wasn't long before the government began to insist that he and the others return to their northern lands. Standing Bear initially resisted. He said many in the group missed their relatives and did not want to be separated from them again. He said some of them didn't care if they lost their land up north, they just wanted to stay with their relatives. He said they had now fought for a dozen years to reclaim their lands, that every government investigation had promised to return them, and yet they still had no paper proving they were the rightful owners. Finally, government agents told him the northern lands would soon be allotted—and if they didn't return, they would lose them all. So in the summer of 1890, Standing Bear once again made the six-hundred-mile journey between the new lands and the old ones. While he and the others made their way back home in the hot days of July, the Northern Ponca who had remained on the Niobrara began to select their allotments—individual plots carved from the ancestral homeland, plots they could now legally claim as their own.

The law that had carved up the Great Sioux Reservation into six smaller ones a year earlier had also specified how the old Ponca homeland was to be allotted. Under the new law, the Northern Ponca were to select allotments based on age and family position. Each family head would get 320 acres and each single Ponca over eighteen could select 160 acres. Each orphan under eighteen also would get 160 acres and all others under eighteen could claim eighty acres. "The most of them took kindly to this measure and manifested great interest, and for the most part exercised sound judgment, in selecting their lands," reported the Reverend John E. Smith, the Ponca Agency missionary.

On August 18, 1890, Standing Bear and a number of his followers finally made it back to the Niobrara. "This wily and crafty chief," the missionary noted in his annual report, "seeing the emoluments of his office slipping away from him because of the growing intelligence of the Poncas, too lazy to work, but not too proud to beg, hatched in his idle brain the scheme of selling this land and removing his immediate followers to Indian Territory, leaving the rest to starve for aught he cared, to spend his remaining days in the pleasures of the dance and harem. He has been and returned, a sadder and seemingly a wiser man."

Late that summer—twenty-two years after his homeland had been given away to the Lakota, eleven years after a federal judge set him free with nowhere to go, ten years after the Great Father pledged to return all their lands, nine years after Congress approved the Ponca Relief Bill, three years after the Dawes Act, a year after the Great Sioux Reservation was dismantled—Standing Bear received Allotment No. 146: a 297.8-acre parcel of rich, dark soil hugging a bend on the west bank of the Running Water. The sixty-two-year-old chief had been among the last to receive his land and, in the end, when the last allotment had been made, when they were all totaled up, the individual parcels amounted to 27,202 acres of what was once a 96,000-acre reservation.

In short order, in going from a tribally owned reservation to individual allotments, the Northern Ponca had lost 70 percent of their original homeland.

For the rest of the decade the aging chief stayed close to the land he could now legally claim as his own with papers on file in the county courthouse. It was fertile land with good drainage and lots of pasture, and it wasn't long before his property sported healthy fields of corn and wheat, a sizeable vegetable garden, and a fair number of cattle. He fenced his pastures and put up a number of outbuildings and built a solid wooden home and lived quietly on his farm with his two wives, Susette and Lottie, an infant son, Fisher, their three daughters—Lucy, Fanny, and Jennie—and two orphaned grandsons. As had been true for many years, he got along well with his many white neighbors and it wasn't unusual for them to occasionally see him tending his fields in breechcloth, moccasins, and a hat, the bear claw necklace visible against his bare chest.

One day in the late spring of 1906, a visitor made his way to the lush farm nestled on the west bank of the Niobrara. He was surprised to see how white the landowner's hair had become. The visitor had come with some news, had come to tell him that Carl Schurz was dead. After hearing the news, Standing Bear stood quietly, smoking in silence for a full minute. When he finished, he looked up and offered the visitor a one-word response: "Good."

Back then, in the early years of a new century, whenever the oldman chief looked out across his fields in late autumn, whenever he padded down the rows of tender, green corn shoots in the early spring, whenever he reflected back on his own long life, he could roam over eight decades that had meandered, much like the Niobrara, across a diverse, adaptable, and enduring landscape. A life that had begun in obscurity along this same river and, by and by, had branched off into back channels of sweltering stockades and elegant hotels, frozen haystacks and formal courtrooms, a lonely island in the middle of the Great Plains, and a bustling street corner at the crossroads of the world. He could remember rummaging for field corn in the Kansas snow and sipping tea with a famous Boston poet. The burial dress of his daughter and the mosquitoes and disease that took the babies and children in the cold tents in the Warm Country. He knew it was rare to have survived it all and to have lived to old age.

And he could never forget the last words of his son, and what he had said to the judge and all the others, and what the judge had said about him and all those like him. At one time, he could imagine, he may have been the best known of all the people like him and now he could tend to his corn and his wheat and his cattle, walk his farmland, visit with neighbors, venture into town, chop wood and fish the river, and no one really knew who he was. No one much cared. No one remembered. But his fathers were in the hills and the bluffs to the north and west and so was his son, and his daughters were safe in the sturdy house he had built and, although it had been a long and difficult journey, he was back with all of them, the only place he had ever wanted to be.

On September 6, 1908, a single paragraph, buried amid the day's other news, appeared in the back pages of some of the nation's newspapers: "Standing Bear, a famous Ponca Indian chief, is dead at Niobrara. He was once exploited in Boston and other Eastern cities by Thomas Tibbles, former Vice Presidential candidate. Mr. Tibbles claimed the Indian chief was a martyr to Government persecution."

Most every summer, Larry Wright Jr. carefully packs his beaded moccasins, leggings, eagle wing fan, embroidered vest, bells, bone choker, gourd rattles, and roach, and drives to the Niobrara for the annual Northern Ponca Powwow. A century after Standing Bear's death, Wright, the new chairman of his people, comes to dance, to eat, to talk and mingle with the others, to try to do his part to sustain the cultural traditions of his small, fragmented tribe—and to remember. Nine months of the year, he teaches American history at Lincoln High School in Lincoln, Nebraska, and he wants his students to know some of the things that he knows, the things the elders have passed down to him. "I know it's important that we have our stories of George Washington and the cherry tree and Honest Abe the rail-splitter. Those are all important stories," he likes to say. "But there are some other stories worth knowing, too. What's more American than loving your country, your homeland this much? What's more American than loving your son and the traditions of your people so much that you would risk everything to honor a promise? What's more American than preferring death in a freedom flight home to dying slowly as a prisoner in a place you hate, a place you have no connection to? I mean, this was a man who took on the U.S. government on a different kind of battlefield— and he won. When you think about it, it's one of the best American stories we have."

Janet Saiz remembers, too. She remembers being a young girl in the 1940s and taking the train north out of Omaha with her sister, and how her grandfather would pick them up at the station in his buckboard and take them back to his farm near the Niobrara. She remembers coming over a hill and seeing the fields of wheat and corn and oats, and all of his pigs and horses and chickens, and then the large vegetable garden and all the vibrant marigolds and zinnias. Leander Penisca was born near the river in 1889 and lived there for all of his seventy-nine years. When the chief died in the early fall of 1908, Grandpa Lee was a young man and a part of the small, close-knit community. That day, he and all the others went to the funeral, to a place on Standing Bear's land where they laid the chief to rest in a family plot with his wife and two grandsons. Years later, he would tell the story of the funeral along the river to Janet's mother.

Saiz remembers visiting the area with her mother in the high hard heat of a summer day near the end of the last century, and how they stood on a knoll overlooking the broad valley, her mother motioning to a distant hill where three of their chiefs were buried side by side. Later that day, she remembers her mother pointing to the area where another chief lay buried, a place across the valley from the bones of the son, not far from where the ancient cottonwood still stands, its roots sunk deep into the soil of the homeland, a peaceful spot not far from the high chalk bluffs of the Running Water.

Bibliography

1. BOOKS

Bourke, John G. *On the Border With Crook.* New York: Charles Scribner's Sons, 1981.

———*Scatalogic Rites of All Nations.* Washington: W. H. Lowdermilk & Co., 1981.

———*With General Crook in the Indian Wars.* Palo Alto, California: Lewis Osborne, 1968.

Brown, Dee. *Bury My Heart at Wounded Knee: An Indian History of the American West.* New York: Washington Square Press, 1981.

Buildings of the 80's in Omaha. Omaha: Standard Blue, 1976.

Cash, Joseph H., and Gerald W. Wolff. *The Ponca People.* Phoenix, Arizona: Indian Tribal Series, 1975.

Dando-Collins, Stephen. *Standing Bear Is a Person: The True Story of a*

Bibliography

Native American's Quest for Justice. Cambridge, Massachusetts: Da Capo Press, 2004.

DeConde, Alexander. *This Affair of Louisiana.* New York: Charles Scribner's Sons, 1976.

Fuss, Claude Moore. *Carl Schurz: Reformer (1829–1906).* New York: Dodd, Mead & Company, 1932.

Green, Norma Kidd. *Iron Eye's Family.* Lincoln: Nebraska State Historical Society Foundation, 1969.

Grossman, Mark. *The Native American Rights Movement.* Santa Barbara, California: ABC-CLIO, Inc., 1996.

Hostetler, Eldon E. *The Way It Was: A Collection of Short Histories.* Crete, Nebraska: Dageforde Publishing, Inc., 2004.

Howard, James H. *The Ponca Tribe.* Lincoln: University of Nebraska Press, 1995.

Jablow, Joseph. *Ponca Indians: Enthohistory of the Ponca.* New York: Garland Publishing Inc., 1974.

Jackson, Helen. *A Century of Dishonor.* New York: Indian Head Books, 1993.

Kastor, Peter J. *The Nation's Crucible: The Louisiana Purchase and the Creation of America.* New Haven, Connecticut: Yale University Press, 2004.

Kruse, Lowen V. *Omaha: The Prairie Blossoms: Accounts of Religious Initiative in Relation to Social Change.* Omaha, Nebraska: Paradise Publishing, 2001.

La Flesche, Francis. *The Middle Five: Indian Schoolboys of the Omaha Tribe.* Lincoln: University of Nebraska Press, 1978.

Larsen, Lawrence H., and Barbara J. Cottrell. *The Gate City: A History of Omaha.* Lincoln: University of Nebraska Press, 1997.

Leach, A. J. *A History of Antelope County Nebraska: From Its First Settlement in 1868 to the Close of the Year 1883.* Neligh, Nebraska: Antelope County Historical Society, 1909.

Luebke, Frederick C. *Nebraska: An Illustrated History.* Lincoln: University of Nebraska Press, 1995.

Lyon, E. Wilson. *Louisiana In French Diplomacy: 1759–1804.* Norman: University of Oklahoma Press, 1934.

Mathes, Valerie Sherer, and Richard Lowitt. *The Standing Bear Contro-*

versy: Prelude to Indian Reform. Champaign: University of Illinois Press, 2003.

Mulhair, Charles. *Ponca Agency.* Niobrara, Neb.: Charles Mulhair, 1992.

Nabokov, Peter, ed. *Native American Testimony: A Chronicle of Indian-White Relations from Prophecy to Present, 1492–1992.* New York: Viking Penguin, 1991.

Pitot, James. *Observations on the Colony of Louisiana from 1796 to 1802.* Translated by Henry C. Pitot. Baton Rouge: Louisiana State University Press, 1979.

Robinson, Charles M., III. *General Crook and the Western Frontier.* Norman: University of Oklahoma Press, 2001.

Schmitt, Martin F., ed. *General George Crook: His Autobiography.* 2nd ed. Norman: University of Oklahoma Press, 1960.

Schurz, Carl. *The Reminiscences of Carl Schurz.* Vol. 3. New York: Doubleday, Page & Company, 1908.

Tibbles, Thomas Henry. *Buckskin and Blanket Days: Memoirs of a Friend of the Indians.* Lincoln: University of Nebraska Press, 1969.

———*The Ponca Chiefs: An Account of the Trial of Standing Bear.* Lincoln: University of Nebraska Press, 1972.

Waldman, Carl. *Who Was Who in Native American History.* New York: Facts On File, Inc., 1990.

Wallace, Anthony F. C. *Jefferson and the Indians: the Tragic Fate of the First Americans.* Cambridge, Massachusetts: Harvard University Press, 1999.

Wilson, James. *The Earth Shall Weep: A History of Native America.* London: Picador, 1998.

Wishart, David J., ed. *Encyclopedia of the Great Plains.* Lincoln: University of Nebraska Press, 2004.

———*An Unspeakable Sadness: The Dispossession of the Nebraska Indians.* Lincoln: University of Nebraska Press, 1994.

2. ARTICLES AND PERIODICALS

Clark, Stanley. "Ponca Publicity." *The Mississippi Valley Historical Review*, March 1943, 495–516.

Bibliography

Farrar, Jon. "Nebraska Rivers." *NEBRASKAland* Magazine (January–February 1983), 103–113.

Flowerday, Charles A., and R. F. Diffendal, Jr., ed. *Geology of Niobrara State Park, Knox County, Nebraska, and Adjacent Areas—with a Brief History of the Park, Gavins Point Dam, and Lewis and Clark Lake.* Educational Circular 13 of Conservation and Survey Division Institute of Agriculture and Natural Resources. Lincoln: University of Nebraska–Lincoln, September 1997.

"Governor to Sign Chief Standing Bear Day Proclamation," *Ponca Tribe of Nebraska Tribal Newsletter,* May 2001, 1.

"The Journal of Agent Howard," *Antelope County Historical Society Newsletter,* May 2002, 1–7.

King, James T. "'A Better Way': General George Crook and the Ponca Indians." *Nebraska History,* 50, no. 3 (1969): 239–256.

Lake, James A. Sr., "Standing Bear! Who?" *Nebraska Law Review* 60 (1981): 451–503.

McCarthy, Sean. "Standing Bear." *The Reader*, 23–29 September 2004, 8.

The Nation. (22 March 1879), 2.

Placek, Marita. "Ponca Tribe Builds the Old Way," *Nebraska Life,* September/October 2004, 12.

Reilly, Hugh. "First Civil Rights Victory." *Home & Away*, July/August 2004, 19a.

Roeder, James A. "The One Hundred and Second Congress and the Niobrara Scenic River: Old Arguments, New Compromises." *Nebraska History* 85, no. 3 (2004): 116–127.

Sheldon, Robert. "Retracing Discovery: With Lewis and Clark in Mind and Spirit," *Nebraska Magazine* (Winter 1997), 24–29.

Taylor, Quentin. "President Hayes and the Poncas." *Chronicles of Oklahoma* 81, no. 1 (2003): 104–111.

Tibbles, Thomas Henry. "Anecdotes of Standing Bear." *Nebraska History* 13, no. 4 (1933): 271–276.

Bibliography

3. NEWSPAPERS

Boston Daily Advertiser
Chicago Tribune
Frank Leslie's Illustrated Newspaper (New York City, New York)
Lincoln Journal Star (Nebraska)
Lincoln Star (Nebraska)
The Milford Review (Nebraska)
Nebraska Reporter (Seward, Nebraska)
Nebraska Journal-Leader (Ponca, Nebraska)
Neligh News and Reader (Nebraska)
New York Daily Tribune
The New York Times
Niobrara Pioneer Press (Nebraska)
Omaha Daily Bee
Omaha Daily Herald

4. GOVERNMENT DOCUMENTS

Dorsey, James Owen. *The Cehiga Language—Myths, Stories, and Letters.* Washington: GPO, 1890.

"Indians of Nebraska: Omaha" pamphlet. Nebraska Indian Commission, n.d.

"Indians of Nebraska: Ponca" pamphlet. Nebraska Indian Commission, n.d.

Missouri River Basin Project: Niobrara River Basin: Nebraska–Wyoming–South Dakota. Denver, Colorado: Bureau of Reclamation, Region 7, September 1952.

"Niobrara National Scenic River" pamphlet. National Park Service, n.d.

Royce, Charles C. *Indian Land Cessions in the United States.* Washington: GPO, 1900.

"Spirit Mound Historic Prairie" pamphlet. Spirit Mound Trust, National Park Service, and South Dakota Department of Game, Fish and Parks, July 2002.

Bibliography

Supplemental Treaty between the United States of America and the Ponca Tribe of Indians; Concluded March 10, 1865; Ratification advised March 2, 1867; Proclaimed March 28, 1867. 14 Stat. 675 (1865).

Treaty between the United States and the Ponca Tribe of Indians. Concluded at Washington, March 12, 1858. Ratified by the Senate, March 8, 1859. Proclaimed by the President of the United States, April 11, 1859. 12 Stat. 997 (1858).

Treaty between the United States of America, and the Yancton Tribe of Sioux, or Dacotah Indians. Concluded at Washington, April 19, 1858. Ratified by the Senate, February 16, 1859. Proclaimed by the President of the United States, February 26, 1859. 11 Stat. 743 (1858).

A Treaty of Peace and Friendship: Made and concluded between William Clark and Auguste Chouteau, commissioners on the part and behalf of the United States of America, of the one part, and the undersigned chiefs and warriors of the Poncarar tribe of Indians, on the [their] part and of their said tribe of the other part. 7 Stat. 155 (1817).

Treaty With the Poncar Tribe. 7 Stat. 247 (1825).

U.S. Army Signal Service. Meteorological Record. Syracuse, Nebraska: January 1877–March 1877.

———Meteorological Record. Syracuse, Nebraska: January 1879–March 1879.

U.S. Department of the Interior. *Annual Report of the Commissioner of Indian Affairs to the Secretary of the Interior for the Year 1877.* Washington, DC: GPO, 1877.

———*Annual Report of the Commissioner of Indian Affairs to the Secretary of the Interior for the Year 1878.* Washington: GPO, 1878.

———*Annual Report of the Commissioner of Indian Affairs to the Secretary of the Interior for the Year 1879.* Washington: GPO, 1879.

———*Annual Report of the Commissioner of Indian Affairs to the Secretary of the Interior for the Year 1880.* Washington: GPO, 1880.

———*Annual Report of the Commissioner of Indian Affairs to the Secretary of the Interior for the Year 1881.* Washington: GPO, 1881.

U.S. Senate, 46th Congress, 2d Session. *Report No. 670: Removal of the Ponca Indians.* Washington: GPO, 1880.

Bibliography

U.S. Senate, 46th Congress, 3d Session. *Mis. Doc No. 49: Testimony Before the Select Committee on Removal of Northern Cheyennes as to the Removal and Situation of the Ponca Indians.* Washington: GPO, 1881.

———*Ex. Doc. No. 14: Letter from the Secretary of the Interior.* Washington: GPO, 1881.

———*Ex. Doc. No. 30: A Report of the commission appointed December 18, 1880, to ascertain the fact in regard to the removal of the Ponca Indians.* Washington: GPO, 1881.

U.S. Senate, 54th Congress, 1st Session. *Report No. 427: Mr. Allen, from the Committee on Indian Affairs, Report.* Washington: GPO, 1896.

U.S. Circuit Court, District of Nebraska. *Standing Bear v. Crook.* May 12, 1879.

5. CONGRESSIONAL ACTS AND APPROPRIATIONS (BY DATE)

An Act to provide for an exchange of lands with the Indians residing in any of the states or territories, and for their removal west of the river Mississippi. 4 Stat. 411.

An Act making Appropriations for fulfilling Treaty Stipulations with the Ponca Indians, and with certain Bands of Indians in the State of Oregon and Territory of Washington, for the Year ending June thirtieth, eighteen hundred and sixty. 12 Stat. 4.

An Act making Appropriations for the current and contingent Expenses of the Indian Department, and for fulfilling Treaty Stipulations with various Indian Tribes, for the Year ending June thirtieth, eighteen hundred and sixty-one. 12 Stat. 44.

An Act making Appropriations for the current and contingent Expenses of the Indian Department, and for fulfilling Treaty Stipulations with various Indian Tribes, for the Year ending June thirty, eighteen hundred and sixty-two. 12 Stat. 221.

An Act making Appropriations for the current and contingent Expenses of the Indian Department, and for fulfilling Treaty Stipulations with various Indian Tribes, for the Year ending June thirtieth, eighteen hundred and sixty-three. 12 Stat. 512.

Bibliography

An Act making Appropriations for the current and contingent Expenses of the Indian Department, and for fulfilling Treaty Stipulations with various Indian Tribes, for the Year ending June thirtieth, eighteen hundred and sixty-four. 12 Stat. 774.

An Act making Appropriations for the current and contingent Expenses of the Indian Department, and for fulfilling Treaty Stipulations with various Indian Tribes, for the Year ending June thirtieth, eighteen hundred and sixty-five, and for other Purposes. 13 Stat. 161.

An Act making Appropriations for the current and contingent Expenses of the Indian Department, and for fulfilling Treaty Stipulations with various Indian Tribes for the Year ending thirtieth June, eighteen hundred and sixty-seven, and for other Purposes. 14 Stat. 255.

An Act making Appropriations for the current and contingent Expenses of the Indian Department, and for fulfilling Treaty Stipulations with various Indian Tribes for the Year ending June thirty, eighteen hundred and sixty-eight. 14 Stat. 492.

An Act making Appropriations to supply Deficiencies in the Appropriations for contingent Expenses of the Senate of the United States for the fiscal Year ending June thirtieth, eighteen hundred and sixty-seven, and for other Purposes. 15 Stat. 7.

An Act making Appropriations for the current and contingent Expenses of the Indian Department, and for fulfilling Treaty Stipulations with various Indian Tribes for the Year ending thirtieth June, eighteen hundred and sixty-nine, and for other Purposes. 15 Stat. 198.

An Act making Appropriations for the current and contingent Expenses of the Indian Department, and for fulfilling Treaty Stipulations with various Indian Tribes for the Year ending June thirtieth, eighteen hundred and seventy. 16 Stat. 13.

An Act making Appropriations for the current and contingent Expenses of the Indian Department and for fulfilling Treaty Stipulations with various Indian Tribes for the Year ending June thirty, eighteen hundred and seventy-one, and for other Purposes. 16 Stat. 335.

An Act making Appropriations to supply Deficiencies in the Appropriations for the Service of the Government for the fiscal Years ending June thirty, eighteen hundred and seventy, and June thirty, eighteen hundred and seventy-one and for former Years, and for other Purposes. 16 Stat. 515.

An Act making Appropriations for the current and contingent Expenses of the Indian Department, and for fulfilling Treaty Stipulations with various Indian Tribes, for the Year ending June thirty, eighteen hundred and seventy-three, and for other Purposes. 17 Stat. 165.

An Act making Appropriations for the current and contingent Expenses of the Indian Department, and for fulfilling Treaty Stipulations with various Indian tribes, for the Year ending June thirtieth, eighteen hundred and seventy-four, and for other purposes. 17 Stat. 437.

An Act making Appropriations for the current and contingent expenses of the Indian Department, and for fulfilling treaty stipulations with various Indian tribes, for the year ending June thirtieth, eighteen hundred and seventy-five, and for other purposes. 18, Part 3 Stat. 146.

An Act making Appropriations to supply deficiencies in the appropriations for fiscal years ending June thirtieth, eighteen hundred and seventy-five, and prior years, and for other purposes. 18, Part 3 Stat. 402.

An Act making Appropriations for the current and contingent expenses of the Indian Department, and for fulfilling treaty-stipulations with various Indian tribes, for the year ending June thirtieth, eighteen hundred and seventy-six, and for other purposes. 18, Part 3 Stat. 420.

An Act making Appropriations for the current and contingent expenses of the Indian Department, and for fulfilling treaty-stipulations with various Indian tribes, for the year ending June thirtieth, eighteen hundred and seventy-seven, and for other purposes. 19 Stat. 176.

An Act making Appropriations for the current and contingent expenses of the Indian Department, and for fulfilling treaty-stipulations with various Indian tribes, for the year ending June thirtieth, eighteen hundred and seventy-eight, and for other purposes. 19 Stat. 271.

An Act making Appropriations for the current and contingent expenses of the Indian Department, and for fulfilling treaty stipulations with various Indian tribes, for the year ending June thirtieth, eighteen hundred and seventy-nine, and for other purposes. 20 Stat. 63.

Bibliography

An Act making Appropriations for the current and contingent expenses of the Indian Department, and for fulfilling treaty stipulations with various Indian tribes, for the year ending June thirtieth, eighteen hundred and eighty, and for other purposes. 20 Stat. 295.

An Act making Appropriations for the current and contingent expenses of the Indian Department, and for fulfilling treaty stipulations with various Indian tribes, for the year ending June thirtieth, eighteen hundred and eighty-one, and for other purposes. 21 Stat. 114.

An Act making Appropriations to supply deficiencies in the appropriations for the fiscal year ending June thirtieth, eighteen hundred and eighty-one, and for prior years, and for those certified as due by the accounting officers of the Treasury in accordance with section four of the act of June fourteenth, eighteen hundred and seventy-eight, heretofore paid from permanent appropriations, and for other purposes. 21 Stat. 414.

An Act making Appropriations for the current and contingent expenses of the Indian Department, and for fulfilling treaty stipulations with various Indian tribes, for the year ending June thirtieth, eighteen hundred and eighty-two, and for other purposes. 21 Stat. 285.

An Act making Appropriations for the current and contingent expenses of the Indian Department, and for fulfilling treaty stipulations with various Indian tribes, for the year ending June thirtieth, eighteen hundred and eighty-three, and for other purposes. 22 Stat. 68.

An Act making Appropriations to supply deficiencies in the appropriations for the fiscal year ending June thirtieth, eighteen hundred and eighty-two, and for prior years, and for those certified as due by the accounting officers of the Treasury in accordance with section four of the act of June fourteenth, eighteen hundred and seventy-eight, heretofore paid from permanent appropriations, and for other purposes. 22 Stat. 257.

An Act making Appropriations for the current and contingent expenses of the Indian Department, and for fulfilling treaty stipulations with various Indian tribes, for the year ending June thirtieth, eighteen hundred and eighty-four, and for other purposes. 22 Stat. 433.

Bibliography

An Act making Appropriations for the current and contingent expenses of the Indian Department, and for fulfilling treaty stipulations with various Indian tribes, for the year ending June thirtieth, eighteen hundred and eighty-five, and for other purposes. 23 Stat. 76.

An Act making Appropriations for the current and contingent expenses of the Indian Department, and for fulfilling treaty stipulations with various Indian tribes, for the year ending June thirtieth, eighteen hundred and eighty-six, and for other purposes. 23 Stat. 362.

6. ARCHIVES

"Burial of Standing Bear." Nebraska State Historical Society, 1951–1952.

The Diary of John Gregory Bourke, microform, 1846–1896.

"The General Crook House Museum: Tour Guide" pamphlet. Douglas County Historical Society, 2001.

La Flesche, Susette. *Autograph Book.* Nebraska State Historical Society.

"Pleas Before the Honorable Elmer S. Dundy." Nebraska State Historical Society, May 1879.

Poppleton, Andrew J. "Character: Its Development and Exaltation the True End of Education: An Address Delivered before the University of Nebraska, at the Fifth Annual Commencement." Lincoln: University of Nebraska, 27 June 1877.

———*Reminiscences.* Lincoln: Nebraska State Historical Society, 1915.

Poppleton, Caroline L. "The War Bonnet." Lincoln: Nebraska State Historical Society, 15 January 1915.

Sheldon, A. E. "Bright Eyes: Data for Sketch." Nebraska State Historical Society, 1902.

"Writ of Habeas Corpus." Nebraska State Historical Society, 11 April 1879.

7. WEB RESOURCES

Carl Schurz. <http://www.spartacus.schoolnet.co.uk/USAschurz.htm> (4 June 2005).

Bibliography

Cunningham, Nobel E., Jr., "Jeffersonian Democracy." *The Reader's Companion to American History.* <http://college.hmco.com/history/reader scomp/rcah/html/ah_047600_jeffersonian.htm> (2 February 2005).

Lewis, M.D., Michael R. "Scrofula." *eMedicine.* 5 November 2004. <http://www.emedicine.com/ent/topic524.htm> (14 March 2005).

Major General Carl Schurz. <http://www.russscott.com/~rscott/26thwis/cshurz.htm> (4 June 2005).

"Malaria." *Center for Disease Control and Prevention.* <http://www.cdc.gov/malaria> (17 March 2005).

"Niobrara's History." *Village of Niobrara* <http://www.niobrarane.com/historyl.htm#Niobrara> (2 February 2005).

Northern Virginia Community College, "The Age of Jeffersonian Democracy." *Sage History.* <http://www.sagehistory.net/history121/part2/topics/JeffersonianDem.htm> (2 February 2005).

"President Jefferson's letter to William Henry Harrison, February 27, 1803." *Indiana Historical Bureau.* <http://www.statelib.lib.in.us/www/ihb/publications/jeffharrison.html> (2 February 2005).

"Scrofula." *University of Maryland Medical Center.* <http://www.umm.edu/ency/article/001354.htm> (14 March 2005).

"Thomas Jefferson on Politics & Government." *Electronic Text Center at the University of Virginia Library.* <http://etext.lib.virginia.edu/jefferson/quotations/jeffcont.htm> (2 February 2005).

"The Treaty of Fontainebleau (Treaty of Paris), February 10, 1763." *The Solon Law Archive.* <http://www.solon.org/Constitutions/Canada/English/PreConfederation/Treaty_of_Paris_1763.html> (12 February 2005).

"Treaty of San Ildefonso, October 1, 1800." *The Avalon Project at Yale Law School.* <http://www.yale.edu/lawweb/avalon/ildefens.htm> (12 February 2005).

"Transcript of Dawes Act (1887)." *Our Documents.* <http://www.ourdocuments.gov/doc.php?doc=17&page=transcript>(12 February 2005).

"Transcript of Jefferson's Secret Message to Congress Regarding the Lewis & Clark Expedition (1803)." *Our Documents.* <http://www

Bibliography

.ourdocuments.gov/doc.php?doc=17&page=transcript> (12 February 2005).

"Transcript of Louisiana Purchase Treaty (1803)." *Our Documents.* < http://www.ourdocuments.gov/doc.php?doc=18&page=transcript> (12 February 2005).

"Transcript of President Andrew Jackson's Message to Congress 'On Indian Removal' (1830)." *Our Documents.* <http://www.ourdocuments .gov/doc.php?doc=25&page=transcript>http://vvw.ourdocuments.gov/ doc.php?doc=25&page=transcript (12 February 2005).

8. ENCYCLOPEDIAS

American National Biography, 1999, s.v. "Schurz, Carl."
Encyclopedia of American Biography, Second Edition, 1996, s.v. "Schurz, Carl."

9. BOOK REVIEW

Zebolsky, Kirk H. Review of *Susan La Flesche Picotte, M.D.: Omaha Indian Leader and Reformer,* by Benson Tong. *Grassroots Nebraska* (May 2000): 4, 18.

10. DISSERTATIONS

Froehling, Oliver Raymond. "Allotment in Severalty on the Northern Ponca Reservation—The Geography of Dispossion." M.A. thesis, University of Nebraska–Lincoln, 1993.
Price, David H. "The Public Life of Elmer S. Dundy: 1857–1896." M.A. thesis, University of Nebraska at Omaha, 1971.

11. PONCA INTERVIEWS

Judi Morgan gaiashkibos
Rosetta Le Clair

Mark Peniska
Debbie Robinette
Gary Robinette
Janet Saiz
Bill Smith
Shawna Smith
Sandy Taylor
Nancy Velasquez
Phil Wendzillo
Parrish Williams
Larry Wright Sr.
Larry Wright Jr.

12. PONCA TRIBAL RECORDS

The Standing Bear Files—Folders 1–5.

Index

251

Index

Index

Index

Index

Index

Index